SACRAMENTO BASEBALL

FRONT COVER: This c. 1924 photograph shows Earl McNeeley, a Sacramento native born in 1898 and one of Sacramento's great ballplayers. Known for his speed, he played center field for the Washington Senators and was the hero of the 1924 World Series when he drove in the winning run of Game 7 in the 12th inning. He played for Pacific Coast League (PCL) Sacramento in 1922 and part of 1924 then played in the American League for eight years. When he returned to Sacramento in 1932, he became the Sacramento Senators manager and eventually the team's owner. (Courtesy of Sacramento Public Library, Sacramento Room Special Collections.)

COVER BACKGROUND: The Sacramento Solons posed for this photograph at Edmonds Field in 1949. After finishing in last place in the Pacific Coast League in 1948, the team returned in 1949 to finish third. They year 1949 was the first year the Solons played at their new ballpark following the July 1948 fire. (Courtesy of Sacramento Public Library, Sacramento Room Special Collections.)

BACK COVER: This photograph shows the 1921 Heeseman Clothiers Winter League team. Pictured are, from left to right, (first row) Howard Foote (pitcher), Danny Wright (pitcher), Bill Keenan (pitcher), Bobby Schang (right field), Frank Tobin (catcher), and Clif Derringer (second base); (second row) Al Hutchinson (manager), Bob Nixon (left field), Guy Wright (center field), Earl Kunz (pitcher), Arthur Luddy (third base), Tommy White (short stop), George Gibson (pitcher), Reese Peek (pitcher), and Frank Gerig (first base). (Courtesy of GoodOldSandlotDays.com.)

SACRAMENTO BASEBALL

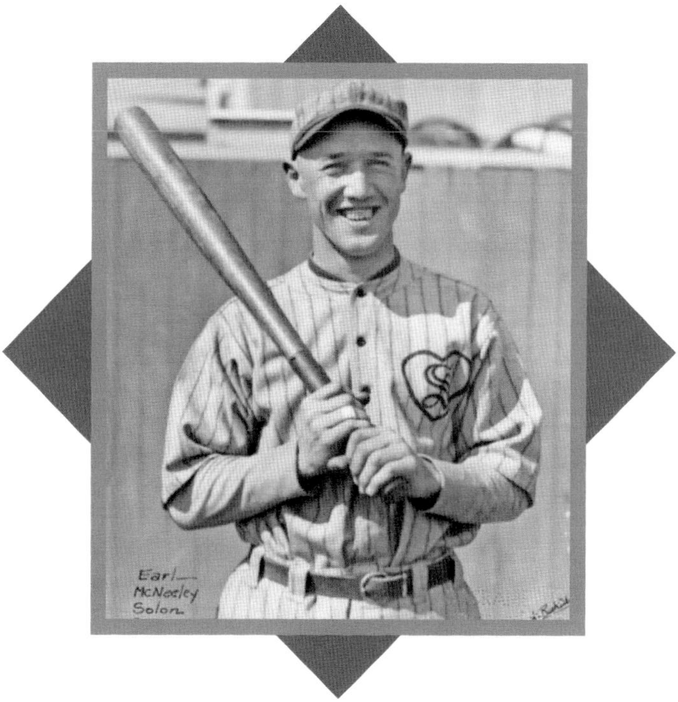

William D. McPoil

ARCADIA
PUBLISHING

ISBN 978-1-4671-1710-4

Published by Arcadia Publishing
Charleston, South Carolina

Printed in the United States of America

Library of Congress Control Number: 2016945811

For all general information, please contact Arcadia Publishing:
Telephone 843-853-2070
Fax 843-853-0044
E-mail sales@arcadiapublishing.com
For customer service and orders:
Toll-Free 1-888-313-2665

Visit us on the Internet at www.arcadiapublishing.com

To Myles and Mason Hammond, baseball players, fans, and fantastic grandsons

CONTENTS

ACKNOWLEDGMENTS

I now understand why so many authors acknowledge their spouse at the beginning of a book. My wife, Gayle, has encouraged and supported me from the proposal submission to completion. I cannot thank her enough.

The images in this book, and the descriptions that go with them, came to me from many sources. I got started with photographs from the Sacramento Room at the Sacramento Public Library. Amanda DeWilde and the other librarians provided me with photographs dating from the Gilt Edge through the Sacramento River Cats. Tim Armstrong, the grandson of Tony Freitas, gave me photographs and information about Freitas and the Sacramento Solons that I am sure I could not have found anywhere else. Alan O'Connor, Sacramento's true baseball historian, helped me populate the chapters on the early days of Sacramento baseball and the chapter on the Sacramento Solons. Kerry Yo Nakagawa, director of the Nisei Baseball Research Project, helped me start on the chapter about Nisei baseball with images and provided me with historical information I used throughout that chapter. Norman Blackwell Sr. provided me photographs of the Golden Seniors, amateur and semipro baseball, and several of the photographs of equipment. Julie Thomas at California State University (CSU), Sacramento Special Collections was a tremendous help with the CSU–Sacramento photographs and several of the photographs in the Nisei chapter. Sacramento River Cats general manager Chip Maxson gave his support from the very beginning, and Erin O'Donnell and Amanda Holland at the Sacramento River Cats opened the River Cats photograph archives to me. I spent too many hours to count at the Arden Fair Apple store where Katja, Marquita, River, Stephanie, and Sherelle answered many questions when I was composing the photographs and text. The others, too numerous to include here, deserve to be thanked and have been both personally and by crediting their photographs in the following pages.

Of course, Alyssa Jones, the acquisitions editor who worked so hard to help me get the project approved, and Henry Clougherty, my title manager, who worked with me through many e-mails and telephone conversations to bring the book to publication, deserve special thanks.

INTRODUCTION

Although organized and recreational baseball had been played in the Sacramento area since the Gold Rush, according to Sacramento baseball historian Alan O'Connor, the *Sacramento Daily Union* published the first written record of professional baseball in the capitol city in 1859. Ten years later, in September 1869, the Cincinnati Red Stockings, the first recognized professional baseball team in America, came to Northern California and played against the Pacifics, a local team in San Francisco, and then went to Sacramento, where a team was organized to play against them. Although the game was enjoyed by the crowd that turned out, the local squad lost by a score of 50-6.

A decade after that, in 1879, the California League was established. It is recognized as the first professional league in the state. It was comprised of teams from San Francisco and Oakland—Oakland Pioneers, San Francisco Athletics, San Francisco Californias, and the San Francisco Mutuals. Seven years later, in 1886, the league was expanded. With that expansion, the league now included the Oakland Greenhood and Morans, the San Francisco Haverlys, the San Francisco Pioneers, the San Francisco Star, and the Sacramento Altas. The Altas played at Agricultural Park in downtown Sacramento and later at Snowflake Park, still in the downtown grid but a few blocks south and east.

In 1890, the Altas were renamed the Senators as a reference to their location in the state's capital. They competed for a couple of years, but unfortunately for baseball fans, Sacramento did not field a team in the middle of the decade. However, in 1898, a local brewery, Ruhstaller Brewery, sponsored a new team, naming it after their best-selling lager, Gilt Edge, and bringing organized baseball back to town. The Gilt Edge posted impressive numbers in their first three years, winning league championships in 1898, 1899, and 1900. In 1901, the team was again renamed the Senators and finished third in a four-team league.

A new league, the Pacific Coast League, was formed in 1903, becoming the West Coast's answer to major league baseball's two eight-team leagues in the East. The league was formed as an independent league, and the Sacramento Senators was one of the six founding members that represented cities from Los Angeles to Seattle. As if the name change was not confusing enough, in 1906 and 1907, the team's name became the Sacramento Cordovas, having been named for Cordova wine produced by the California winery. The name changed back to the Senators in 1908, and that team became the 1909 Pacific Coast League Senators and stayed that way until 1936.

In 1936, the team was purchased by the St. Louis Cardinals. Branch Rickey, the Cardinals' business manager, expanded player development and pioneered the minor league farm system we recognize today as affiliates of major league clubs. Since "Solons" had been used casually by sports writers since before World War I, the name was changed officially with the purchase by the Cardinals, and the Sacramento Solons name stayed with the team until they left in 1960 and again for the brief period in the 1970s when they returned.

Organized fun is a term I chose for any baseball where the competitors are not being paid. That said, they were and continue to be competitive. Whether it was teams sponsored by businesses, hardball leagues, softball leagues, high schools and colleges, or Little League, competitive amateur baseball has been part of Sacramento baseball for more than a century. In the early decades of the 20th century, businesses sponsored teams to help advertise their wares, and in 1925, American Legion Baseball was organized for boys between 13 and 19. After World War II, boys between the ages of 9 and 13 were organized into Little League teams and competed for the right to advance as far as the Little League World Series in Williamsport, Pennsylvania, which was won by a Sacramento team in 1969. High school teams have played against other high schools for decades, several of which are noted in the following pages.

Prior to World War II, Japanese Nisei teams organized and traveled throughout California, competing against each other and local community teams. When Executive Order 9066 was signed by Pres. Franklin D. Roosevelt following the declaration of war on Japan, Japanese American citizens from the Sacramento area were moved to assembly centers and then to internment camps. Internment did not stop them from playing baseball; the teams continued to compete with teams from other camps. Even though the camps were fenced with barbed wire and under guard by the US Army, in most cases the fields and fans' viewing areas were built outside the compound. When the teams traveled, they traveled in small guarded groups to other camps to compete, and competition was fierce.

Buffalo Park was built at the corner of Riverside Boulevard and Broadway in 1910 for the Senators—later renamed the Solons—and remained there until 1960. When the Solons left Sacramento and became the Hawaiian Islanders, Edmonds Field was demolished, and a Gemco department store was built on the site. Sacramento's baseball fans believed baseball was gone forever; with the Giants now 90 miles away in San Francisco and games being broadcast on television, the prospect of a team drawing enough attendance to be profitable seemed remote. However, in 1974, the Eugene (Oregon) Emeralds moved to Sacramento and became the Solons, but the team and Sacramento professional baseball was short-lived. Without a proper ballpark, the Solons played at Hughes Stadium, the football and track and field facility for Sacramento City College, and attendance was never what was hoped. After two seasons, the team moved again, this time to San Jose.

Throughout 1980s and 1990s, baseball fans continued to dream of professional baseball in Sacramento. Steering committees were formed to try to discover away to build a ballpark and either lure the Oakland Athletics to Sacramento or find another minor league team to call their own. Finally, in 2000, Art Savage purchased the Vancouver Canadians and moved them to Sacramento. A joint-powers agency, spearheaded by Christopher Cabaldon during his first term as mayor of West Sacramento, was formed between the City of West Sacramento, Sacramento County, and Yolo County. The purpose of that agency was to build a ballpark for the Canadian team that had become the Sacramento River Cats. The naming rights for the facility were sold to Raley's supermarket chain. The ballpark is one of the few professional sports facilities in the nation built without a public sector contribution.

For the first 15 years, the River Cats were the Triple-A team for the Oakland Athletics. In 2015, the affiliation changed to the San Francisco Giants.

1

The Early Years
Amateur and Professional Baseball, 1870–1935

For 70 years before the Solons became Sacramento's home team, organized baseball encompassed amateur, semiprofessional, and professional baseball; in fact, recreational and organized baseball had been played in the Sacramento area since the Gold Rush. But it was not until 1879, when the California League was established, that true professional baseball became a part of Sacramento. It was that year the California League was established in the San Francisco Bay area and recognized as the first professional league in the state. In 1886, the league was expanded, and with that expansion, the Sacramento Altas joined teams from Oakland and San Francisco and began playing weeklong stands against each other.

In 1890, the Altas, named for a Northern California race horse, were renamed the Senators as a reference to their location in the state's capital; they played at Agricultural Park in downtown Sacramento and later at Snowflake Park, a few blocks south and east but still in the downtown grid. During this time as the Senators, they only played for three years—1890, 1891, and 1893, with breaks in 1892 and from 1894 to 1897. In 1898, Ruhstaller Brewery, a local brewery, sponsored a new team, naming it after their best-selling lager, Gilt Edge, and bringing professional baseball back to town. Gilt Edge lasted only three years, but in each of those years the team won California League championships.

In 1903, the Pacific Coast League was formed, and with that, a new era in West Coast baseball began. The league was formed as an independent league, with the Sacramento Senators as one of the six founding members that represented cities from Los Angeles to Seattle.

As if the name change during this time was not confusing enough, in 1906 and 1907, the Senators name became the Sacramento Cordovas, having been named for Cordova wine produced by the California Winery. In 1908, the name changed to back to the Senators. That team then became the 1909 Pacific Coast League Senators and stayed that way through the 1935 season.

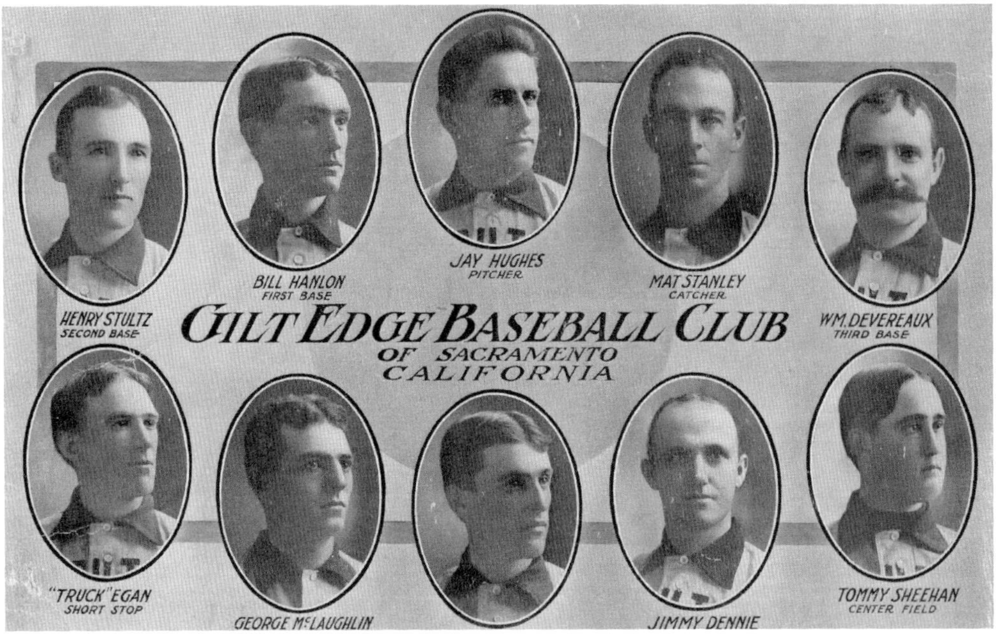

In 1897, a semiprofessional team from Sacramento, the Gilt Edge Baseball Club, played in the San Francisco Examiner tournament and did so well, it joined the professional California League the following year. The team, like many other teams of the period, was sponsored by a brewery; in this case, the Ruhstaller Brewery. The team was named for the brewery's best-selling beer. As a professional team, the Gilt Edge went on to win the California League championship in 1898, 1899, and 1900. In 1901, the team changed its name to the Senators to be recognized as the state capital's team. (Courtesy of Sacramento Public Library, Sacramento Room Special Collections.)

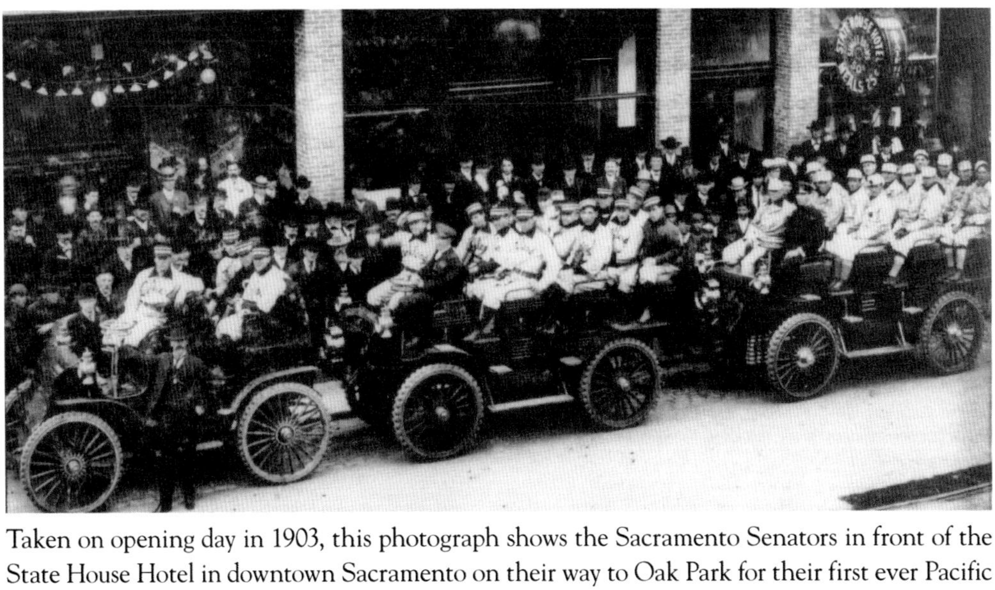

Taken on opening day in 1903, this photograph shows the Sacramento Senators in front of the State House Hotel in downtown Sacramento on their way to Oak Park for their first ever Pacific Coast league game. Rooms at the hotel at that time were 50¢, and meals could be purchased for 25¢. (Courtesy of Alan O'Connor.)

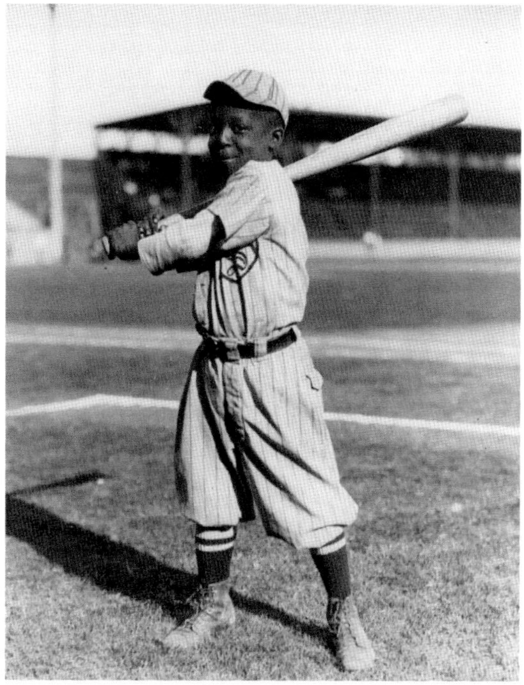

This 1921 photograph shows the Sacramento Senators batboy at Moreing Field. The Senators played at several ballparks, including Agricultural Park between Twentieth and Twenty-Third Streets and E and H Streets, Snowflake Park farther south between Twenty-Eighth and Thirtieth Streets and R and S Streets, and Oak Park (today's McClatchy Park) in what is now the Oak Park neighborhood of Sacramento. In 1910, the team moved to Buffalo Park, which underwent several subsequent name changes, at the corner of Riverside Boulevard and Y Street (today's Broadway), which became a permanent home to Sacramento baseball until 1960. (Courtesy of Sacramento Public Library, Sacramento Room Special Collections.)

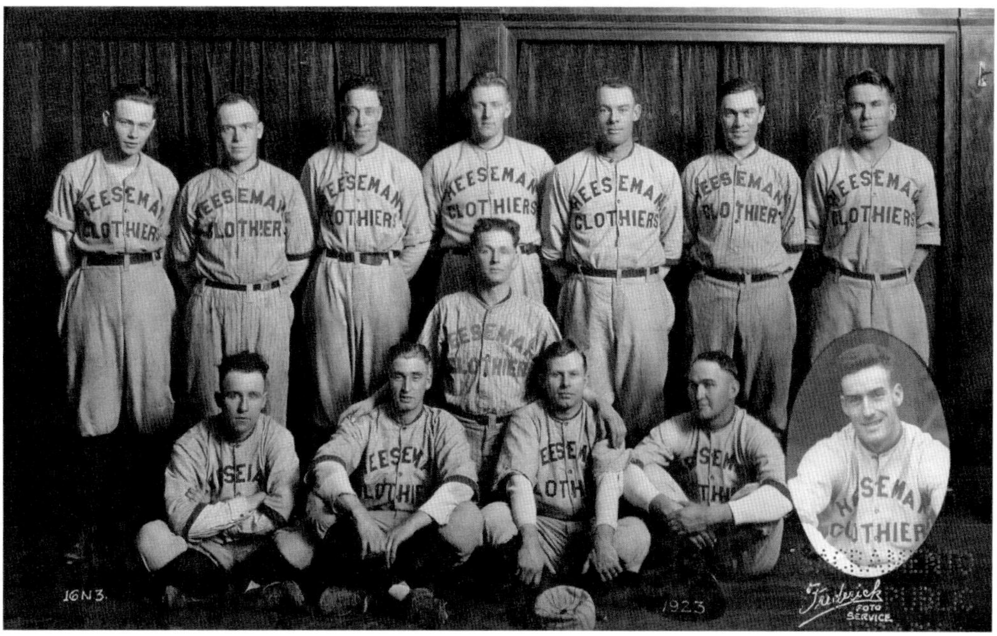

This photograph shows the 1923 Heeseman Clothiers baseball team, which played in the Sacramento City League. Charles Heeseman opened his clothing store in 1916 at 619 K Street, operating at that location for 30 years. In the early 1960s, the store moved to 1022 K Street. The highlighted player in the photograph is Wally McGee, who died from tuberculosis the same year the photograph was taken. Other teams in the league included the Foresters, the Lobners, Thompson-Diggs, and the Acorns. (Courtesy of Sacramento Public Library, Sacramento Room Special Collections.)

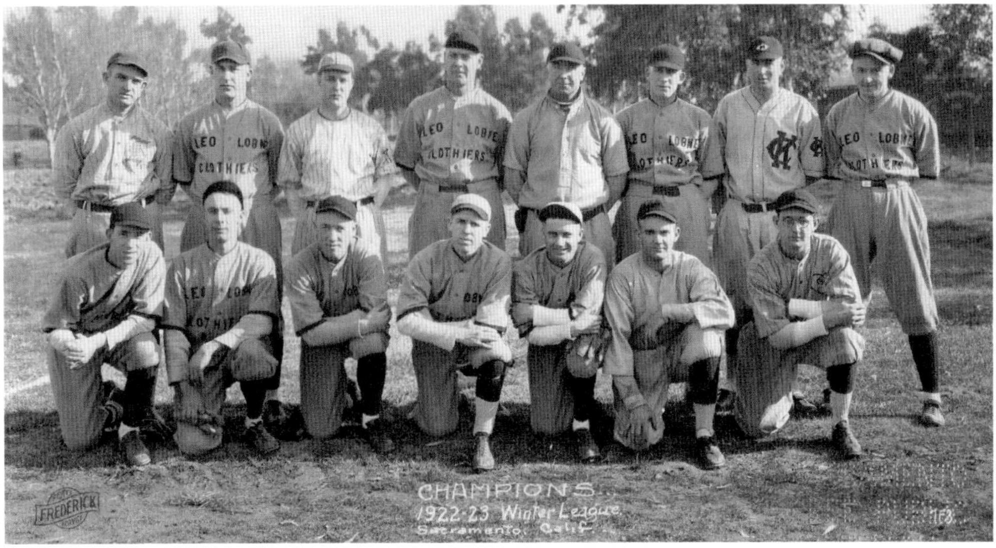

This Leo Lobner Clothiers team portrait was taken in 1923.The Lobner team was the Sacramento Winter League champion for 1922–1923. Ken Penner, pictured in the second row, second from left, was the star of the final game against the Thompson-Diggs team; Lobner defeated them 9-3. In that game, Penner went three for five and scored three runs. The game was played at Moreing Field at Riverside Boulevard and Broadway. (Courtesy of Sacramento Public Library, Sacramento Room Special Collections.)

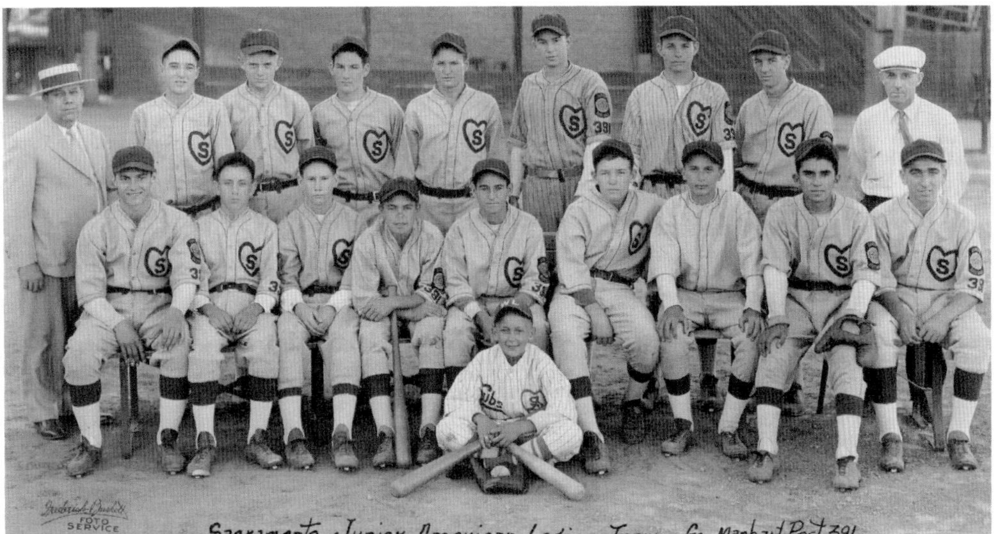

A 1931 photograph shows the Sacramento Junior American Legion team players assembled on a bench in Oak Park. Only a few of the players were identified; Bill Svilich (first row, far left), Victor Pitts (first row, fifth from left), ? Davies (second row, fourth from left), Ellsworth Davies (second row, third from right), and Frank Schreck (second row, second from right). The gentlemen standing at left and right are not identified but are probably the manager and coach. (Courtesy of Sacramento Public Library, Sacramento Room Special Collections.)

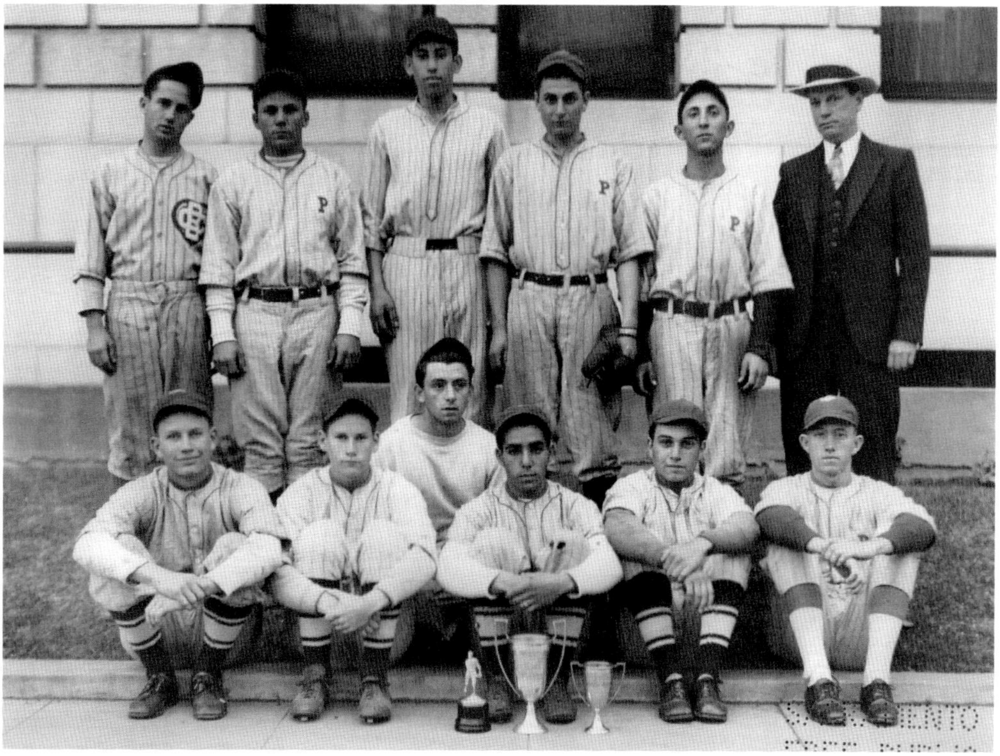

The Sacramento Police Juniors team, pictured here around 1933, participated in the city's recreational league. In 1931, the team won 15 straight games and went on to become the Sacramento Rural League champions. The team was sponsored by the Sacramento Police Department and is shown posing in front of the Hall of Justice located at 813 Sixth Street. (Courtesy of Sacramento Public Library, Sacramento Room Special Collections.)

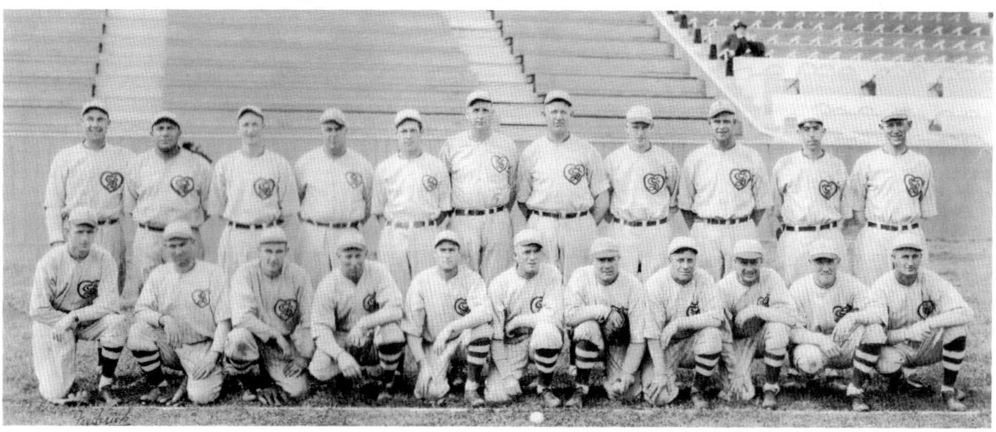

The Sacramento Solons were preceded by the Sacramento Senators, but both teams played at Moreing Park, later named Edmonds Field. In spite of the team's best hitter Wilbur "Bud" Davis's .330 batting average, the 1925 team pictured here finished the year with a record of 82 wins and 119 losses, which was only good enough to place them seventh in a league of eight teams at the end of the season. (Courtesy of Sacramento Public Library, Sacramento Room Special Collections.)

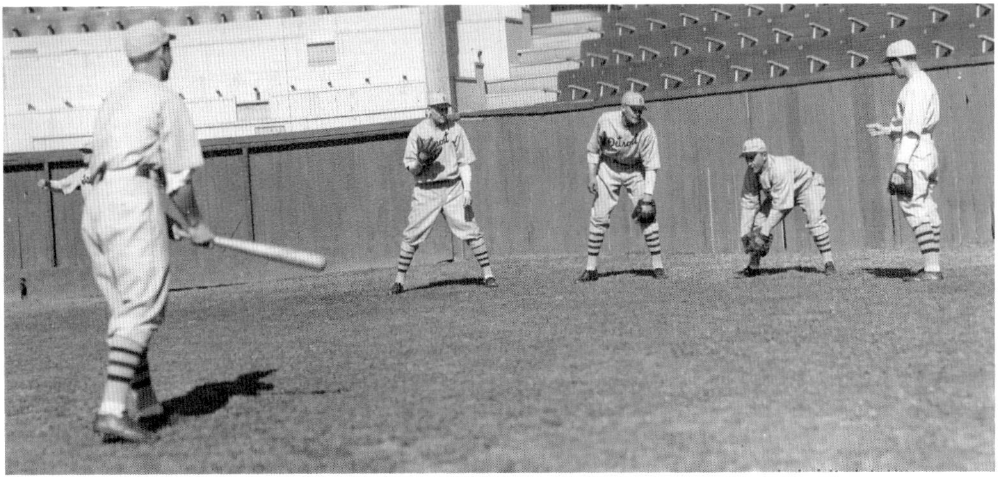

Major league teams located in the East frequently came to California during the winter and spring to begin their training for an upcoming season. In 1931, the Detroit Tigers spent 12 days in Sacramento conducting drills prior to reporting for spring training. Members of the team are seen here playing pepper, where fielders position themselves a few feet from a batter and practice fielding ground balls. From Sacramento, they moved to Woodland for two exhibition games with the Seattle Indians. (Courtesy of Sacramento Public Library, Sacramento Room Special Collections.)

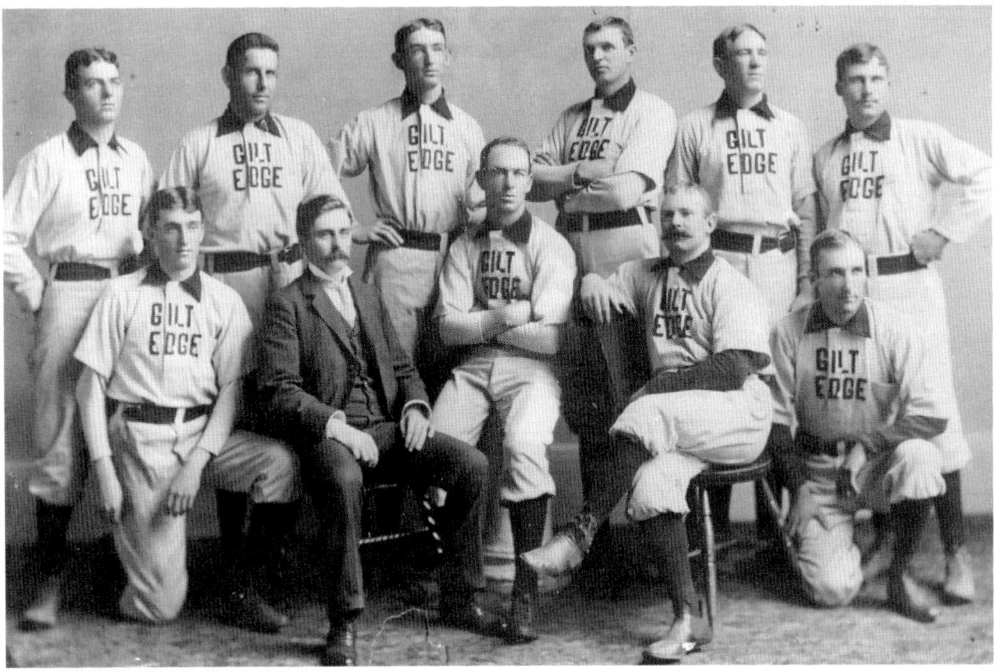

The Gilt Edge was a Sacramento team that only played for three years, from 1898 to 1901. It was sponsored by Ruhstaller Brewery and named for one of its best-selling beers. The team was California League champions in 1898 with a 49-27 record. In 1899, it repeated the championship with the league's top pitcher, "Demon" Doyle, who pitched to a 28-11 record. (Courtesy of Sacramento Public Library, Sacramento Room Special Collections.)

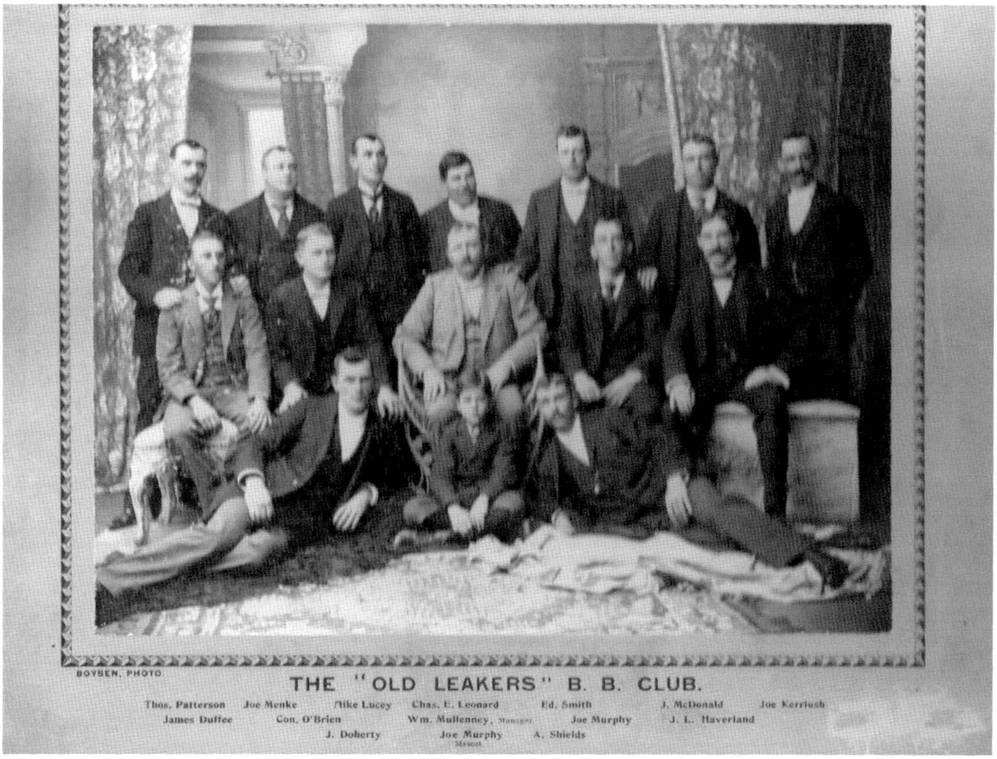

This portrait shows the Old Leakers Baseball Club, which played from 1897 to 1899 at both Thirteenth and S Streets and Snowflake Park at Twentieth and E Streets. An October 4, 1897, *Sacramento Daily Union* article describes a charity game against the Gilt Edge the day before. The proceeds went to the Protestant Orphan Asylum, the Sisters of Mercy Hospital, and the Foundlings Home. The proceeds from the 10¢ and 25¢ tickets, purchased by committees that were not present at the game; reserved seats; and scorecards netted close to $9,980. (Courtesy of Sacramento Public Library, Sacramento Room Special Collections.)

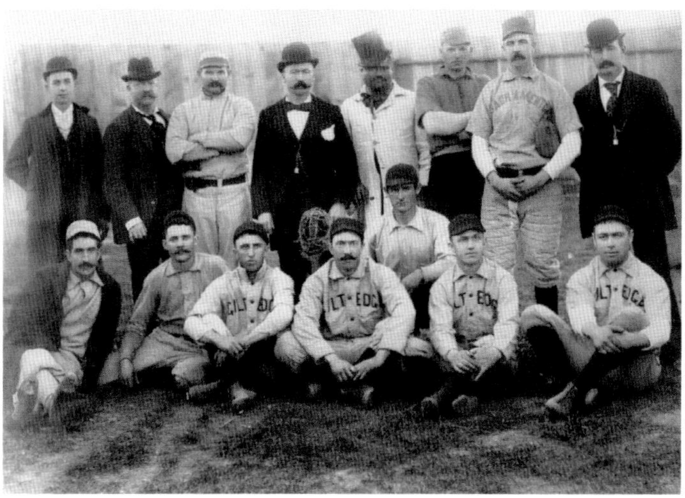

This amateur Gilt Edge team photograph was taken in 1905. It is known to be an amateur team because in 1905, the semipro team no longer existed, the team is wearing uniforms from the previous teams, and at the time, African American players were not allowed into professional baseball. (Courtesy of Alan O'Connor.)

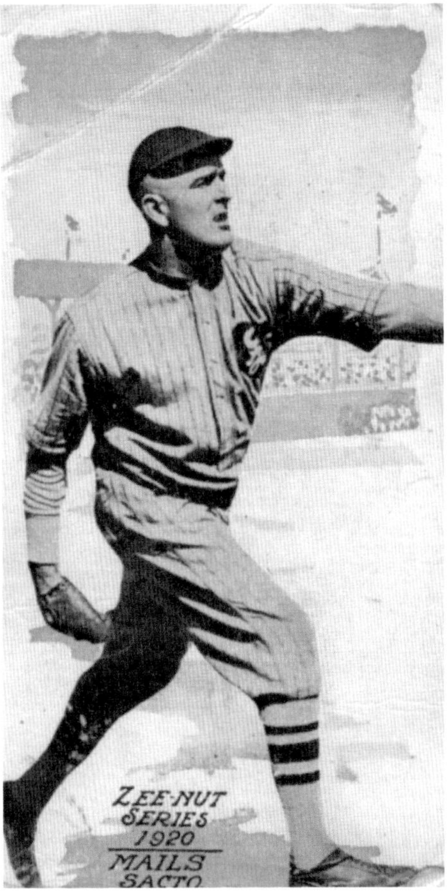

John "Duster" Mails was born October 1, 1894, in San Quentin, California, where his mother worked. He graduated from Sacramento's Christian Brothers High School. He played for several major-league and minor league clubs, including the Sacramento Senators in 1919 and 1920. (Courtesy of Alan O'Connor.)

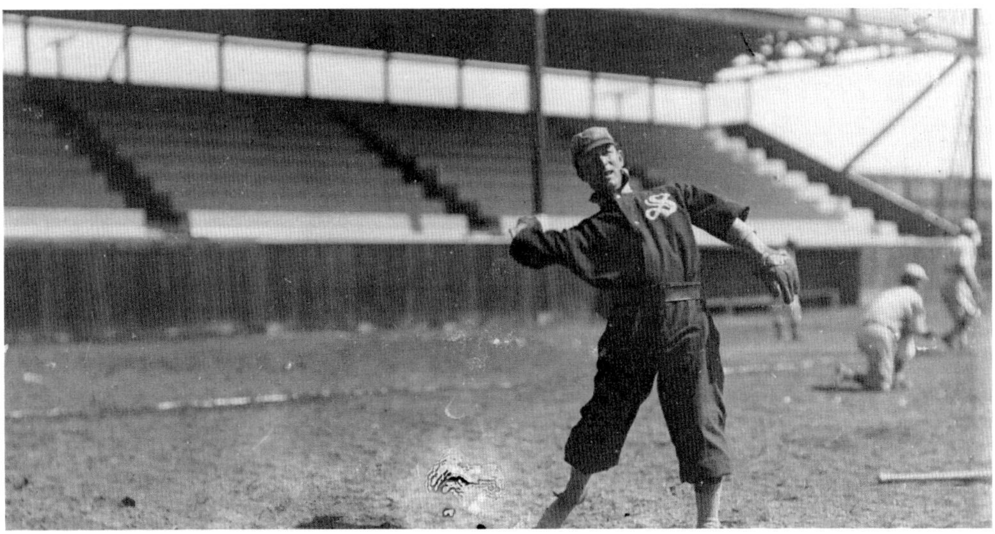

An unidentified Senators player warms up at Buffalo Park, located at Riverside Boulevard and Broadway, before a game in 1913. The Senators played at Buffalo Park between 1910 and 1914 and then again between 1918 and 1921. (Courtesy of Alan O'Connor.)

James "Jay" Hughes was born in Sacramento in 1874. He pitched for local teams in the early 1890s and then started his professional career in 1896 with a Victoria, British Columbia, team in the North West League. Back playing for Gilt Edge in 1897, he was pitching against the National League's Baltimore Orioles Ned Hanlon and was purchased from the Sacramento team and taken east. After several good years, he returned to Sacramento because he preferred to play on the West Coast. (Courtesy of Alan O'Connor.)

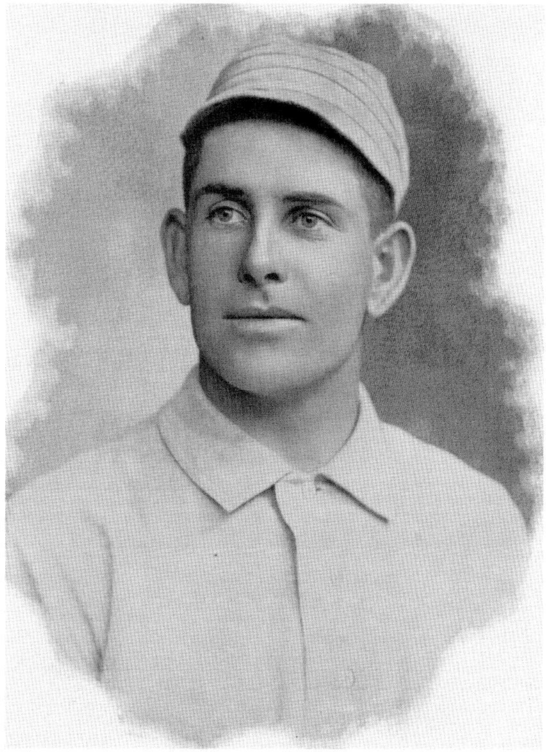

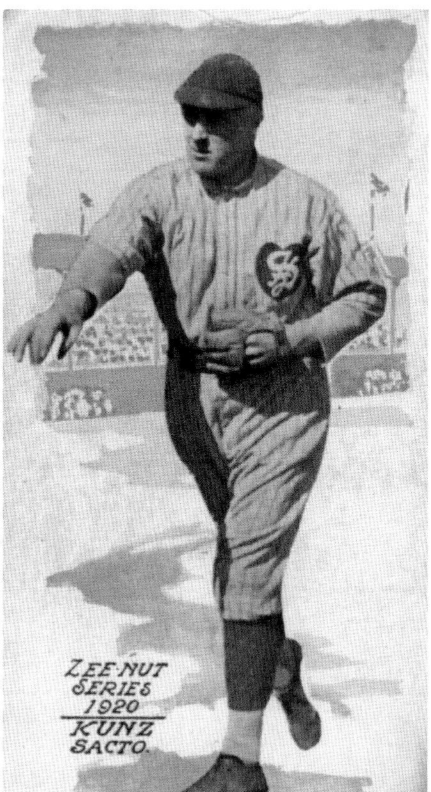

Earl "Pinches" Kunz was born in Sacramento on Christmas Day 1899. He started playing baseball on local sandlots and began his professional career with the Sacramento Senators in 1920, where he played for three seasons before he was picked up by the Pittsburgh Pirates. (Courtesy of Alan O'Connor.)

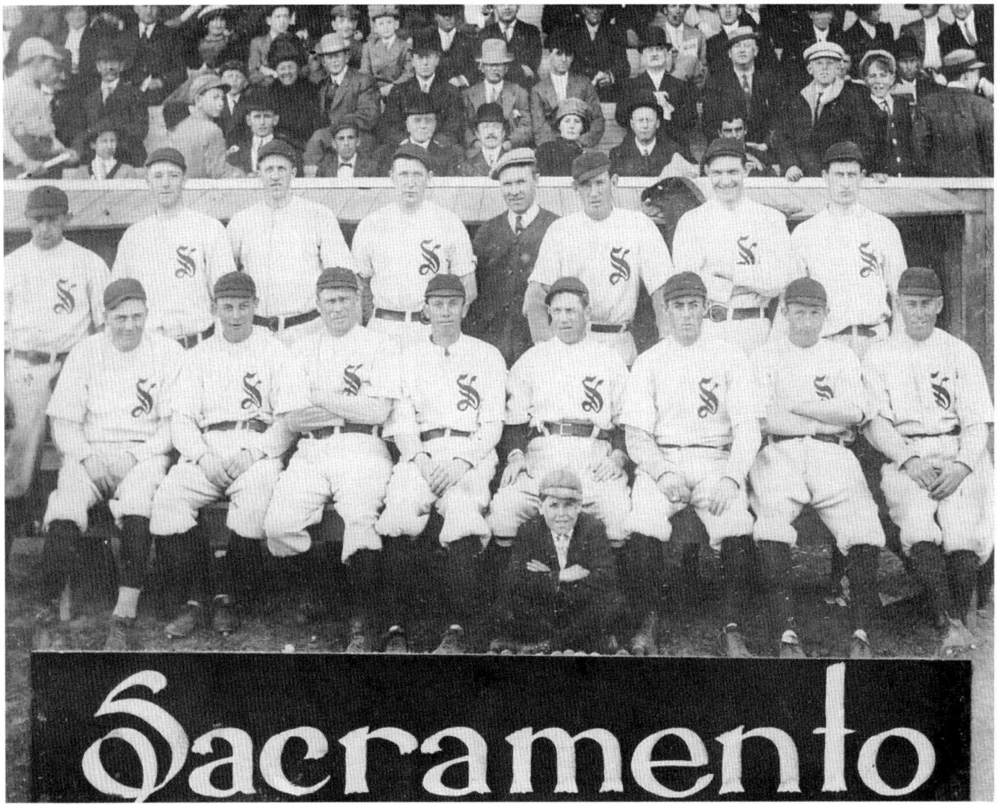

This photograph of the Senators was taken in front of the grandstands at Buffalo Park in 1911. Buffalo Park, located at Riverside Boulevard and Broadway, was renamed Moreing Field in 1922. (Courtesy of Alan O'Connor.)

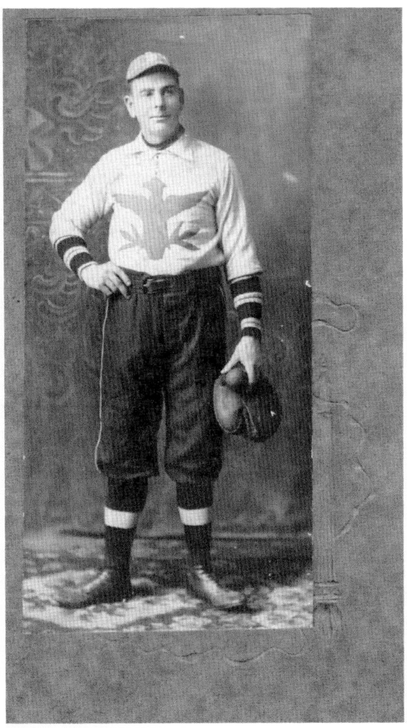

Eugene Mulvey was born in San Francisco in 1872. He moved to Sacramento in 1907 and played catcher for the semipro Sacramento Eagles in 1907 and 1908; they played at Oak Park. He owned the Branch Saloon at 927 K Street from 1908 to 1915 and in 1917 moved back to San Francisco, where he worked as a bartender and a prison guard at San Quentin State Prison. During the 1920s, he worked as a deputy US marshal, enforcing Prohibition under the Volstead Act. (Courtesy of Tom Crisp.)

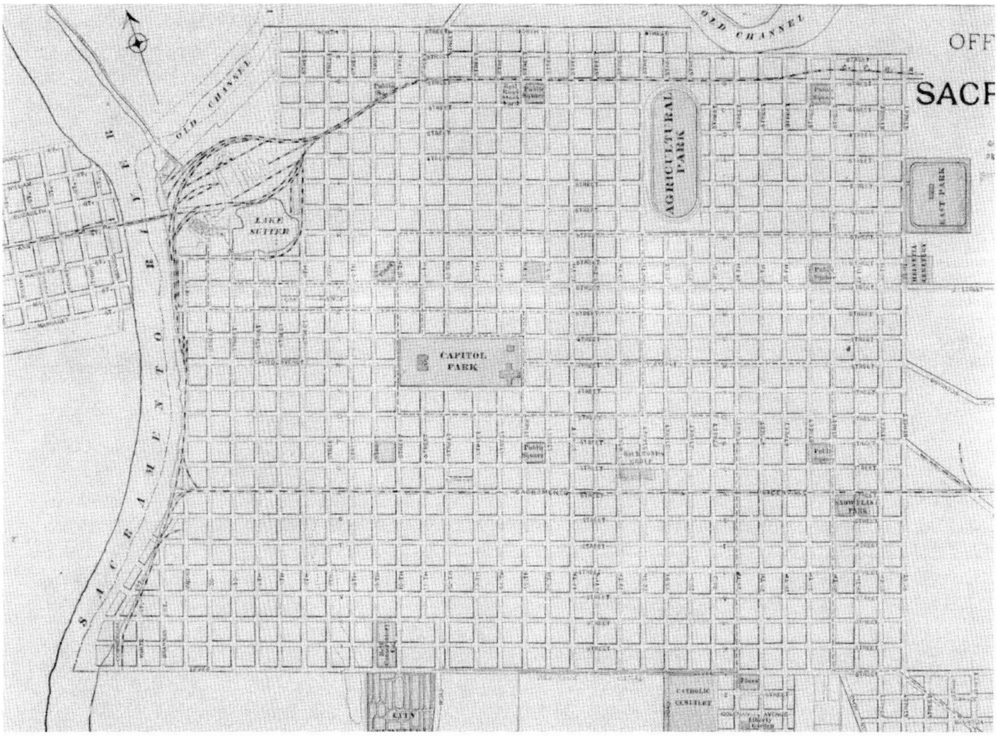

This map of Sacramento shows the various locations where Sacramento professional baseball was played between 1886 and 1898. Agricultural Park, located between Twentieth and Twenty-Third Streets and E and Streets, was utilized by the Altas in 1886 and 1887, and Snowflake Park, situated between Twenty-Eighth and Thirtieth Streets and R and S Streets, was used by the Altas, Senators, and Gilt Edge. (Courtesy of Alan O'Connor.)

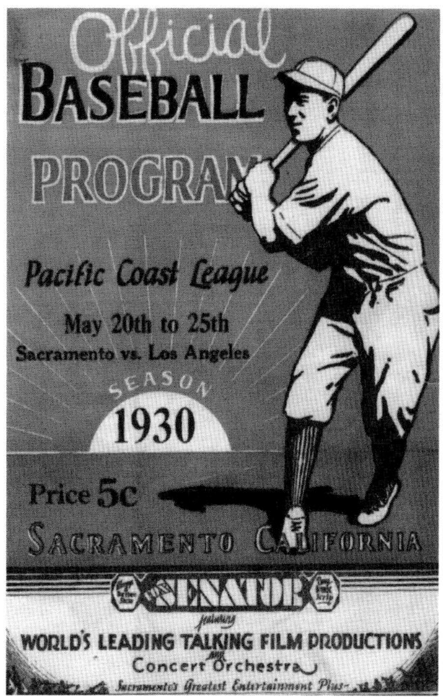

This 1930 program for the week of May 20 to May 25 was sold to fans for 5¢ as they entered the game. Note the advertisement at the bottom hailing the Senator Theater as featuring the "World's Leading Talking Film Productions." (Courtesy of Sacramento Public Library, Sacramento Room Special Collections.)

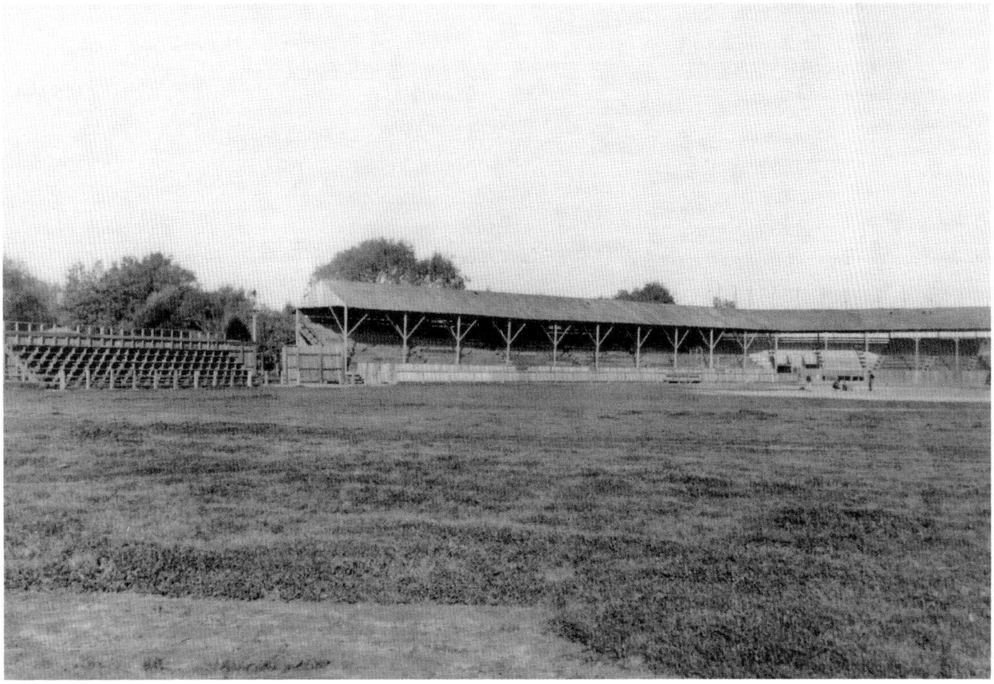

Oak Park (known now as McClatchy Park), located in the Oak Park neighborhood on Fifth Avenue between Thirty-Third and Thirty-Seventh Streets, was where the Gilt Edge played its home games in 1899 and 1900. Following the 1900 season, the team became the Senators and played at that location from 1900 to 1903 and again in 1909. (Courtesy of Alan O'Connor.)

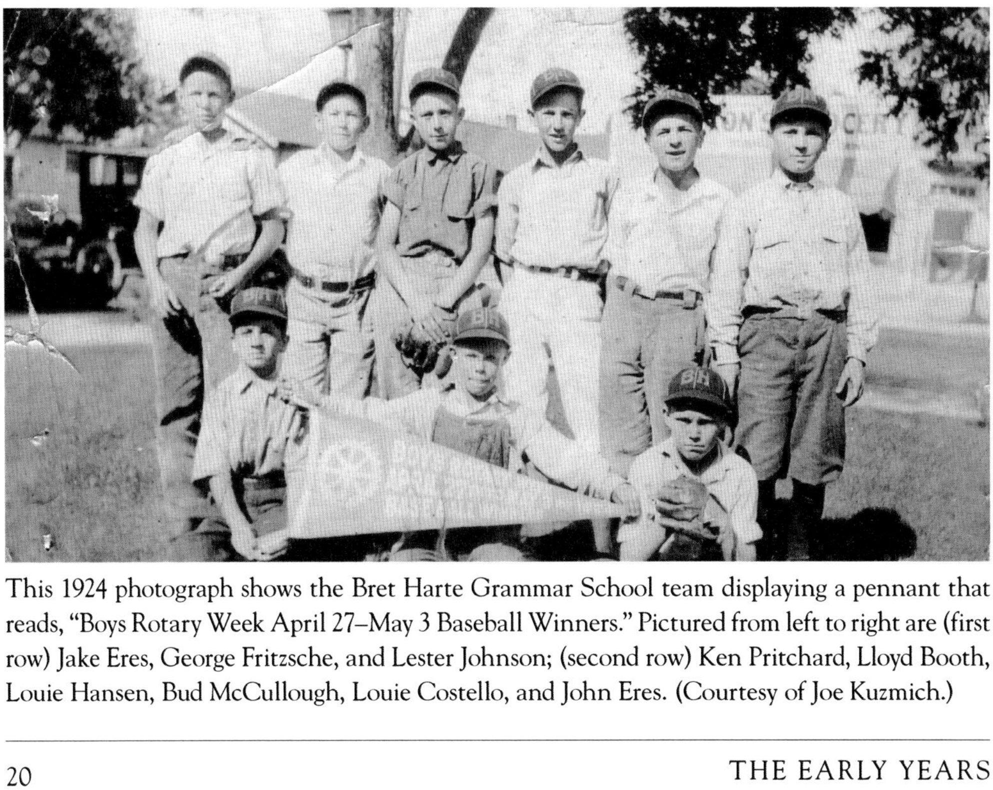

This 1924 photograph shows the Bret Harte Grammar School team displaying a pennant that reads, "Boys Rotary Week April 27–May 3 Baseball Winners." Pictured from left to right are (first row) Jake Eres, George Fritzsche, and Lester Johnson; (second row) Ken Pritchard, Lloyd Booth, Louie Hansen, Bud McCullough, Louie Costello, and John Eres. (Courtesy of Joe Kuzmich.)

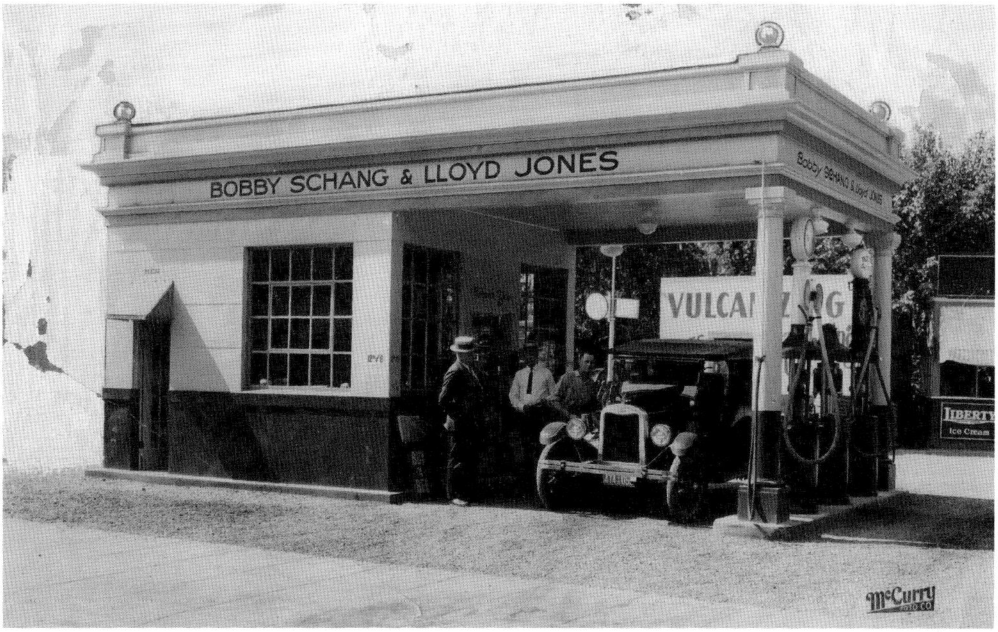

In the early days of professional baseball, most minor league players and many major-league players had second jobs or tended to small businesses they owned in the off-season. Bobby Schang, who played for the Sacramento Senators as a catcher and third baseman from 1919 to 1925, with part of 1923 in Frederick, Maryland, and part of 1925 in Vernon, California, owned this filling station, which sold Shell gasoline, at the corner of Twelfth and C Streets. From left to right in this photograph are Lloyd Jones, "Grandpa" Jones, and Bobby Schang. The man standing to the right of the automobile is unidentified. (Courtesy of Sacramento Public Library, Sacramento Room Special Collections.)

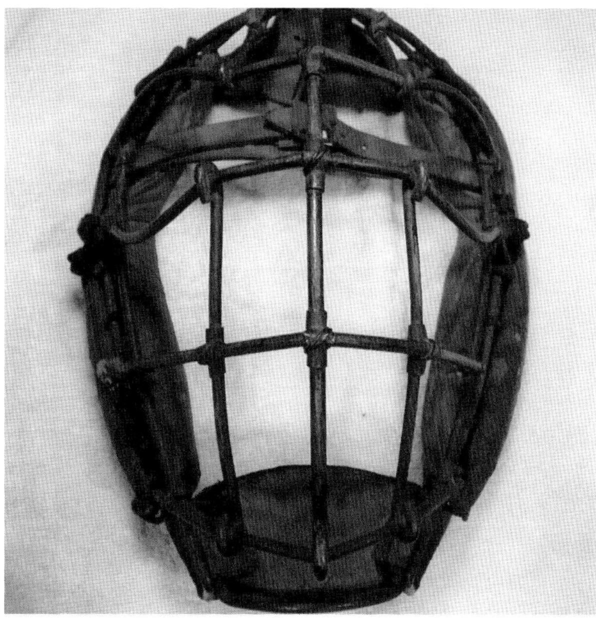

This photograph shows a c. 1900 catcher's mask. According to Chuck Rosciam of SABR (Society for American Baseball Research), the first catcher's mask was invented by Fred Thayer, a Harvard student, when he adapted a fencing mask for the Harvard Nine baseball team. The mask caught on and was widely used in amateur and professional baseball by the 1880s. (Courtesy of Alan O'Connor.)

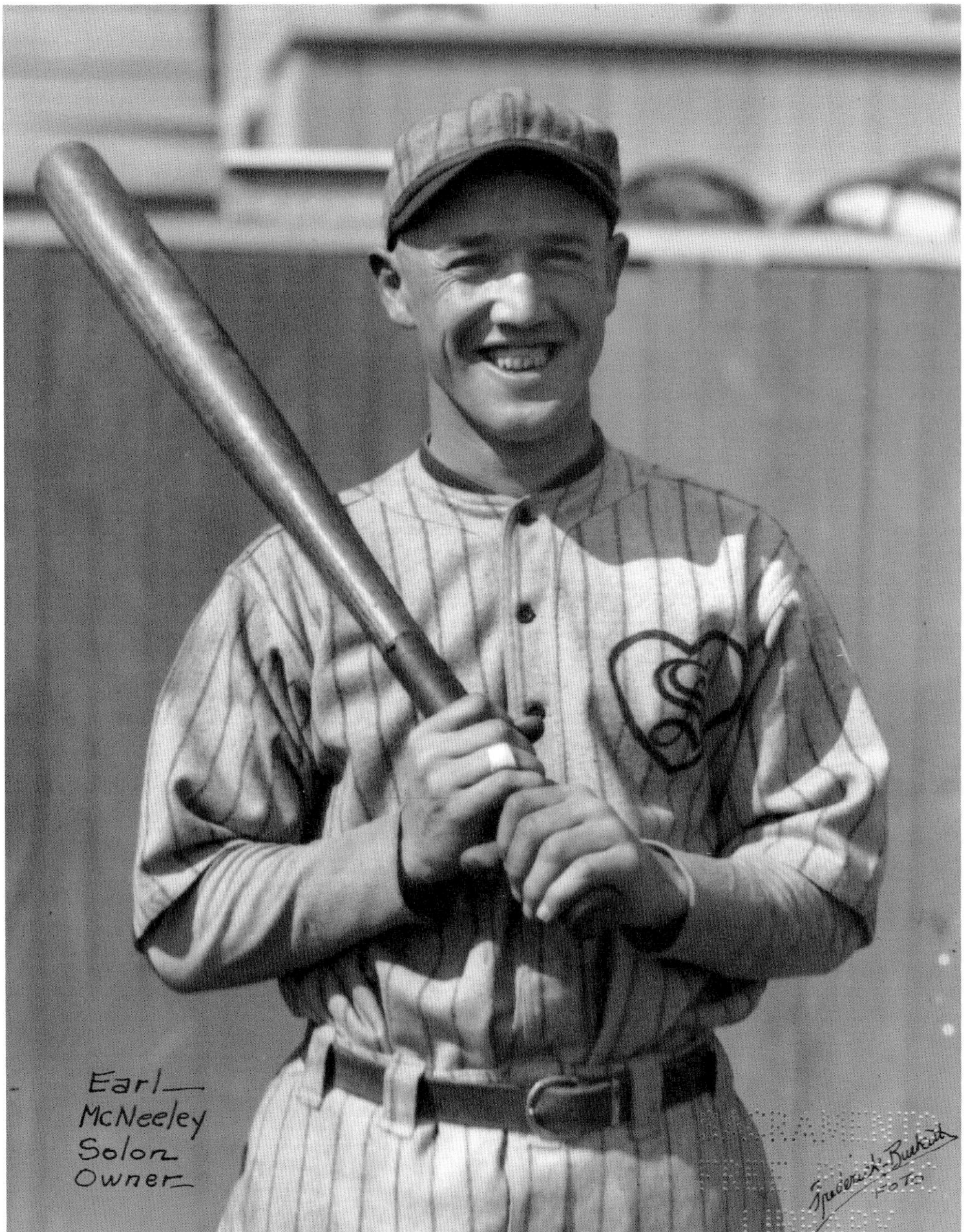

This c. 1924 photograph shows Earl McNeeley, a Sacramento native who was born in 1898 and was one of Sacramento's great ballplayers. Known for his speed, he played center field for the Washington Senators and was the hero of the 1924 World Series when he drove in the winning run of Game 7 in the 12th inning. He played for Sacramento in 1922 and part of 1924, then played in the American League for eight years. When he returned to Sacramento in 1932, he became the Sacramento Senators manager and eventually the team's owner. (Courtesy of Sacramento Public Library, Sacramento Room Special Collections.)

1920-21 HEESEMAN CLOTHIER WINTER LEAGUE BASEBALL CLUB

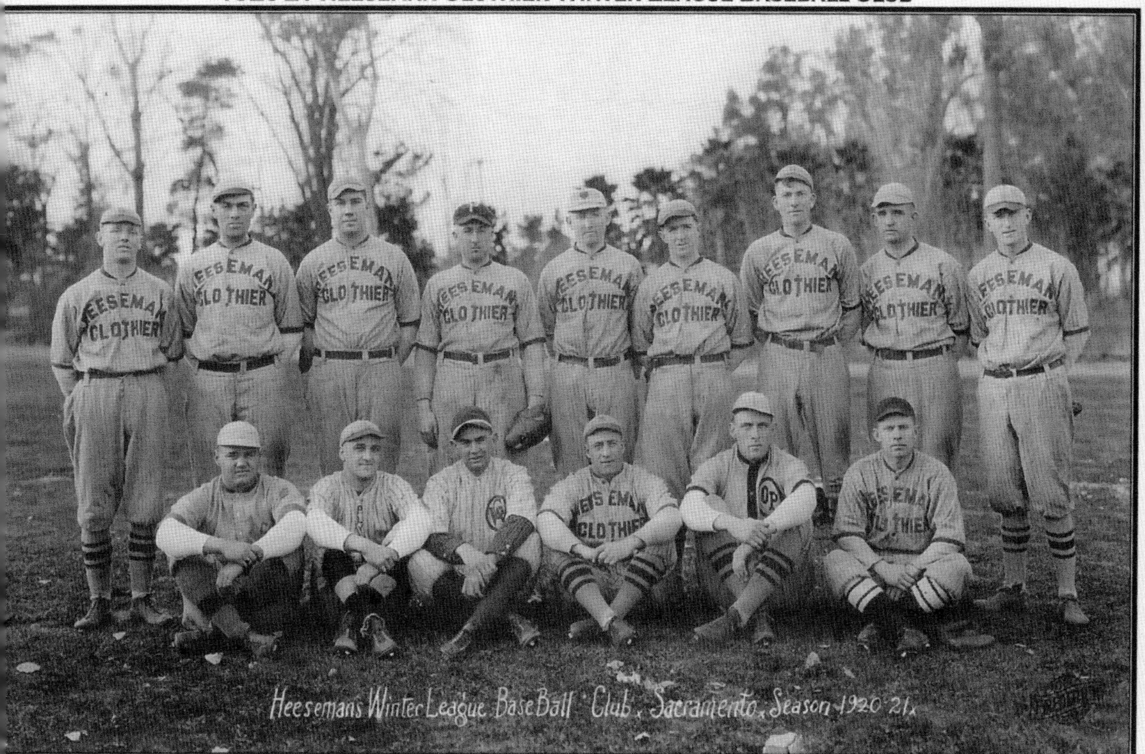

Row (L to R): Mgr. Al Hughson, Bob Nixon (LF), Guy Wright (CF), Earl Kunz (P), Arthur Luddy (3B), Tommy White (SS), George Gibson (P), Reese Peek (P), Frank Gerig (1B

Front Row (L to R): Howard Foote (P), Danny Wright (P), Bill Keenan (P), Bobby Schang (RF), Frank Tobin (C), Cliff Darringer (2B)

This photograph shows the 1921 Heeseman Clothiers Winter League team. Pictured are, from left to right, (first row) Howard Foote (pitcher), Danny Wright (pitcher), Bill Keenan (pitcher), Bobby Schang (right field), Frank Tobin (catcher), and Clif Derringer (second base); (second row) Al Hutchinson (manager), Bob Nixon (left field), Guy Wright (center field), Earl Kunz (pitcher), Arthur Luddy (third base), Tommy White (short stop), George Gibson (pitcher), Reese Peek (pitcher), and Frank Gerig (first base). (Courtesy of GoodOldSandlotDays.com.)

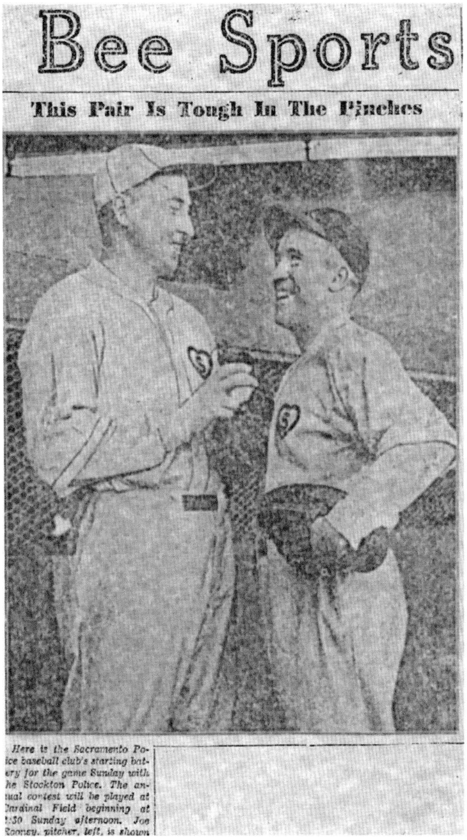

Bee Sports

This Pair Is Tough In The Pinches

Here is the Sacramento Police baseball club's starting battery for the game Sunday with the Stockton Police. The annual contest will be played at Cardinal Field beginning at :30 Sunday afternoon. Joe Rooney, pitcher, left, is shown

This photograph advertises an upcoming game between the Sacramento and Stockton police departments. Pictured at left is pitcher Joe Rooney, and at right is catcher John Lang. (Courtesy of Sacramento Police Officers Association.)

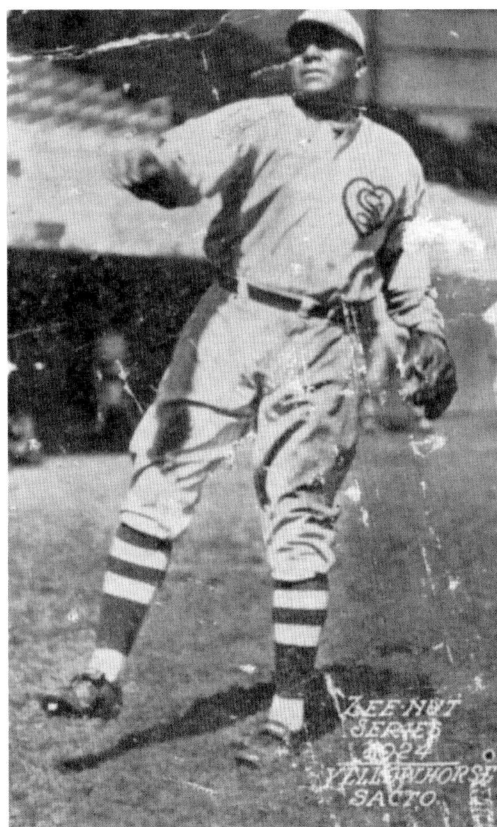

Moses J. Yellow Horse pitched for the Sacramento Senators in 1923. In 1924, he suffered an arm injury and was traded to a Fort Worth, Texas, team but returned after only a few games. He spent two more years with Sacramento before he was sold the Omaha Buffalos, where he retired. (Courtesy of Alan O'Connor.)

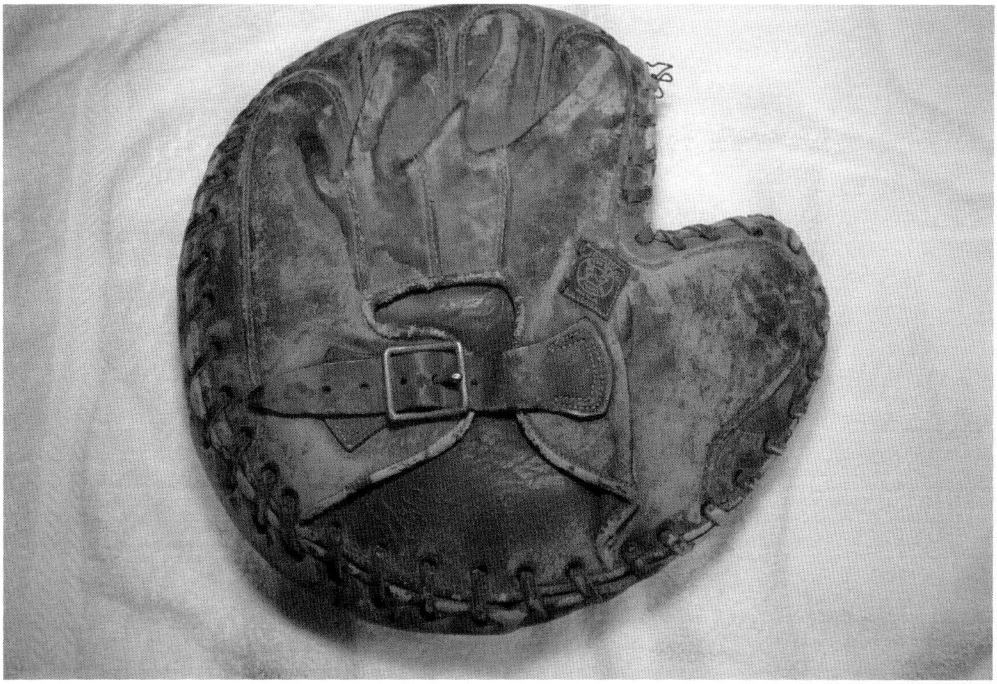

Catcher's gloves—or mitts, as they are often called—like this one, came onto the scene around 1900. Catchers prior to that used padded gloves that resembled a glove used to protect a foundry worker of the period from extreme heat, with the fingertips cut off. (Courtesy of Alan O'Connor.)

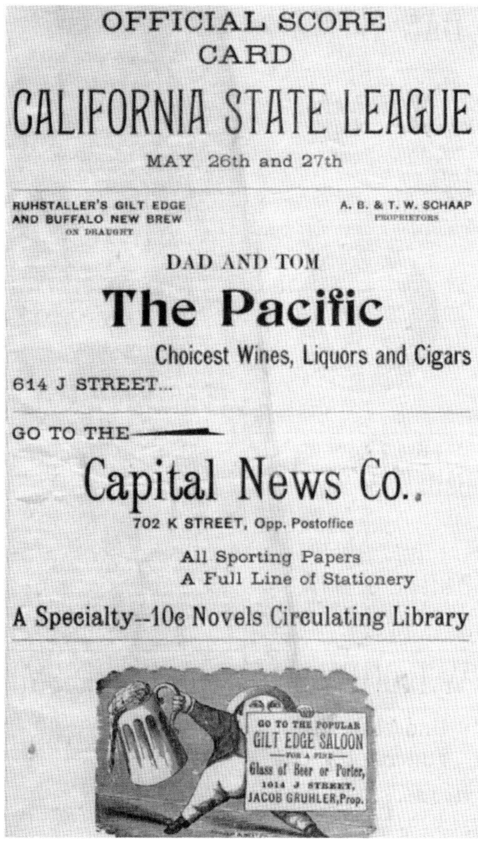

As this 1900 Gilt Edge program shows, advertising has been alive and well in baseball for more than a century. Subsequent programs to this day include advertisements for local businesses. (Courtesy of Alan O'Connor.)

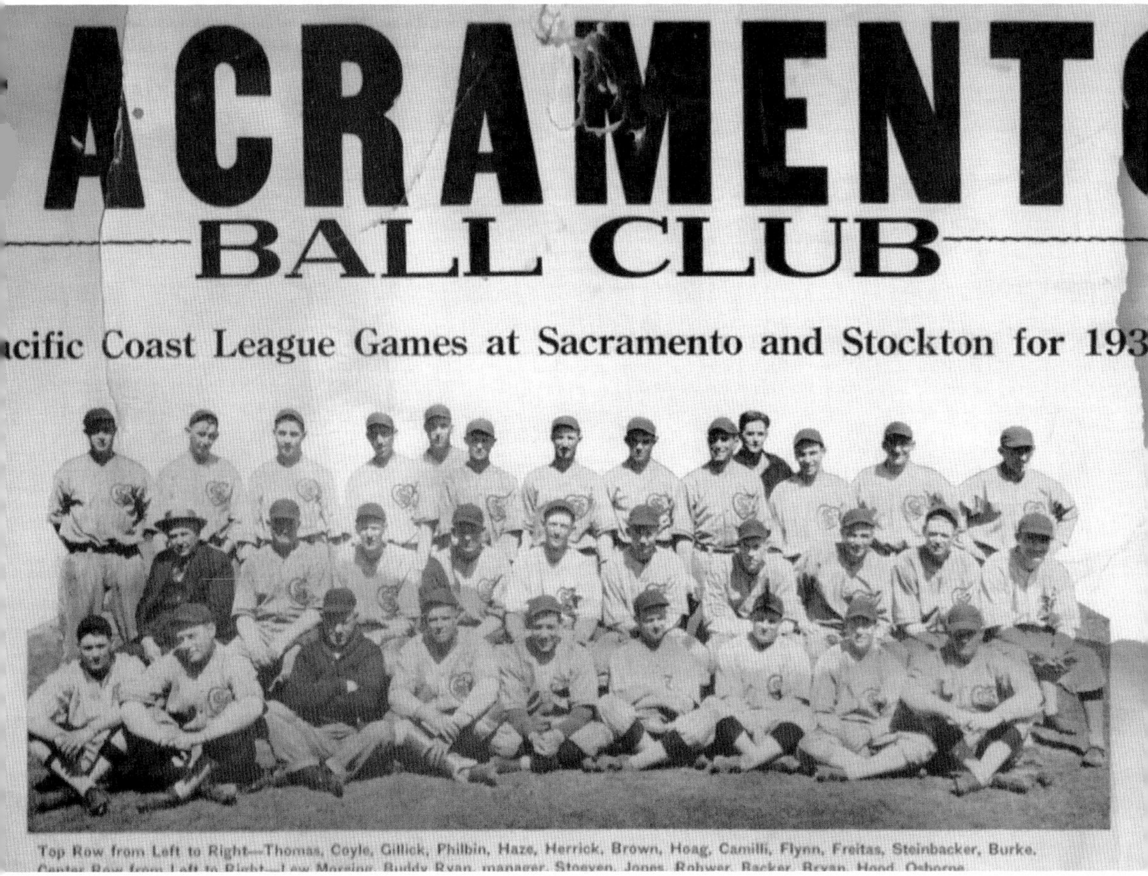

This 1930 photograph shows an advertisement for a game against Stockton. Seated at far left in the second row is Lou Moreing, who owned the team during that period and for whom the ballpark was named. (Courtesy of Alan O'Connor.)

2

Organized Fun

Little League, Softball, and City Leagues

From the late 19th century through at least the 1970s, almost every public park in Sacramento had a baseball diamond, along with makeshift diamonds on vacant lots. The diamonds were used by professional, semiprofessional, and organized amateur teams, as well as adults and youngsters simply looking to have some fun in the beautiful Sacramento climate.

In the first half of the 20th century, amateur teams were usually sponsored by merchants or, in some cases, government entities such as McClellan Air Force Base, Mather Air Force Base, the Sacramento Police Department, and many of the area's fire departments. They competed against each other most often for trophies and bragging rights. In the spring of 1976, after inquiries by local senior citizens, the city recreation department established a softball league for players over 50 years old. As a result of that action, the Sacramento Golden Seniors Softball League was established and continues to thrive.

Little League, founded in Williamsport, Pennsylvania, in 1939 as an organization for young boys, flourished in Sacramento following World War II. In the 1950s, separate leagues were organized in every part of Sacramento. Leagues included Tahoe, which played at Tahoe Park; Fruitridge, which played on Fruitridge Road, south of St. Mary's Cemetery; Land Park, which played at William Land Park; and Old Sacramento Little League, which played on M Street in East Sacramento. As Sacramento grew southward, leagues were chartered near the Sacramento Airport, known now as Sacramento Executive Airport; the Florin Road and Meadowview areas; and Parkway Estates. Leagues expand to the unincorporated areas of Carmichael, Rancho Cordova, and Arden Arcade. In 1972, Pres. Richard Nixon signed Title IX into law, giving greater opportunities to women and girls in athletics. Initially, Little League resisted the entry of girls into the program, but in 1974, following a New Jersey Supreme Court's order to allow girls into the program, Little League Softball was created. Not long after that, other softball programs began to proliferate the Sacramento region, and girls between 8 and 18 years old began playing the sport.

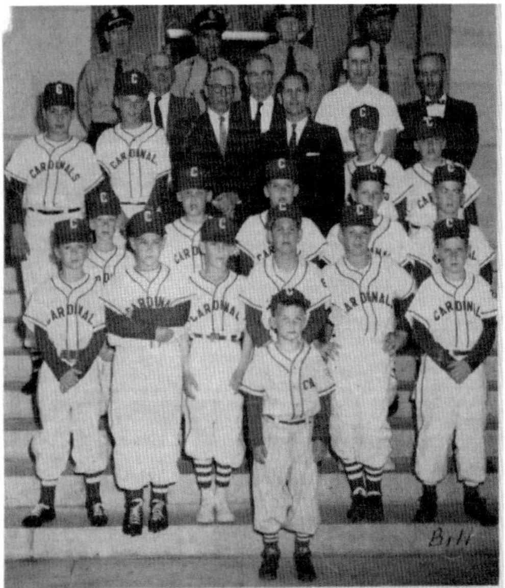

Marking the first time in local history that a law enforcement agency has sponsored a team in any sport activity, California State Police announced they will back the Tahoe Tallac Little League (58th and 8th Ave.) team, the Cardinals. They are pictured above with sponsors and friends. Top row, left to right: Officers Richard Hammond, Albert Martinez, Don Stockwell, and Manuel Gutierrez, (Team Manager). Next Row from top Chief Vincent J. Strei, Justin Childs, Chief of Buildings and Grounds, Harry Pallidini (coach of team), Mr. James Wright (president of Tahoe Tallac Little League).
Next row: Players Alex Gutierrez, Dana Pallidini, Mr. Burt Levitt (Director of Finance), Lt. Governor Glen M. Anderson, Players Creg Ahlstrom, Jack Hall.
Next row: Players Timothy Kemp, Richard Jagula, Richard Ross, David Gargen, Richard Conovan.
Next row: Edmond Wallace, Steu Ahlstrom, Rex Moss, Gerry Smith, Jimmy Nelson, Bil McPail, and the bat boy David Bernt.

This 1959 photograph shows the Tahoe Tallac Little League Cardinals on the steps of the state capitol. The team's manager, Manuel Gutierrez, a member of the California State Police, is pictured in the sixth row at right. Also pictured is California lieutenant governor Glen Anderson and several other dignitaries. (Author's collection.)

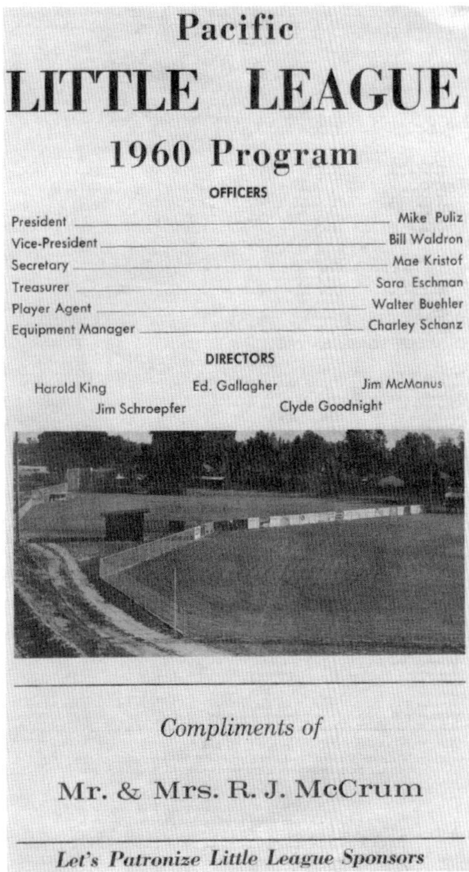

Pacific

LITTLE LEAGUE

1960 Program

OFFICERS

President	Mike Puliz
Vice-President	Bill Waldron
Secretary	Mae Kristof
Treasurer	Sara Eschman
Player Agent	Walter Buehler
Equipment Manager	Charley Schanz

DIRECTORS

Harold King, Ed. Gallagher, Jim McManus, Jim Schroepfer, Clyde Goodnight

Compliments of

Mr. & Mrs. R. J. McCrum

Let's Patronize Little League Sponsors

Pacific Little League played in the Land Park area of Sacramento beginning in 1954. This 1960 program was distributed to team members prior to the beginning of the season to denote the officials of the league and list the many businesses that sponsored the teams. In 1994, Pacific merged with Land Park Little League and then merged again with Curtis Park Little League in 2000. (Courtesy of Alan O'Connor.)

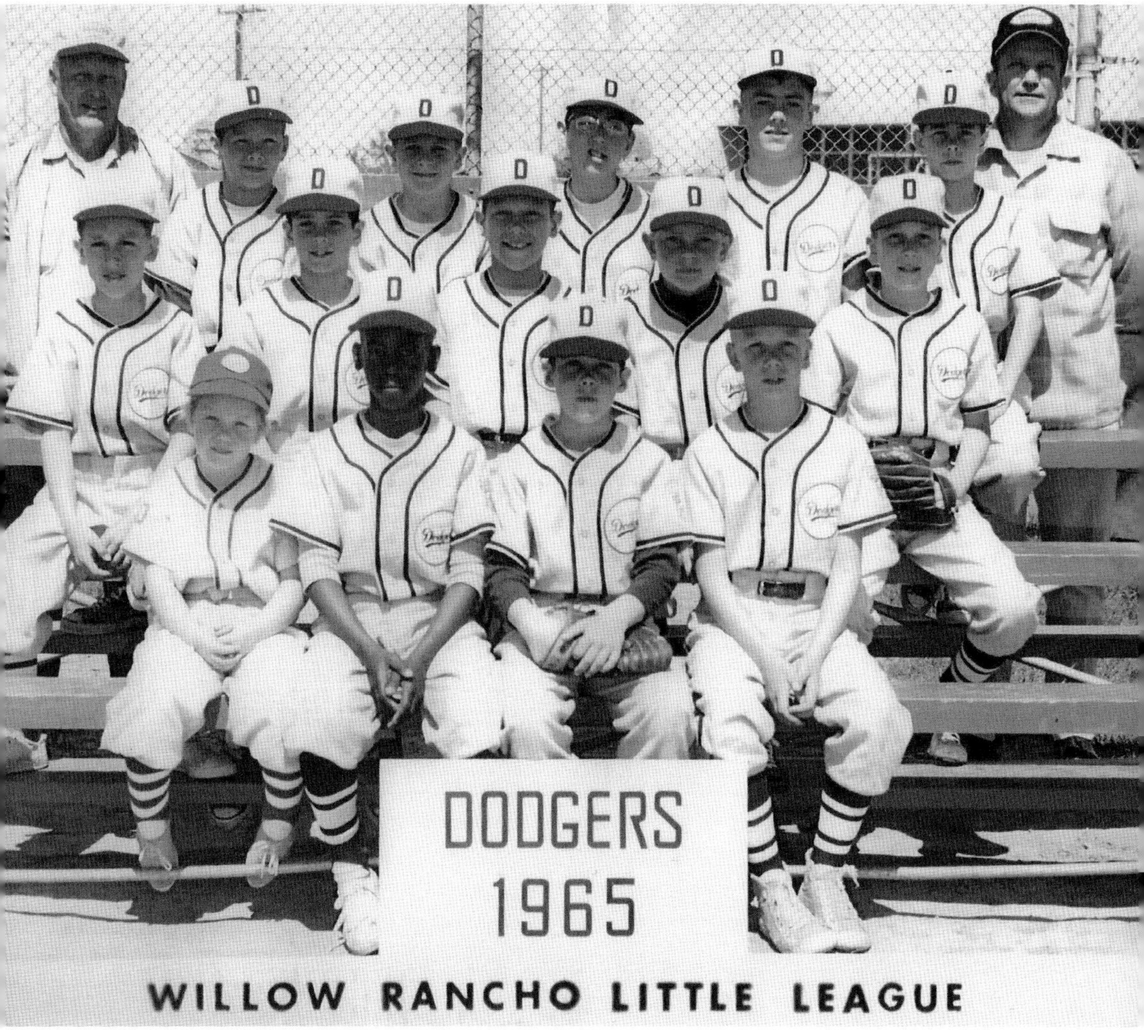

This 1965 portrait shows the Willow Ranch Little League Dodgers. Willow Rancho Little League played in the Meadow View area of Sacramento near Twenty-Fourth Street between Florin Road and Meadow View Road. (Courtesy of Kathy Coyle Brown.)

AIRPORT LITTLE LEAGUE - SENIOR DIVISION

WORLD CHAMPIONS

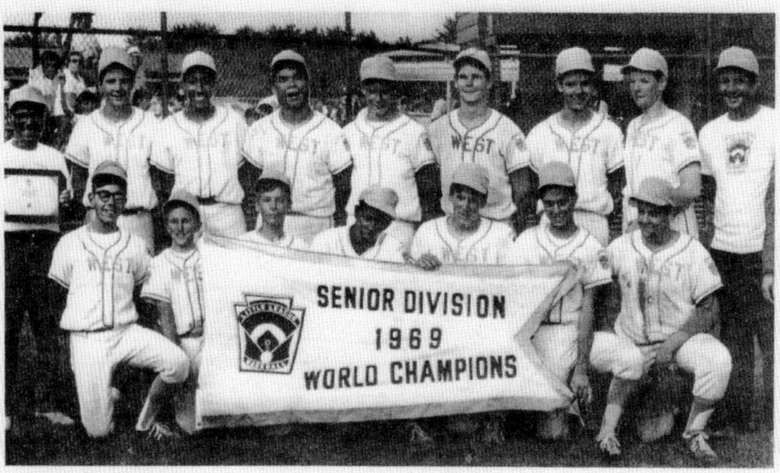

BACK ROW L-R,

ARNIE LA CASSE (MGR.), JIM PETRALLI, GREG SIMS, ZACK VENEGAS, BRAD KLOPP, DANNY MASTERS, DEAN STOTZ, BRUCE RICHARDS, GENE PETRALLI (COACH)

FRONT ROW L-R

PAT ROONEY, TOM WESTLAKE, TERRY SHARP, BOB BUMPERS, RANDY BRUNS, ROCKY LA CASSE, GLEN LEWIS

SCORE	TEAM	PLACE	DATE
18-0	LEMON HILL	SACRAMENTO	7/15
21-4	WILLOW RANCH	SACRAMENTO	7/16
10-0	TAHOE-COLONIAL	SACRAMENTO	7/19
6-0	SEBASTOPOL-L. MOLINA	EAST SACRAMENTO	7/24
1-0	NORTH HIGHLANDS	EAST SACRAMENTO	7/26
1-0	ROSEVILLE	SACRAMENTO	8/1
6-1	CUPERTINO	SACRAMENTO	8/2
2-1	SAN-VAL OF NORTH HOLLYWOOD	SANTA CLARA	8/6
4-1	CAMELBACK OF PHOENIX	SANTA CLARA	8/7
2-1	SAN-VAL OF NORTH HOLLYWOOD	SAN JOSE	8/9
12-2	DE MOINES, IOWA	GARY, IND.	8/12
8-4	LONG ISLAND, N.Y.	GARY, IND.	8/13
5-4	GARY, IND.	GARY, IND.	8/14
9-1	GARY, IND.	GARY, IND.	8/16

The senior division of Little League Baseball is for boys and girls 13 to 16 years old; however, in 1969, it was only available to boys. In 1974, the league rules were revised to allow participation by girls when Little League incorporated softball and senior softball programs. Unlike the 9 to 12 year olds who play on diamonds with 60-foot bases, senior division players use a conventional field with 90-foot bases and pitching distance of 60 feet, 6 inches. The Airport Little League team beat 18 local, regional, and national teams to capture the championship. This photograph shows the 1969 Airport Little League Seniors proudly displaying the Little League World Series championship banner they won in Williamsport, Pennsylvania. Pictured from left to right are (first row) Pat Rooney, Tom Westlake, Terry Sharp, Bob Bumpers, Randy Burns, Rocky LaCasse, and Glen Lewis; (second row) Arnie LaCasse (manager), Jim Petralli, Greg Sims, Zack Veneers, Brad Klopp, Danny Masters, Dean Stotz, Bruce Richards, and Gene Petralli (coach). (Courtesy of Brad Klopp.)

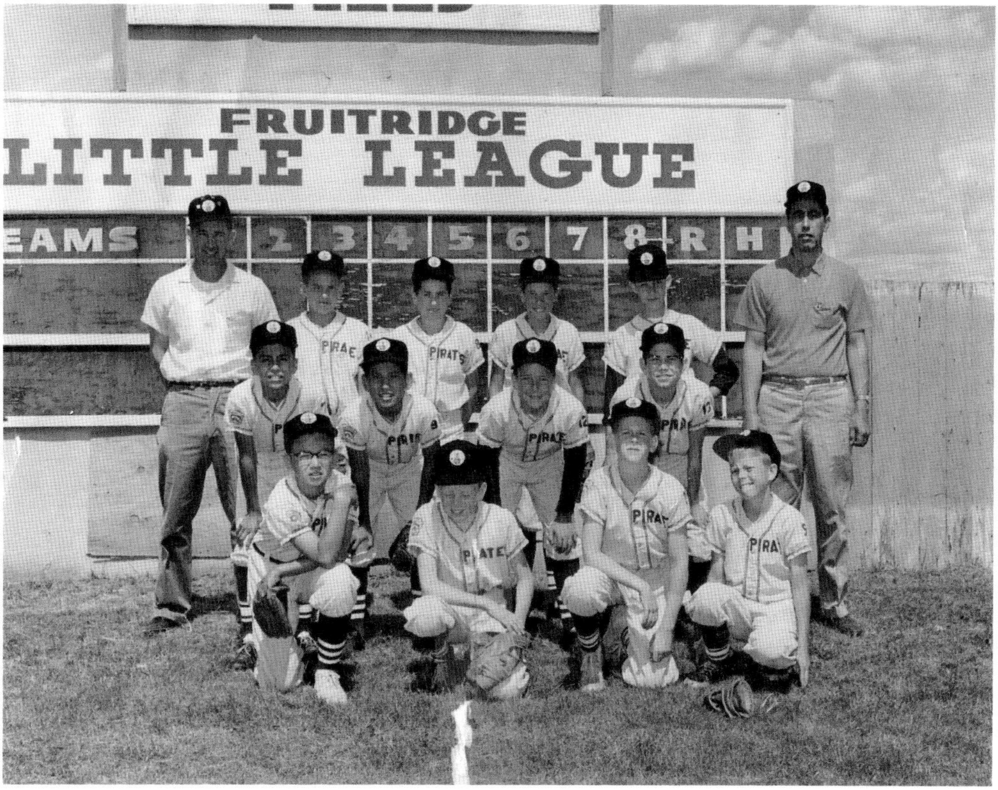

This c. 1960 photograph shows the Fruitridge Little League Pirates. (Courtesy of John "Ric" Cabrera.)

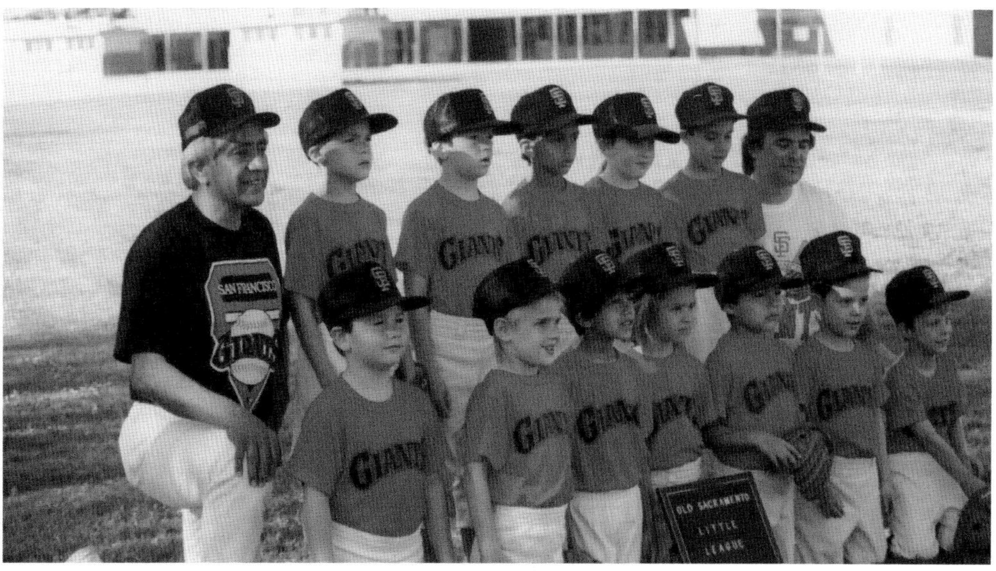

The Old Sacramento Little League Giants are pictured here in May 1989. The Old Sacramento Little League played on M Street between Fifty-Eighth and Sixtieth Streets adjacent to St. Mary's Elementary School. (Courtesy of Joan Pane.)

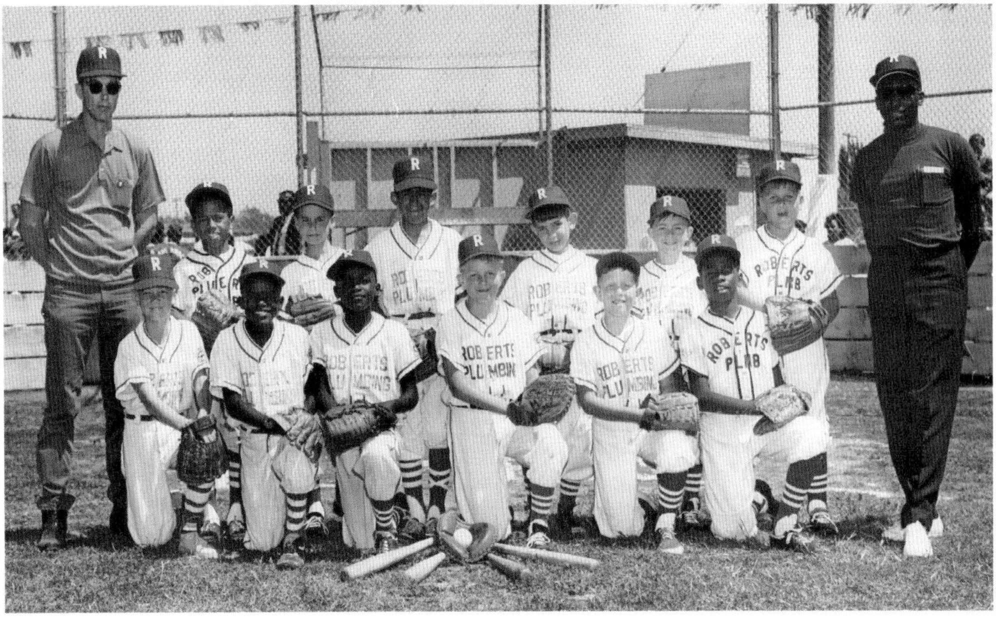

This c. 1963 photograph shows the Oakridge Little League, which played in the southeast area of Sacramento. The league filed for incorporation on May 4, 1954, but is no longer active. (Courtesy of Sacramento Public Library, Sacramento Room Special Collections.)

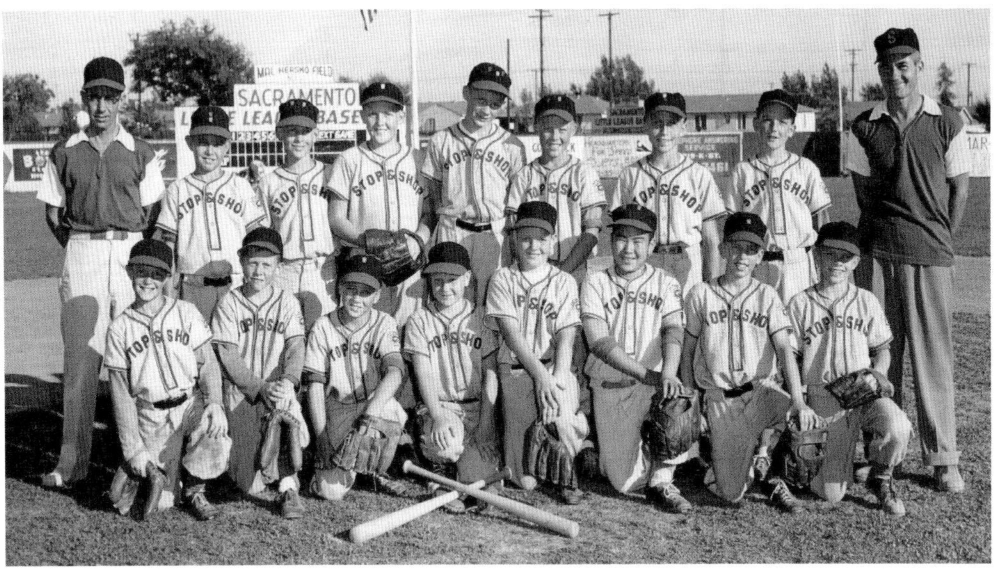

On June 6, 1939, the first ever Little League game was played in Williamsport, Pennsylvania. In the early 1950s, Little League expanded to the rest of the United States, and Sacramento jumped on board. Pictured here is a 1956 Sacramento Little League team sponsored by Stop and Shop Markets. The league played at Malcom Hersko Field, located behind the Sacramento Children's Home on Sutterville Road and named for Malcom R. Hersko, the Sacramento Little League president who died in 1955 at age 26. (Courtesy of Sacramento Public Library, Sacramento Room Special Collections.)

Pictured are the hat pins given to boys when they played Little League and Pony League. Typically, the member would receive the pin at the conclusion of the last game or at a team party, demonstrating that he played the entire season. (Courtesy of John "Ric" Cabrera.)

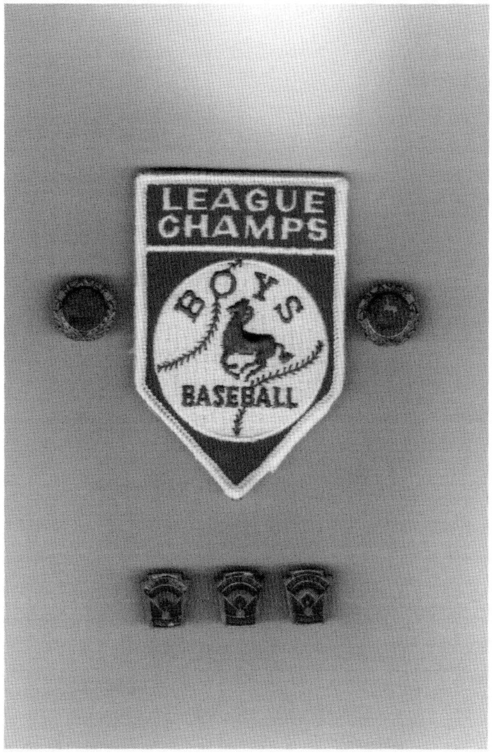

This Southeastern Pony League photograph shows, from left to right, (first row) David Maroni, Steve Broderick, ? Vasquez, unidentified, Dennis Galvon, and two unidentified; (second row) Joe Vasquez (manager), unidentified, Danny Miller, two unidentified, John Cabrera, and unidentified. (Courtesy of John "Ric" Cabrera.)

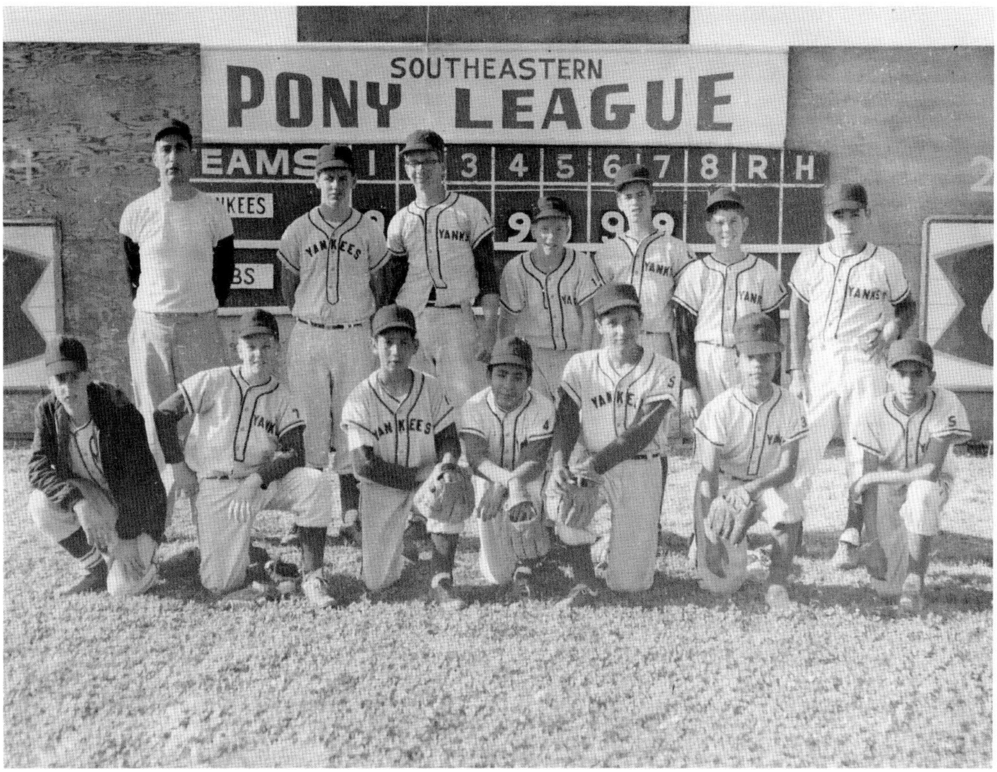

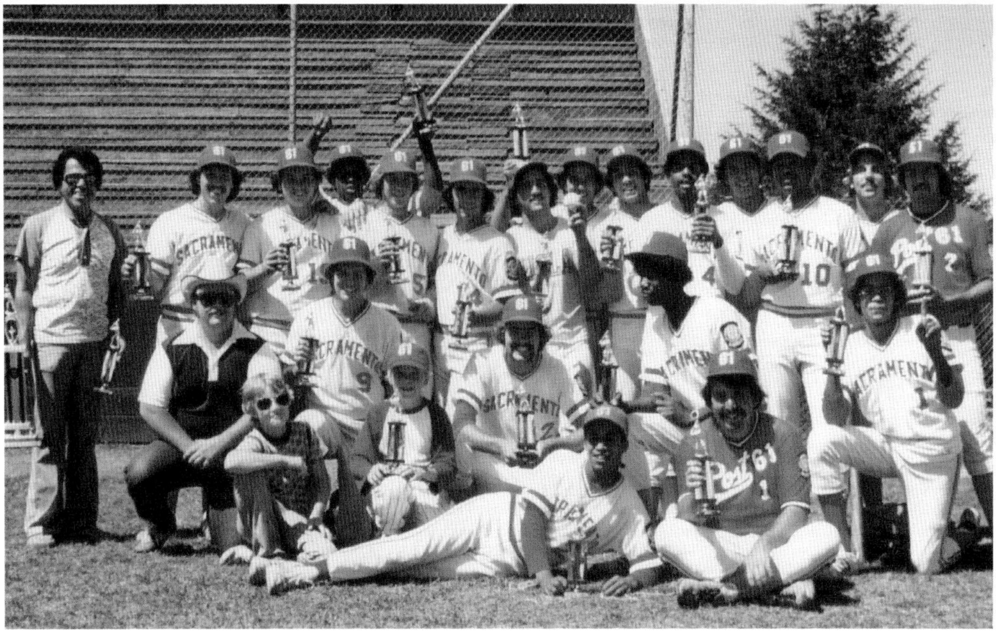

This c. 1970 photograph of American Legion Post 61 was taken after what was probably a regional or state championship. Unfortunately, the tournament and the players, other than Orlando Blackwell, who was drafted by the New York Yankees and is lying in the front of the team, could not be identified. (Courtesy of Keith Davila.)

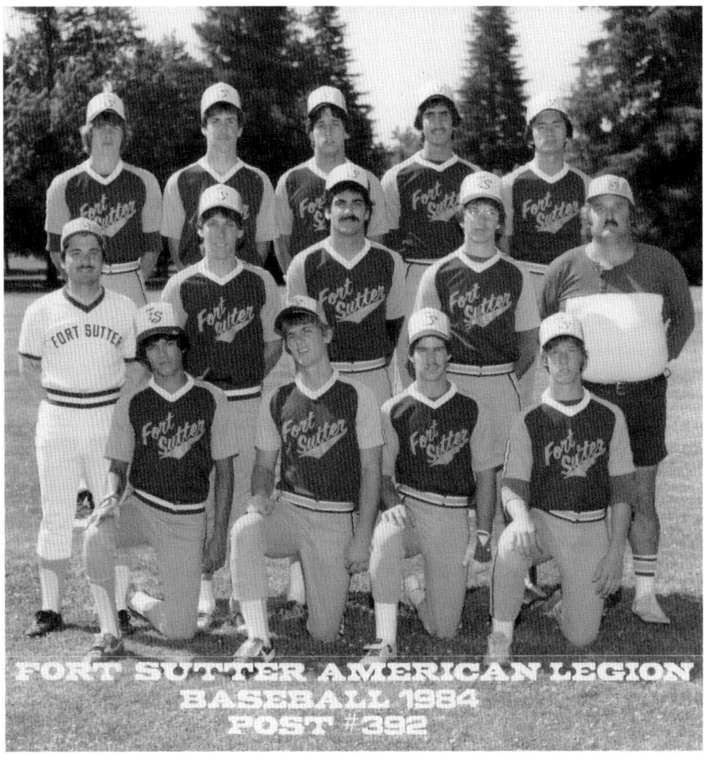

The 1984 Fort Sutter American Legion team included, from left to right, (first row) unidentified, Greg Umfleet, Todd Martin, and Craig Gruber; (second row) an unidentified coach, Ray Riolo, two unidentified, and coach Steve Hammer; (third row) Brian Roberts, Bradd Newton, unidentified, Clark Viegas, and unidentified. (Courtesy of Marion and Gloria Newton.)

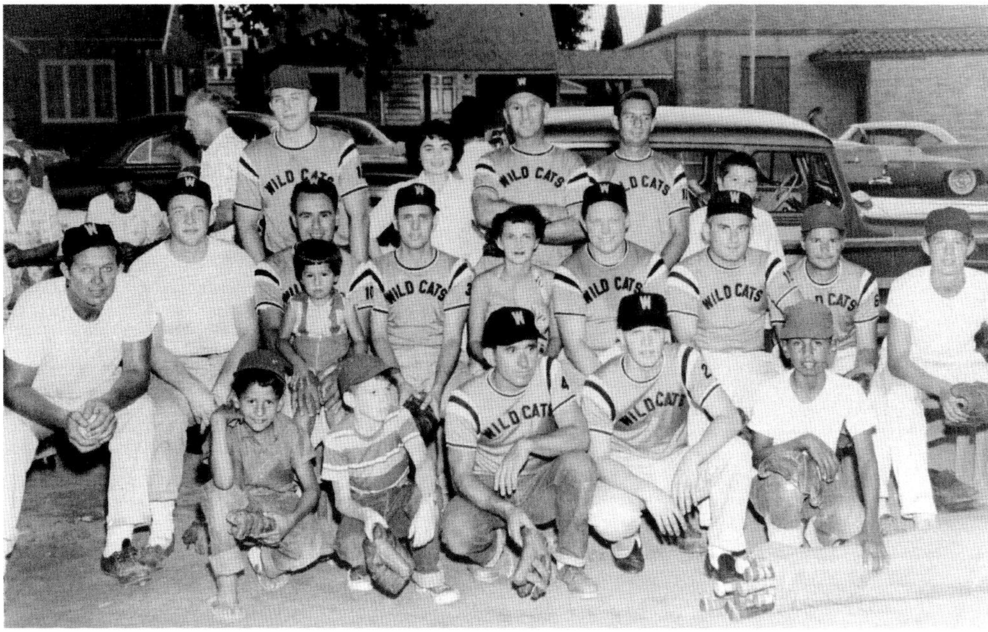

This c. 1959 photograph shows the Wildcats, a typical recreational team prevalent in the 1950s and 1960s. The team probably played in a city parks and recreation league. (Courtesy of Juanita Evans and Bobby Ramirez.)

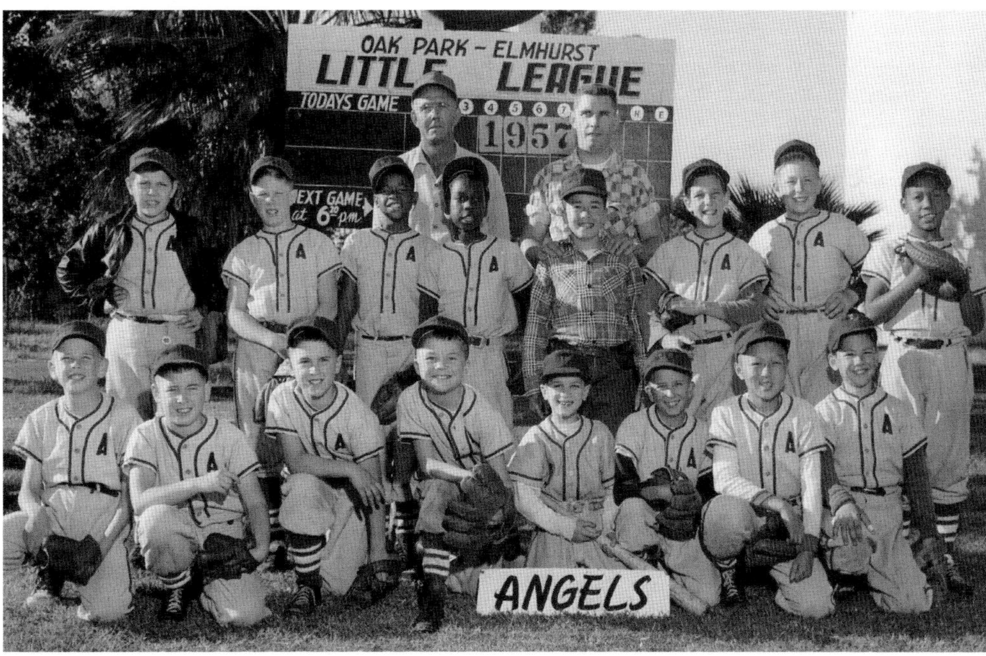

The Oak Park-Elmhurst Little League Angels posed for this team portrait in 1957. With the post–World War II wave of youth baseball excitement, the league received its charter in 1953. The many smiling faces in this photograph are indicative that the players were having a good time. (Courtesy of Sacramento Public Library, Sacramento Room Special Collections.)

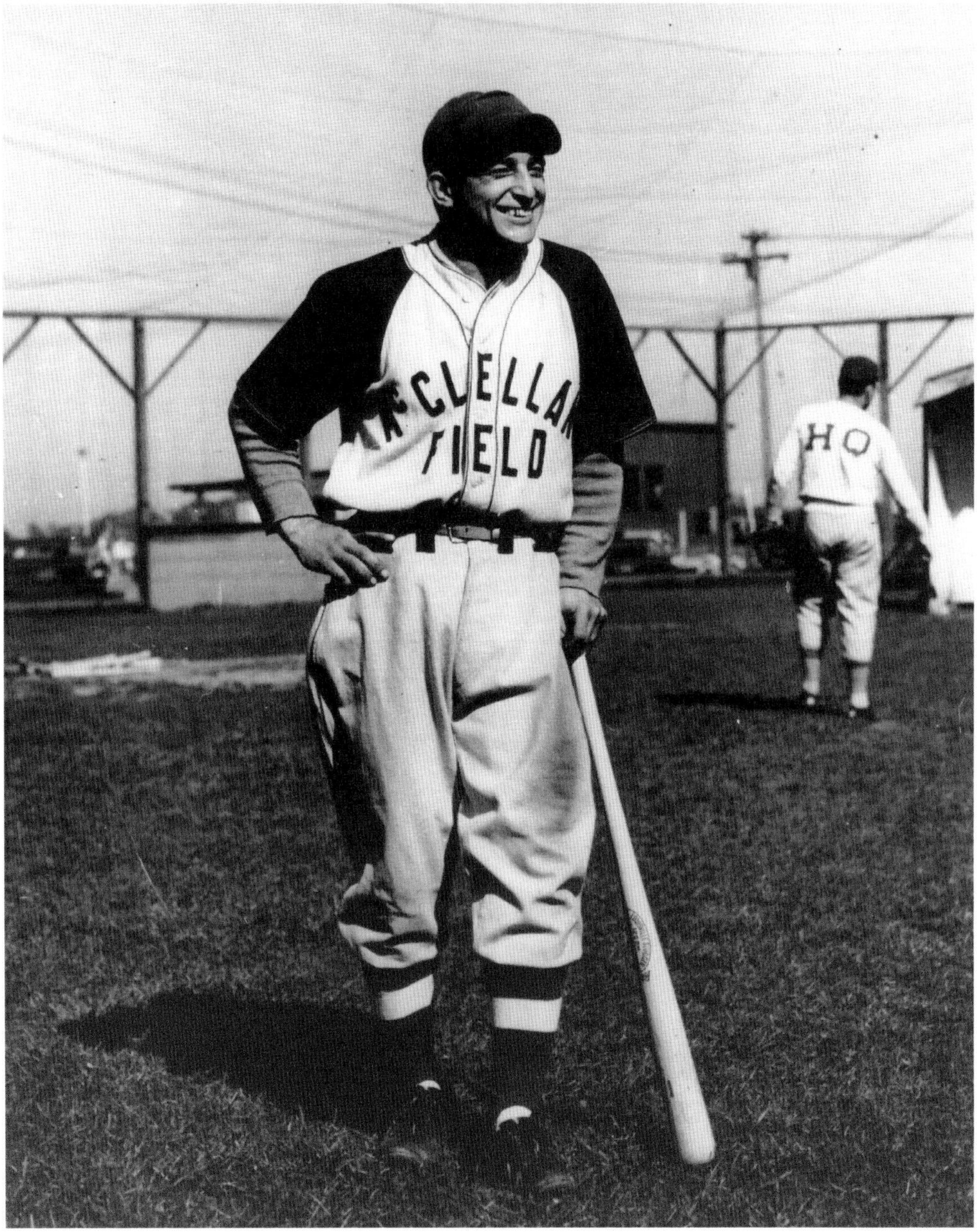

This July 18, 1943, photograph shows McClellan baseball player Al Androcich leaning on a baseball bat. The Sacramento team faced Fresno's Hammer Field US Army Air Corps on this date and the day prior, splitting the contests 11-5 and 5-2, respectively, at Fresno. Both squads were members of the Central California Servicemen's League, a league composed of five teams that included Camp Kohler in Sacramento, Hammer Field in Fresno, Mather Field in Rancho Cordova (Sacramento Solon Joe Marty was a player/manager for the Mather Field team in 1942), McClellan Field in Sacramento, and the Merced Field in Merced. (Courtesy of Sacramento Public Library, Sacramento Room Special Collections.)

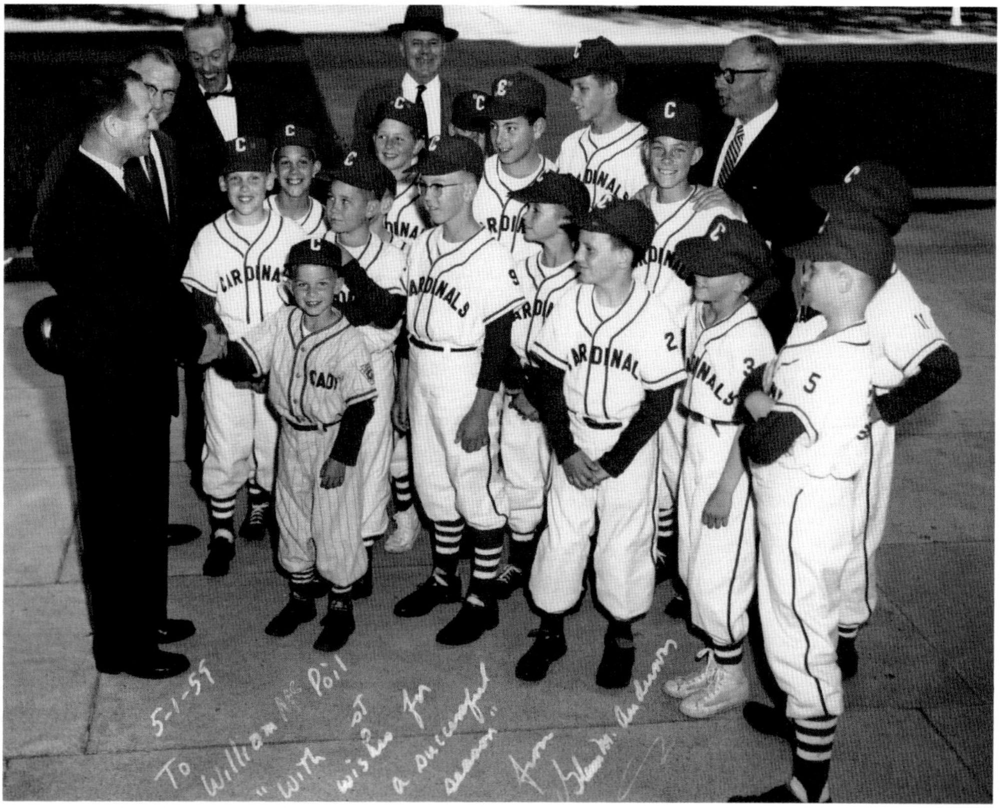

This May 1, 1959, photograph shows the Tahoe Park Little League Cardinals. The gentleman at left shaking hands with the batboy is Glen Anderson, California's lieutenant governor. The team was sponsored by the California State Police Association. In 1995, the California State Police merged with the California Highway Patrol, eliminating the state police, which at the time was the oldest law enforcement agency in California. (Author's collection.)

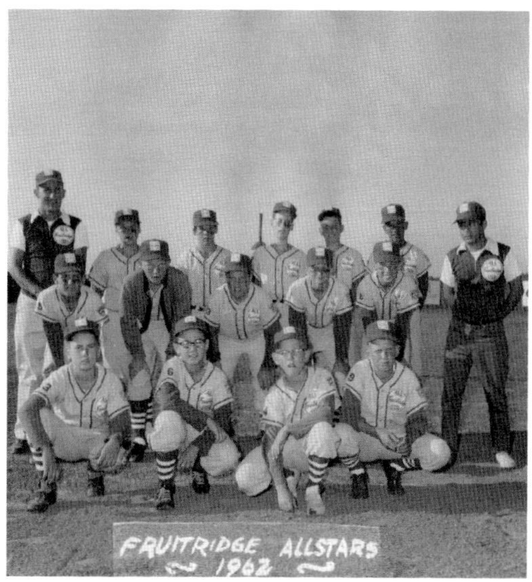

This photograph shows the 1962 Fruitridge Little League All-Stars. Pictured from left to right are (first row) Doug Clark, Joe Ybarra, Steve Valine, and Steven Scherer; (second row) Grant Lotto, Bobby Borsch, Bryan Bush, Bobby Daniels, and Timmy Harper; (third row) Mel Sinkevich Sr. (coach), Randy Bryan, Joe DeLong, David Maroni, Danny Mervin, Tony Ramirez, and Lou Martinez (manager). Borsch later played baseball at Hiram Johnson High School and Sacramento City College and went on to a successful major-league baseball career with the St. Louis Cardinals and Houston Astros. (Courtesy of Greg Dow.)

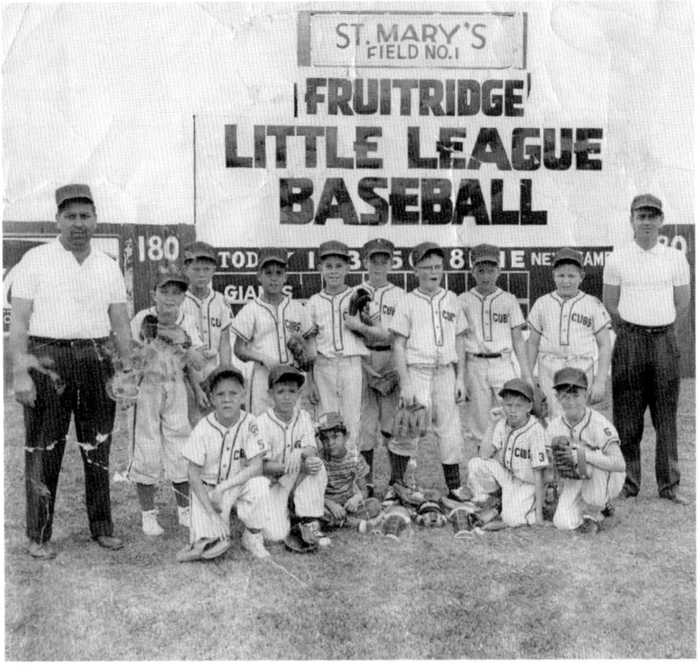

This c. 1960 photograph of the Fruitridge Little League Cubs shows, from left to right, (first row) Charles Monday, Melvin Horst, Gilbert Cabrera (batboy), Terry Monday, and unidentified; (second row) Jesse Cabrera (manager), two unidentified, Douglas Loamier, unidentified, Jesse Thomas Cabrera, unidentified, Butch Whitaker, Lonnie Lundsten, unidentified, and Eddie Fisher (coach). (Courtesy of John "Ric" Cabrera.)

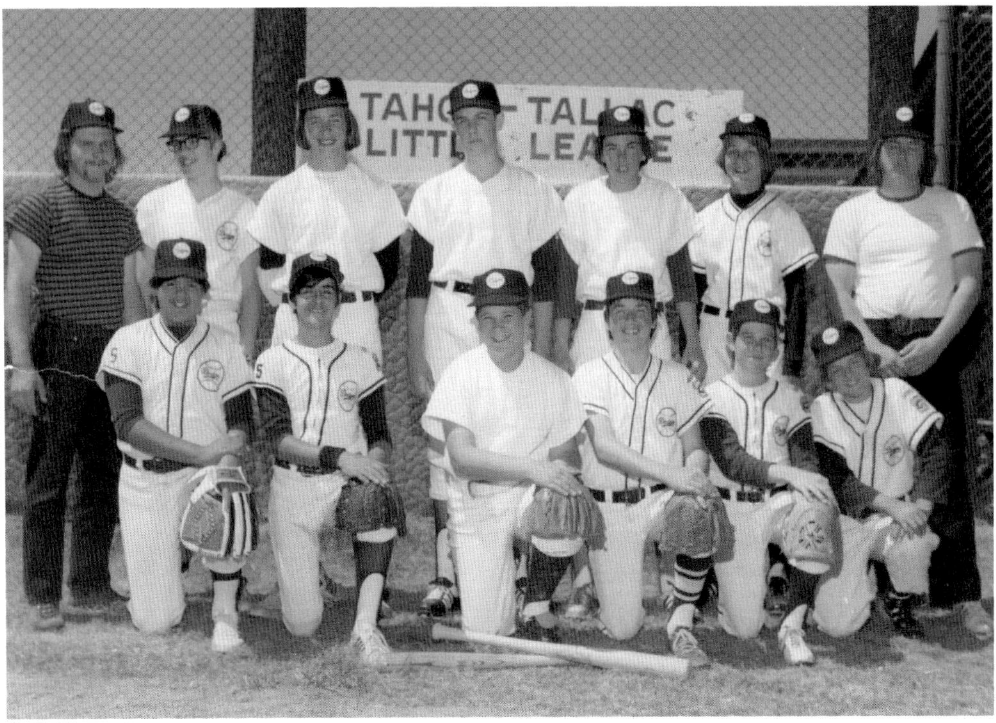

Pictured is the 1973 Tahoe-Tallac Little League Senior Division Dodgers. From left to right are (first row) Mark Martin, Dennis Viegas, Ken Bowen, Tim Snellings, Van Perrin, and Mark Horr; (second row) Bruce Synhorst (manager), Ron Ragen, Tim Lowen, Kevin Twilling, Jeff Lowen, Jeff Ford, and an unidentified coach. (Courtesy of Mark Horr Sr. and Jeff Ford.)

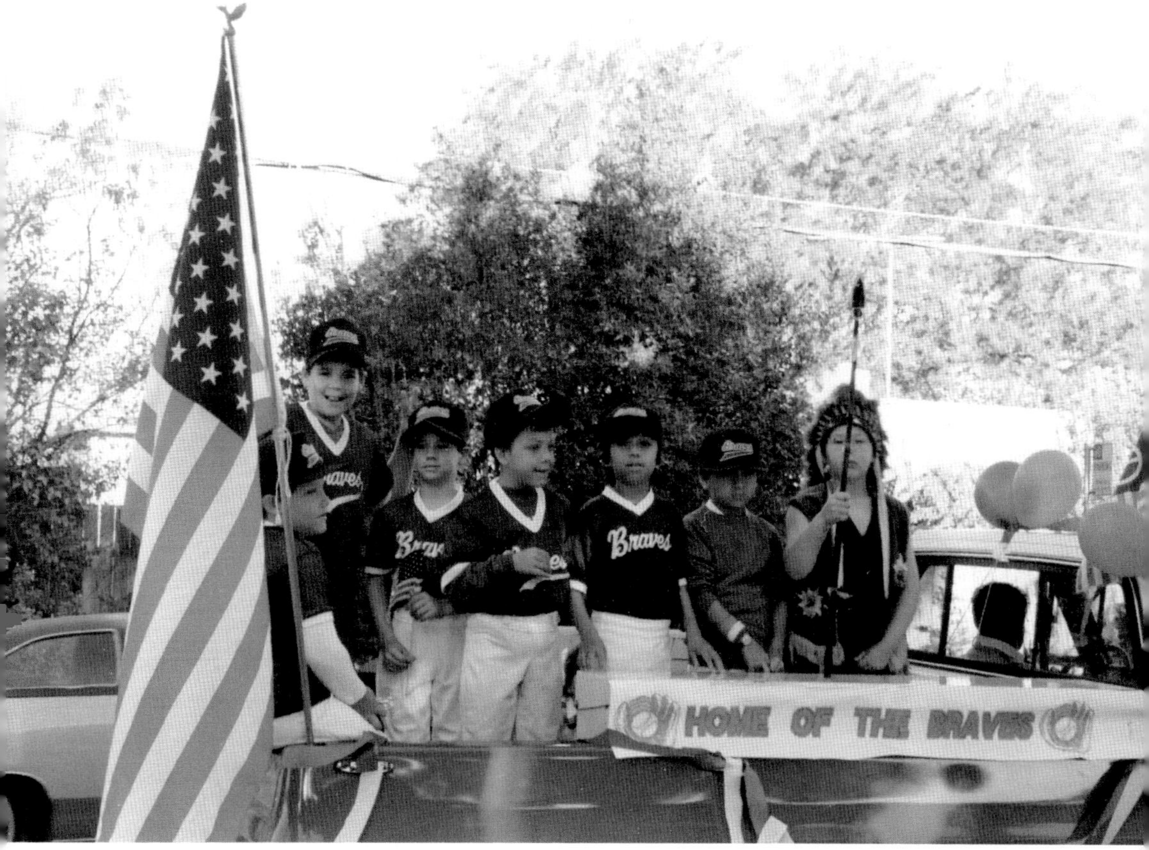

This April 1988 photograph shows seven members of the Braves in the Tahoe-Tallac Little League opening day parade. In the early days of Little League parades, the teams walked the parade route, usually several blocks. They were sometimes escorted by local police cars or fire apparatus. Later, the leagues changed to the boys riding in the back of pick-up trucks. (Courtesy of Joan Pane.)

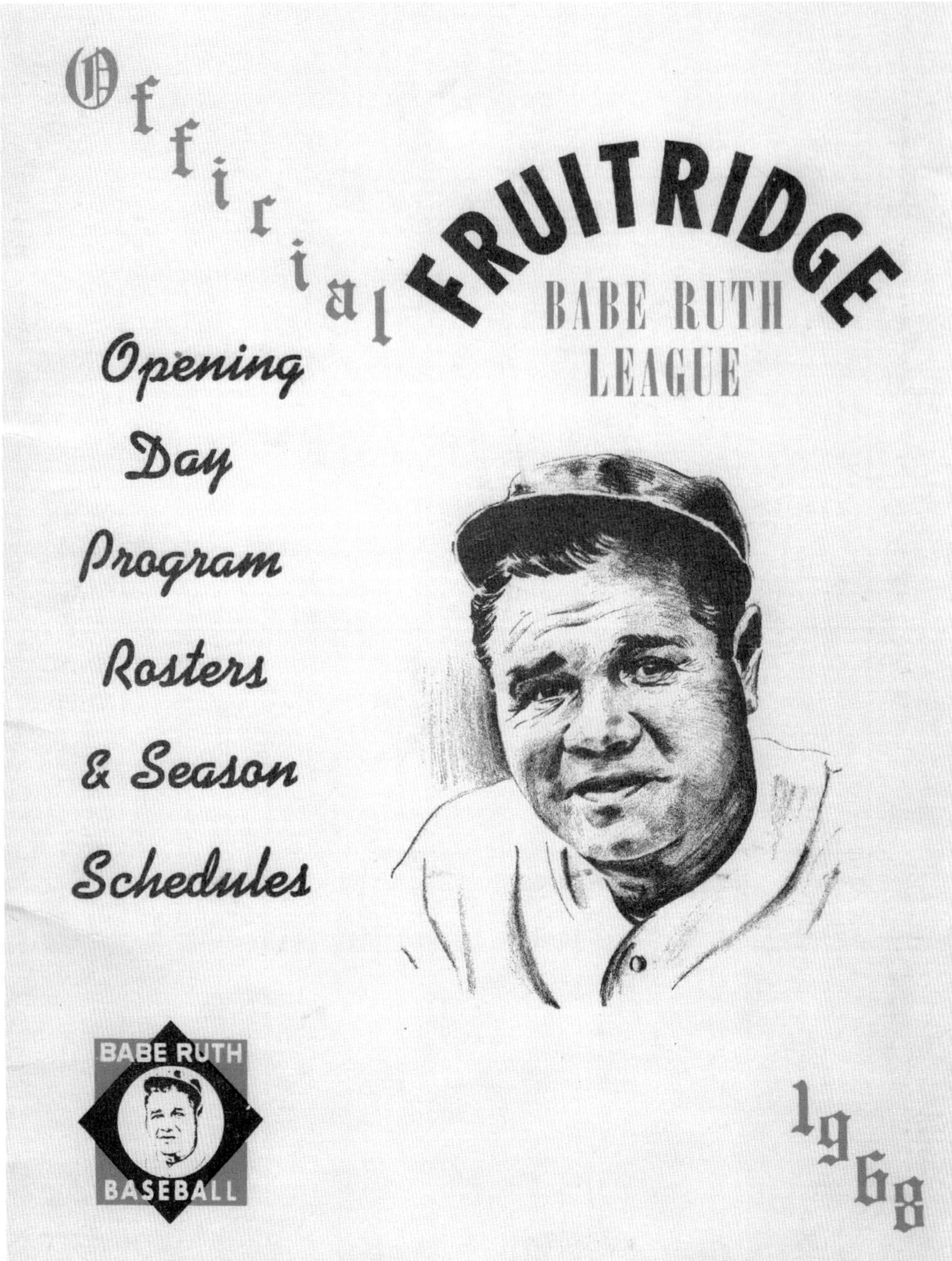

Babe Ruth Baseball was founded in Hamilton, New Jersey, in 1951 as a baseball program for boys between the ages of 13 and 15 years of age. It is currently played in all 50 states and eight other countries. Fruitridge Babe Ruth filed as a corporate entity on Tuesday, February 23, 1960, according to public records filed with California secretary of state. The league played at James Rowell Babe Ruth baseball park, located at 6485 Fruitridge Road, a location now occupied by St. Mary's Cemetery. (Courtesy of Sacramento Public Library, Sacramento Room Special Collections.)

This photograph of a Sacramento Police Department softball team dates to around 1950. The team played in one of the city recreational leagues prevalent at the time. (Courtesy of Sacramento Police Officers Association.)

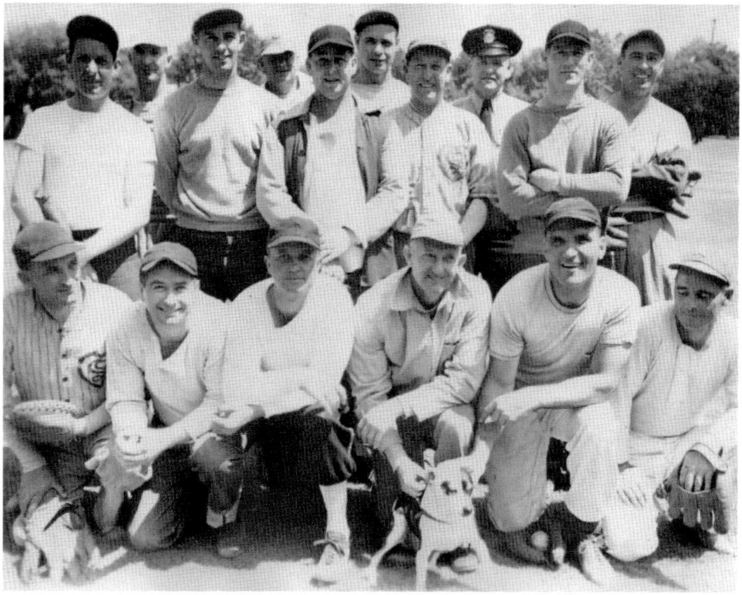

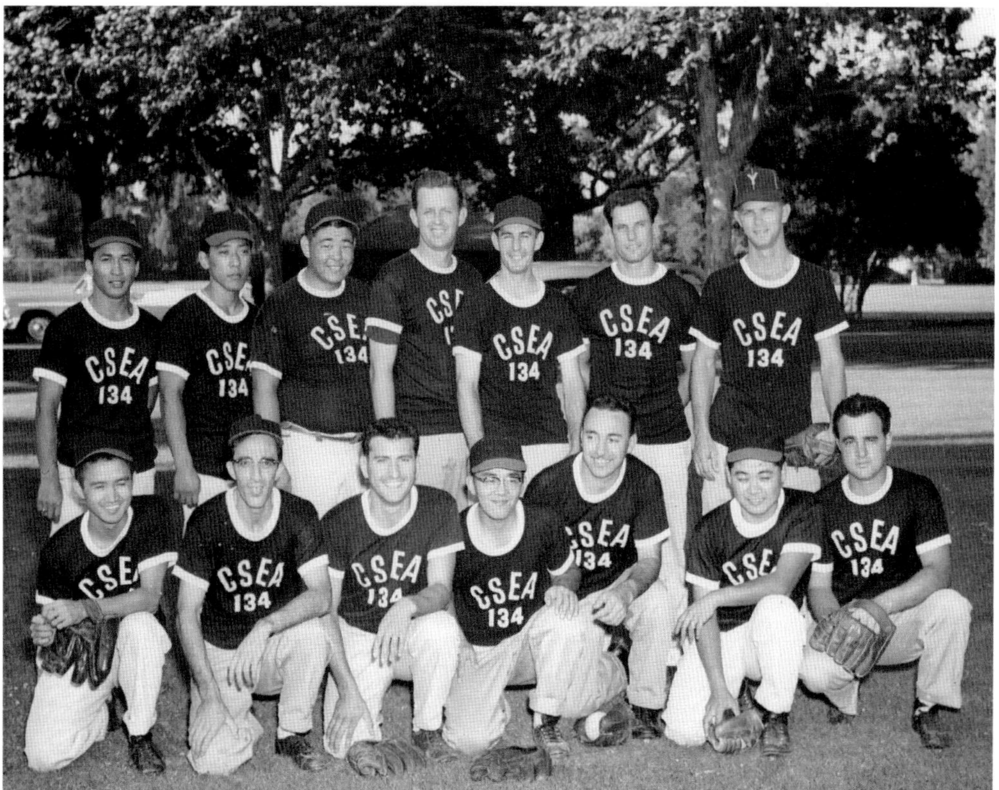

This c. 1960 photograph shows a city recreational team representing the California State Employees' Association, Chapter 134. It is made up of employees from the Department of Motor Vehicles. (Courtesy of Gayle Maita.)

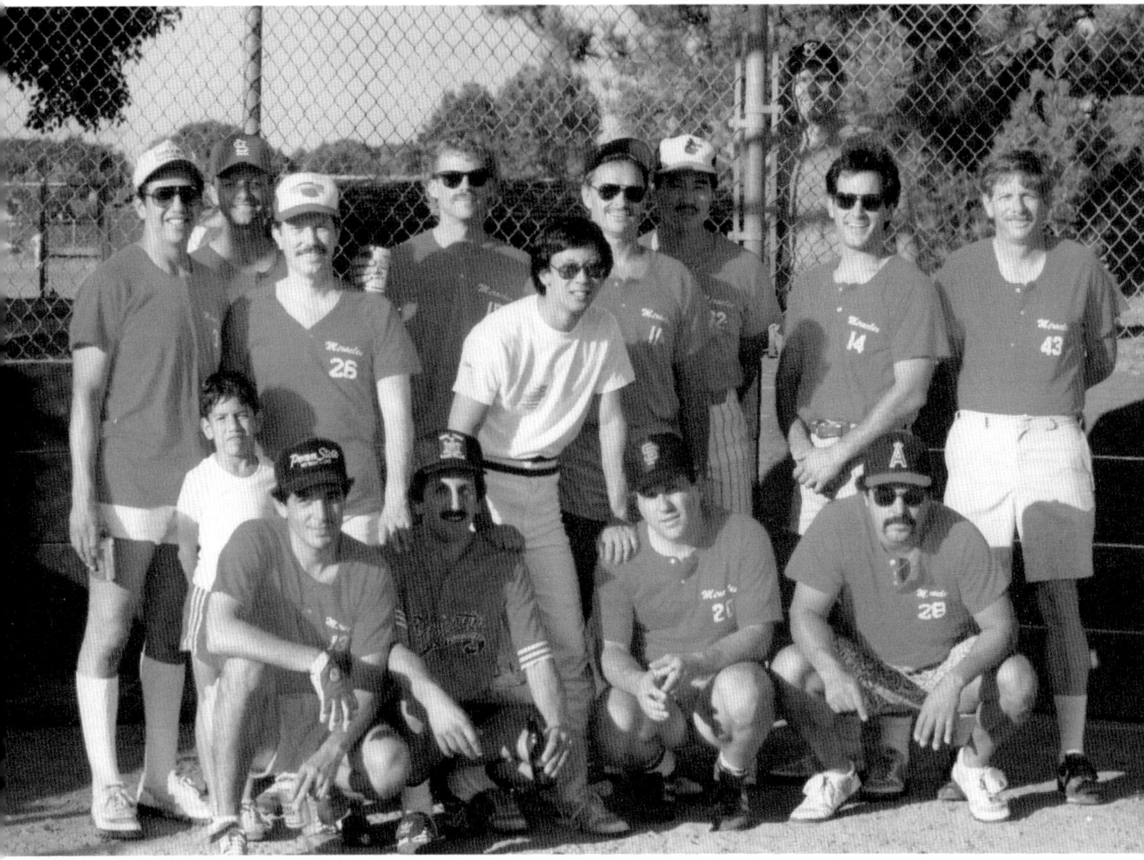

This 1985 photograph shows the Sacramento Police Department Miracles softball team. The photograph was taken following the team's win of the league championship. Pictured are, from left to right, (first row) Angel Delgadillo, Mark Habroe, Ernie Barsotti, and Ron Orich; (second row) Tony Ramirez, Tony's son Jason, John Cabrera, Darrell Fong, Mike Lopez, Pete Willover, Randy Twilling, Greg Twilling, Rich DeBorba, and Ron Mizuno. Standing behind the fence is Rich Gardella, from the losing team. (Courtesy of John "Ric" Cabrera.)

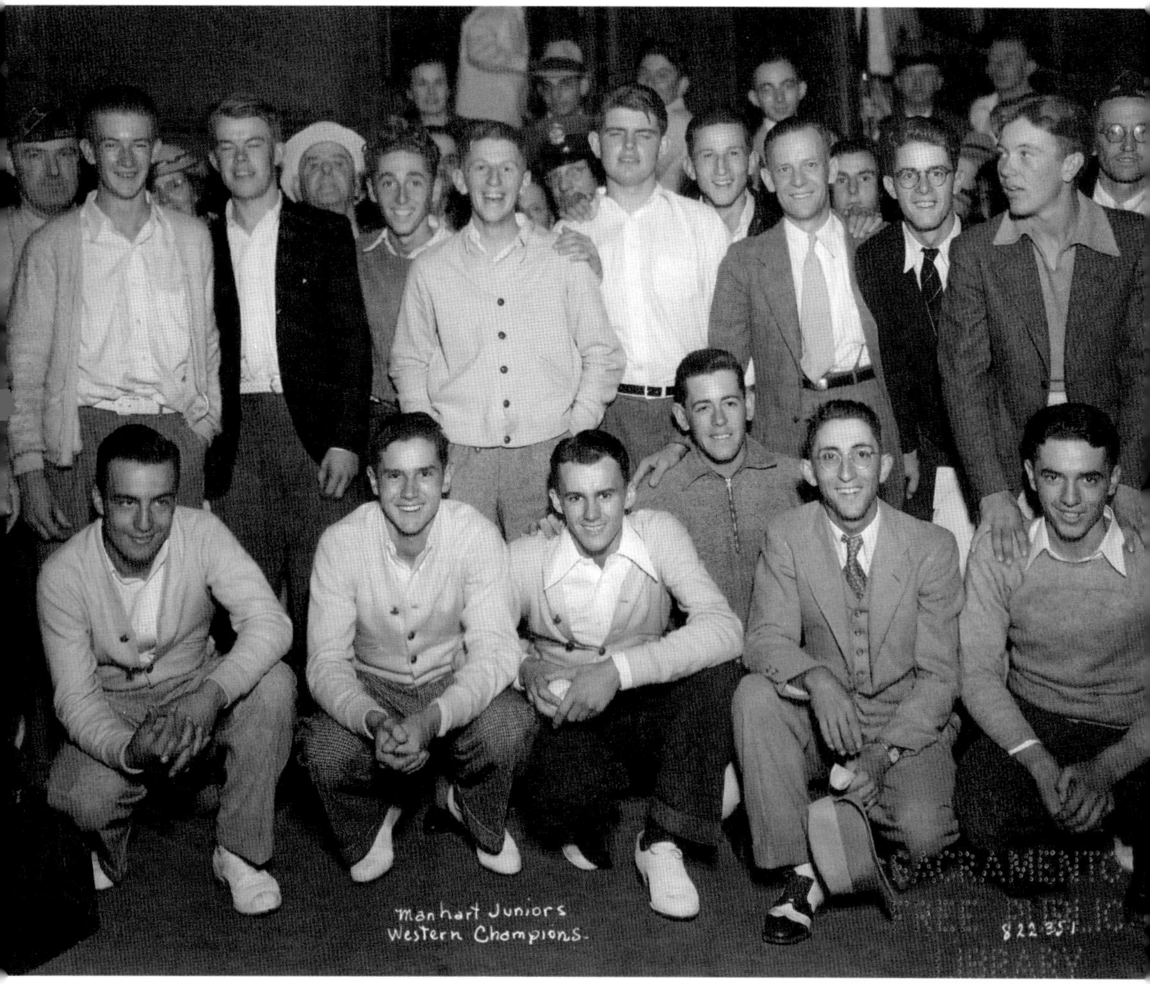

Pictured in this 1935 photograph is the George W. Manhart American Legion junior baseball team. In August, the squad captured the Western States Region championship by defeating a Tucson, Arizona, post by a score of 3-2 at the Oak Park diamond. The star of the game was Jim "Tiny" Hansen (first row, fourth from right). Hansen went on to be honored by entry into the LaSalle Club Hall of Fame in 1985. (Courtesy of Sacramento Public Library, Sacramento Room Special Collections.)

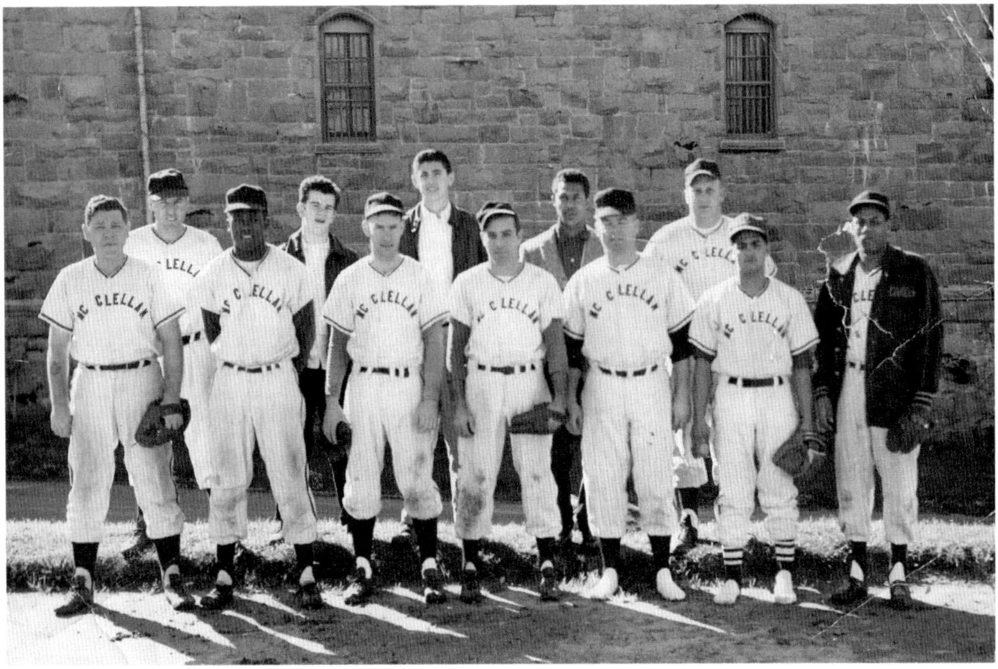

In this c. 1950 photograph of the McClellan Air Force Base team at Folsom Prison are, from left to right, (first row) unidentified, Ray Nelson, Woody ?, ? Shirk, ? Nelson, Delmer Slaughter, and Norm Blackwell; (second row) Al Fry, three unidentified non-players, two unidentified, Don Johnson, and Wally Rath. (Courtesy of Norman Blackwell Sr.)

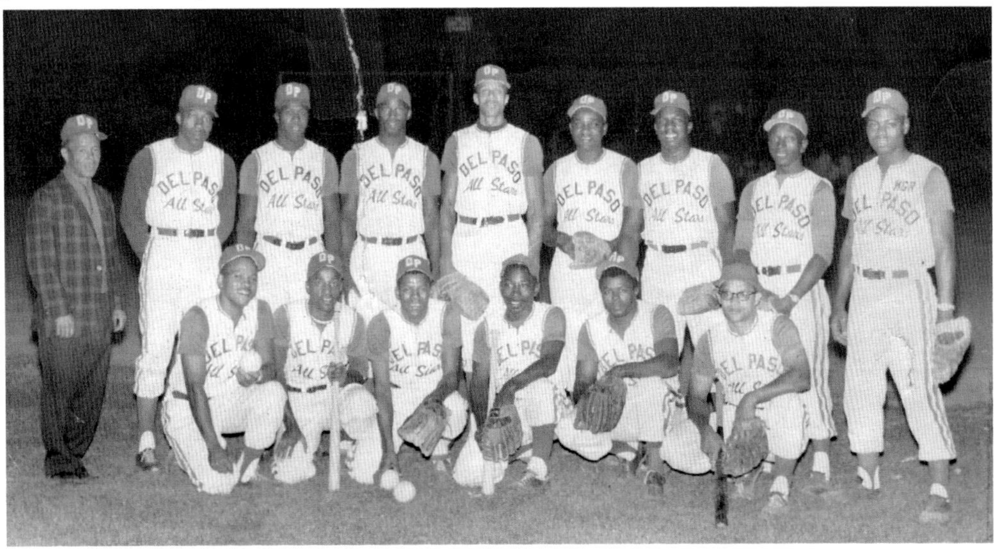

This c. 1970 photograph features the Del Paso All-Stars, a fast-pitch softball team. Pictured are, from left to right, (first row) Al Warren, unidentified, Norm Blackwell, ? Adams, Charlie Massey, and Gabe Grace; (second row) unidentified, Danny Mathews, Fred Blant, John Blackwell, unidentified, ? Core, Joe Brewer, Bob Elder, and the sponsor, only identified as Skip. (Courtesy of Norman Blackwell Sr.)

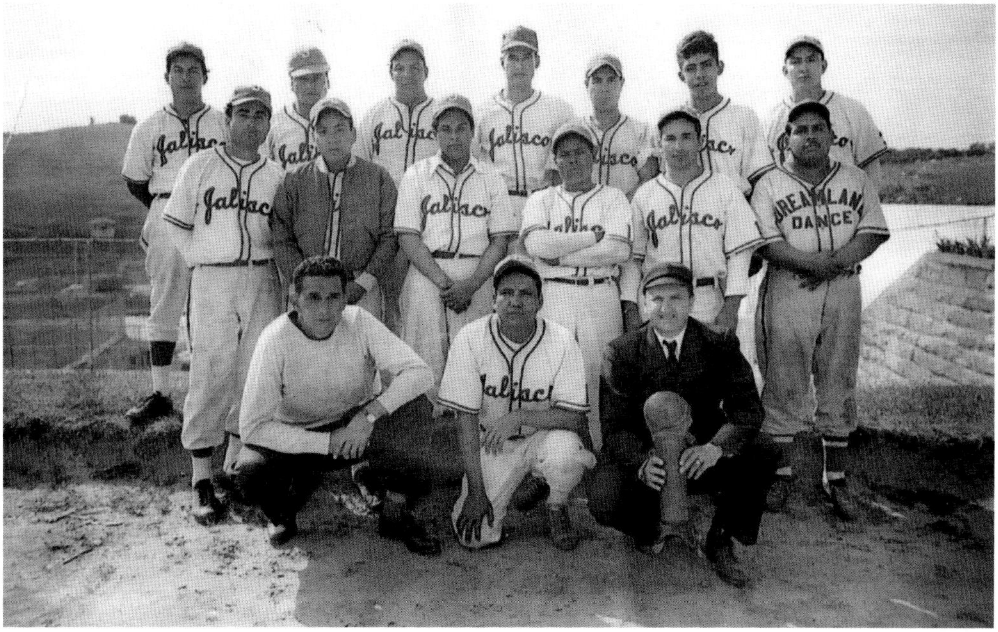

This c. 1950 photograph shows the Jalisco team at an unidentified location probably before a game. An umpire is posing with the team, which was a rare occurrence. (Courtesy of Juanita Evans and Bobby Ramirez.)

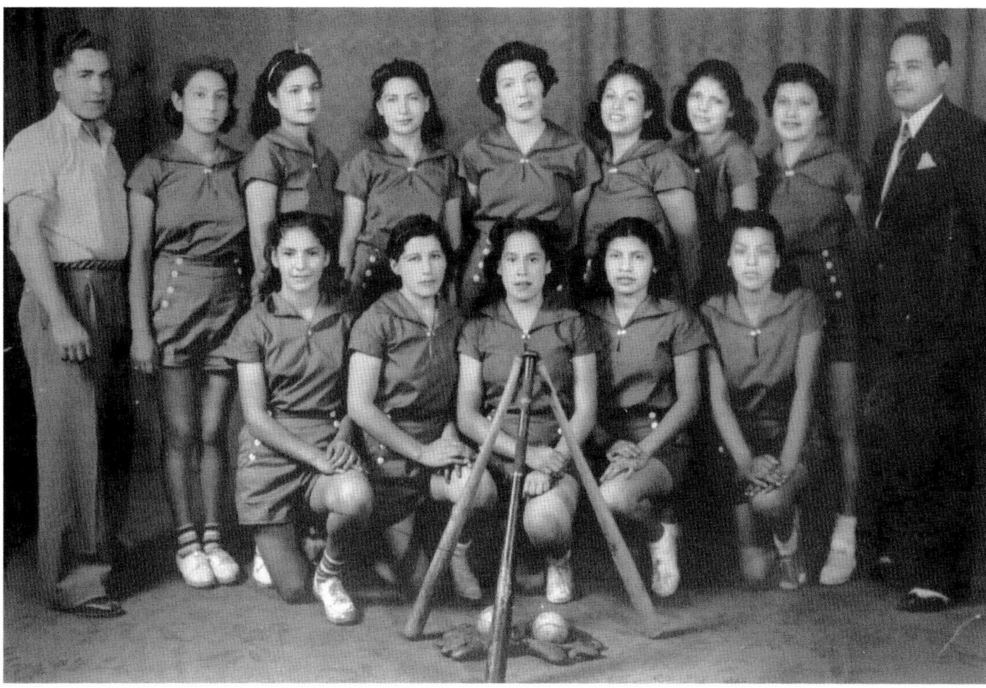

This photograph captures the image of a Mexican American girls' softball team around 1935. The team played primarily at Roosevelt Park between Ninth and Tenth and P and Q Streets. (Courtesy of Juanita Evans and Bobby Ramirez.)

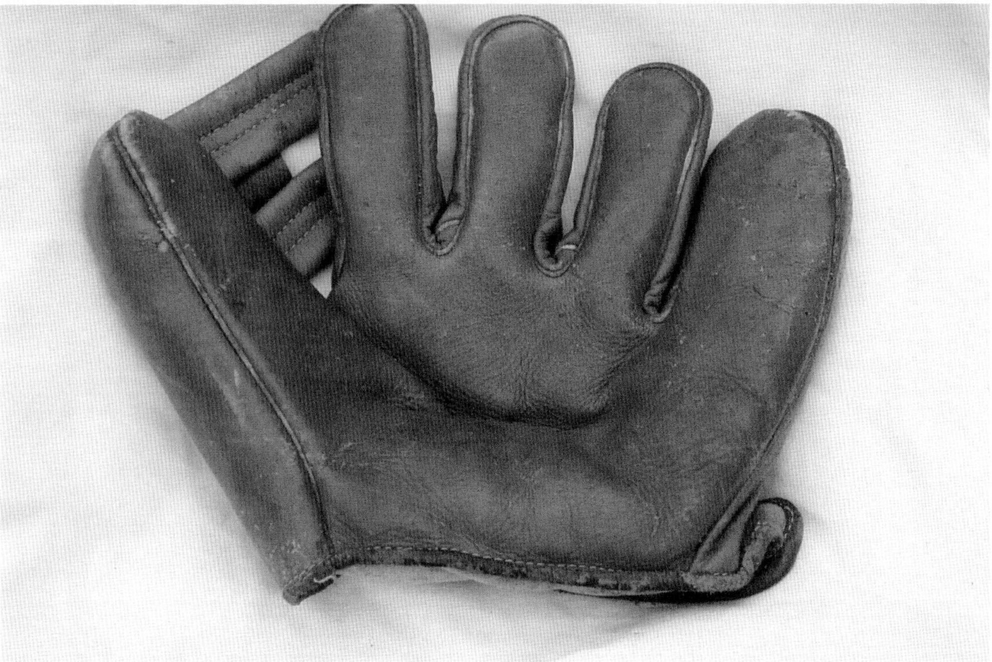

This type of glove, without the fingers stitched together and two strips of webbing, was used from around 1920 to about 1940. (Courtesy of Norman Blackwell Sr.)

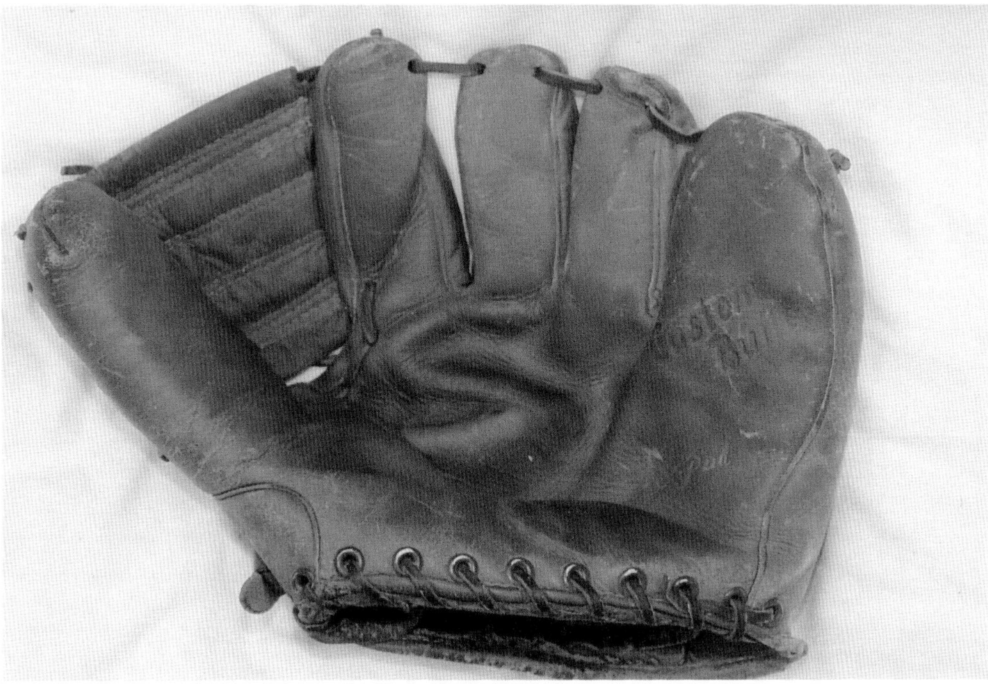

From about 1940 to 1960, gloves were made with a single large web between the thumb and first finger. During this period, glove manufacturers also began tying the fingers together with leather laces. (Courtesy of Norman Blackwell Sr.)

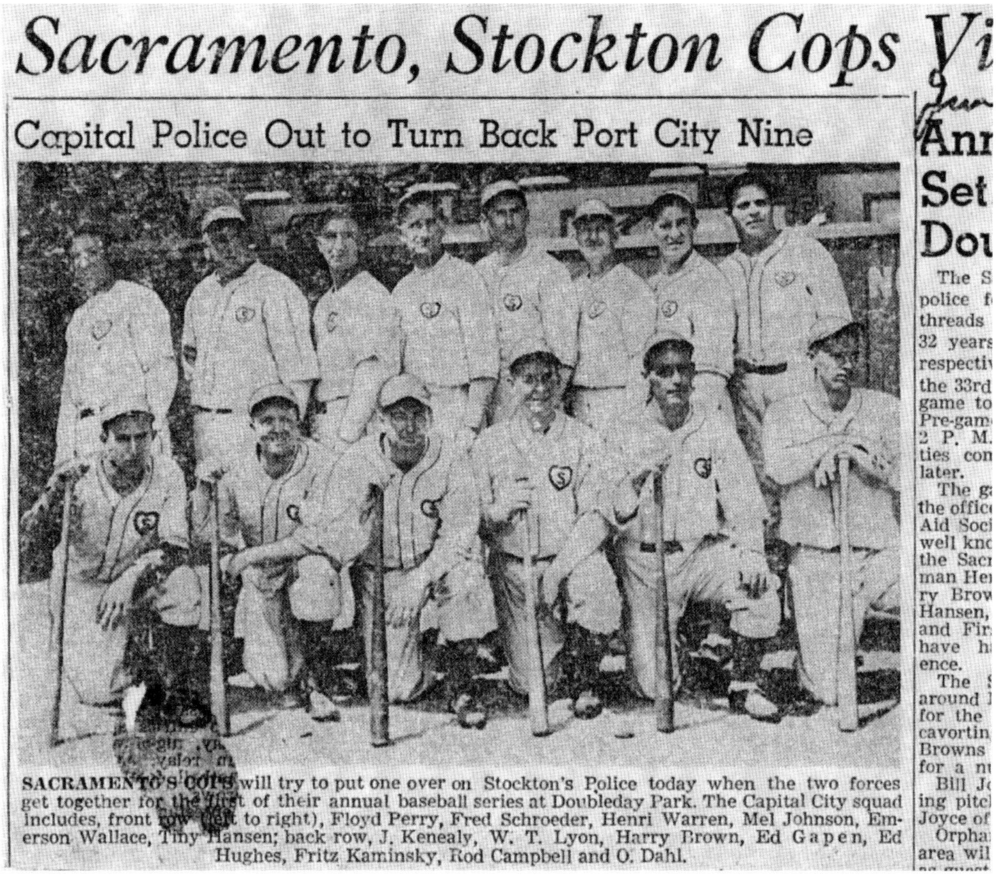

Sacramento, Stockton Cops Vi

Capital Police Out to Turn Back Port City Nine

SACRAMENTO'S COPS will try to put one over on Stockton's Police today when the two forces get together for the first of their annual baseball series at Doubleday Park. The Capital City squad includes, front row (left to right), Floyd Perry, Fred Schroeder, Henri Warren, Mel Johnson, Emerson Wallace, Tiny Hansen; back row, J. Kenealy, W. T. Lyon, Harry Brown, Ed Gapen, Ed Hughes, Fritz Kaminsky, Rod Campbell and O. Dahl.

This June 3, 1945, newspaper article describes the 33rd annual charity game between the Sacramento Police and Stockton Police played at Doubleday Park (later known as Edmonds Field) at Riverside Boulevard and Broadway. The proceeds from the game went to the Police Officers' Widows and Orphans Aid Society, an organization still in existence today. Pictured in the photograph are, from left to right, (first row) Floyd Perry, Fred Schroeder, Henri Warren, Mel Johnson, Emerson Wallace, and Tiny Hansen; (second row) J. Kenealy, W.T. Lyon, Harry Brown, Ed Gapen, Ed Hughes, Fritz Kaminsky, Rod Campbell, and O. Dahl. According to the article, Warren, Brow, Hansen, Perry, and Hughes all had professional baseball experience.

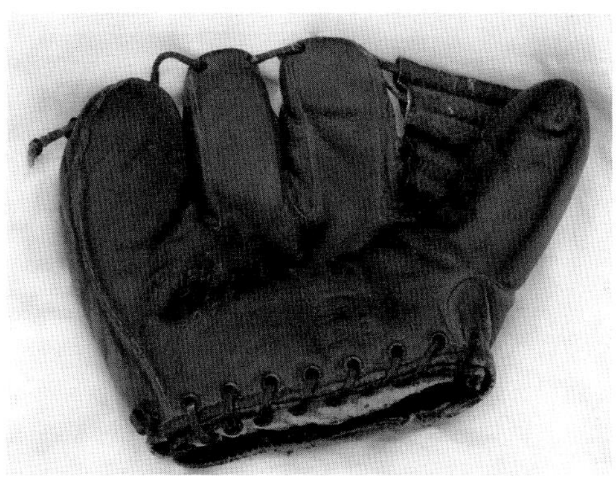

Four-fingered gloves like this one date to the early 1900s and 1910s. This glove was produced and used around 1940. (Courtesy of Norman Blackwell Sr.)

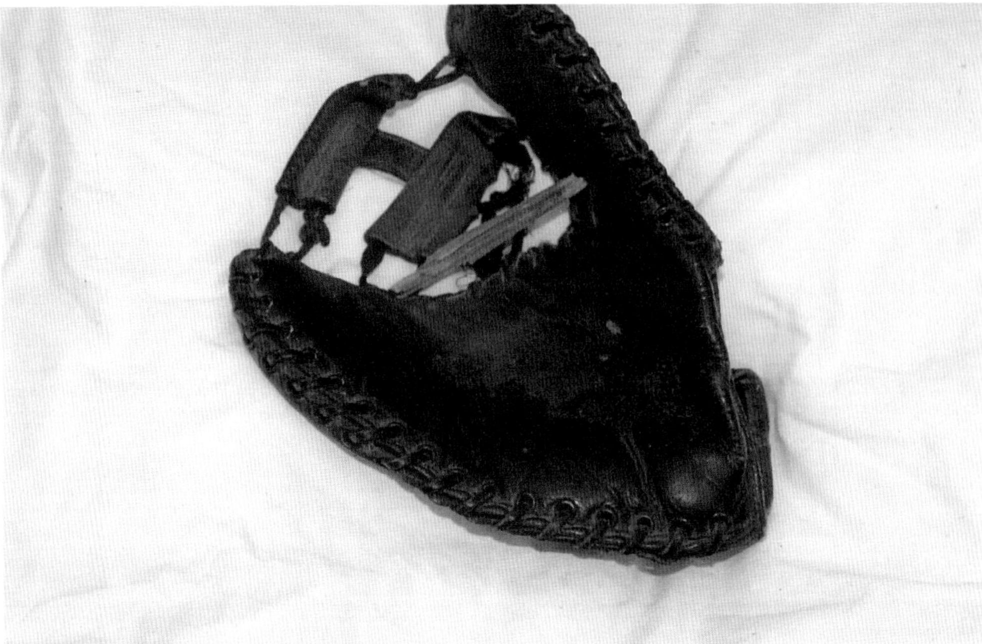

As gloves evolved in the early 20th century, so too did specialty gloves. This c. 1950 photograph shows a first-basemen's glove. (Courtesy of Norman Blackwell Sr.)

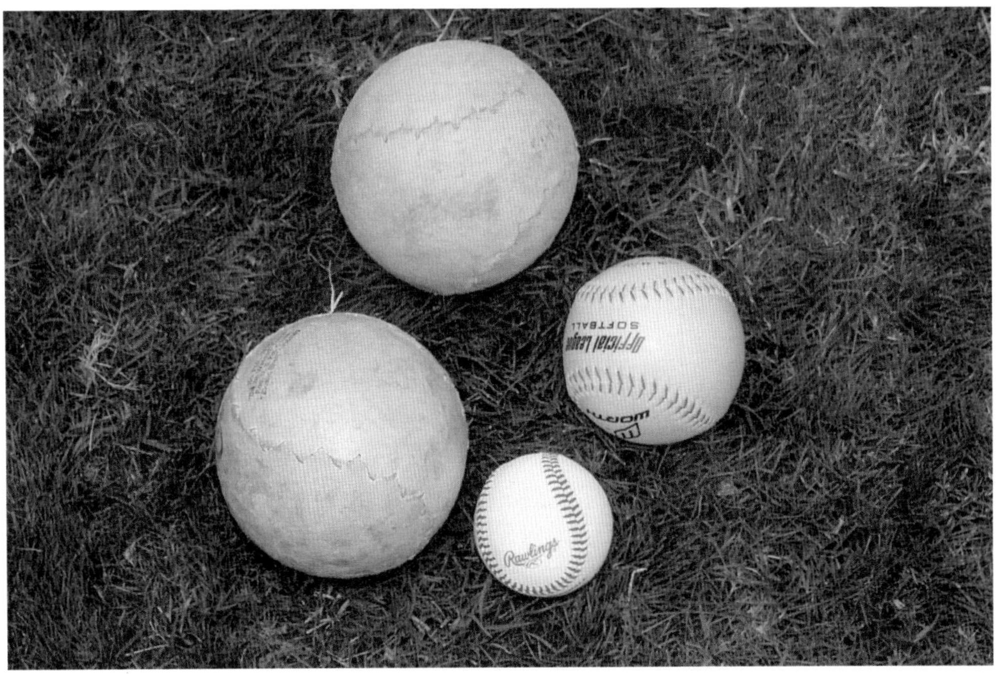

Balls in various sizes were used in different types of play. The two large balls in this photograph are used in indoor softball; the midsize ball is an official outdoor softball, although there is actually nothing soft about it; and the smallest of the balls is the regulation size for amateur and professional baseball. (Courtesy of Norman Blackwell Sr.)

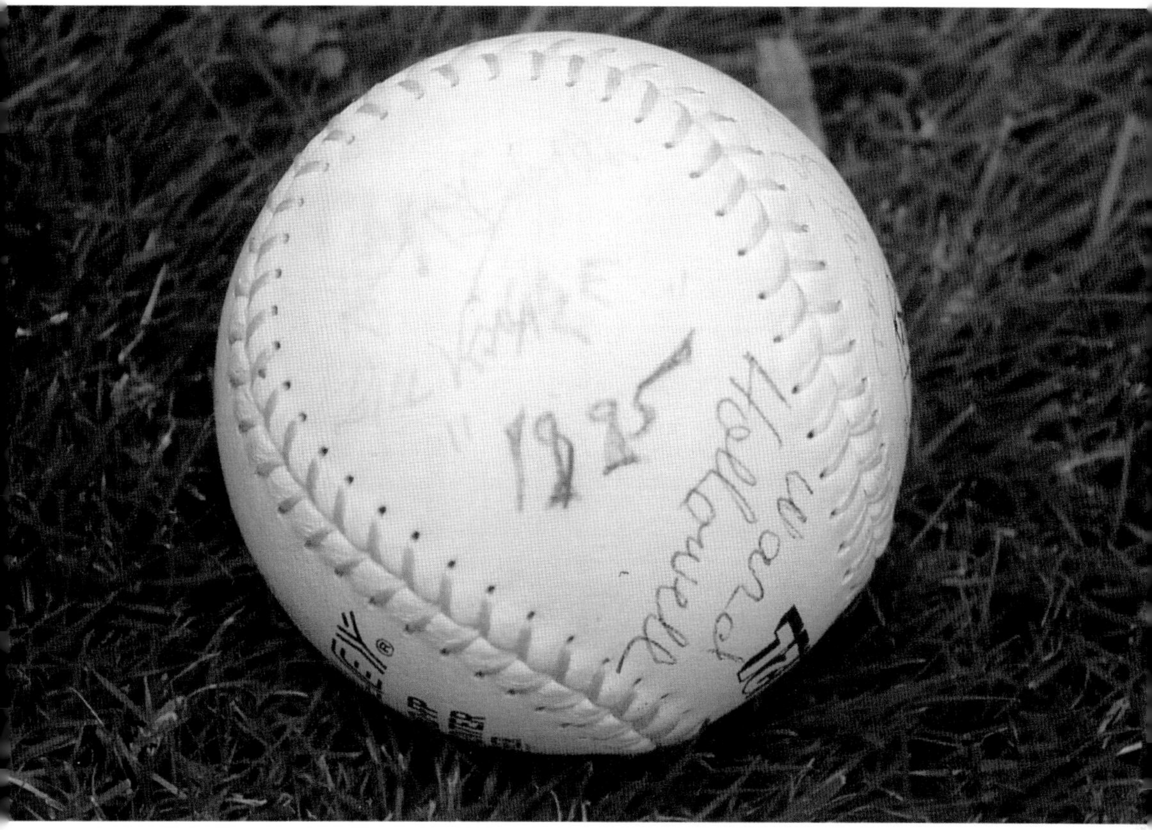

A long-held tradition among amateur players was to have a game ball autographed following a championship game and present it to one of the players or manager as a keepsake of the victory. This ball was presented to Golden Senior player manager Norm Blackwell following the regional championship in 1995. (Courtesy of Norman Blackwell Sr.)

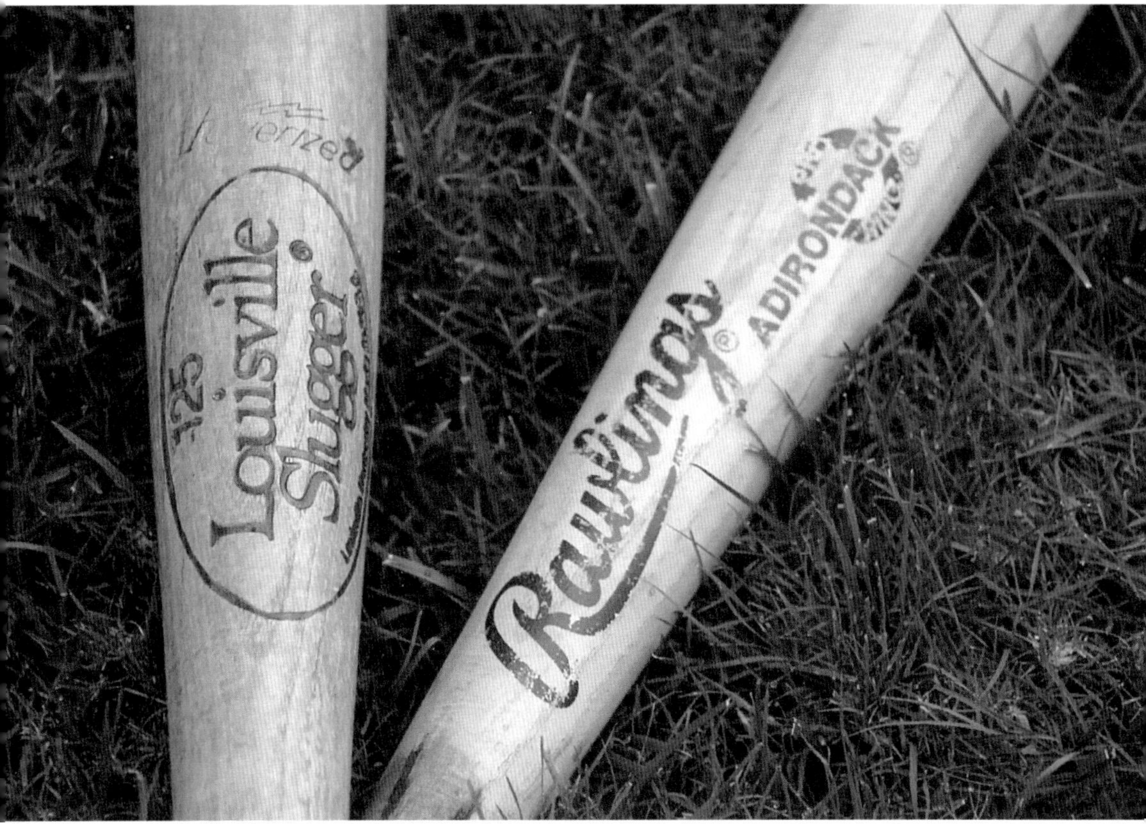

During the first 100-plus years of professional and amateur baseball, wooden bats were the only bats available to players. Easton changed that, however, with the introduction of its aluminum bat in 1970. Aluminum bats are now used almost exclusively in amateur baseball. Although other wooden bat companies manufactured bats, Louisville Slugger and Rawlings were the most popular bats among professional and most amateur players. These bats were used by Juan and Orlando Blackwell, Sacramento High School graduates who played for the San Francisco Giants and New York Yankees organizations. (Courtesy of Norman Blackwell Sr.)

This photograph was taken from one of the frequent histories of the Sacramento Golden Seniors Softball League written and published by the club. It describes the founding of the league in 1976. As the document shows, seniors had been playing softball in Florida since the 1930s. The article boasts the fact that Sacramento has the largest senior league in the nation. (Courtesy of George Hodsdon.)

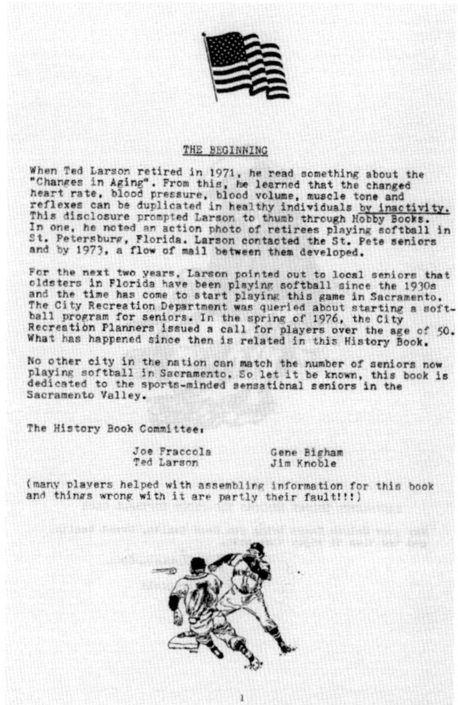

THE BEGINNING

When Ted Larson retired in 1971, he read something about the "Changes in Aging". From this, he learned that the changed heart rate, blood pressure, blood volume, muscle tone and reflexes can be duplicated in healthy individuals by inactivity. This disclosure prompted Larson to thumb through Hobby Books. In one, he noted an action photo of retirees playing softball in St. Petersburg, Florida. Larson contacted the St. Pete seniors and by 1973, a flow of mail between them developed.

For the next two years, Larson pointed out to local seniors that oldsters in Florida have been playing softball since the 1930s and the time has come to start playing this game in Sacramento. The City Recreation Department was queried about starting a softball program for seniors. In the spring of 1976, the City Recreation Planners issued a call for players over the age of 50. What has happened since then is related in this History Book.

No other city in the nation can match the number of seniors now playing softball in Sacramento. So let it be known, this book is dedicated to the sports-minded sensational seniors in the Sacramento Valley.

The History Book Committee:

Joe Fraccola — Gene Bigham
Ted Larson — Jim Knoble

(many players helped with assembling information for this book and things wrong with it are partly their fault!!!)

1

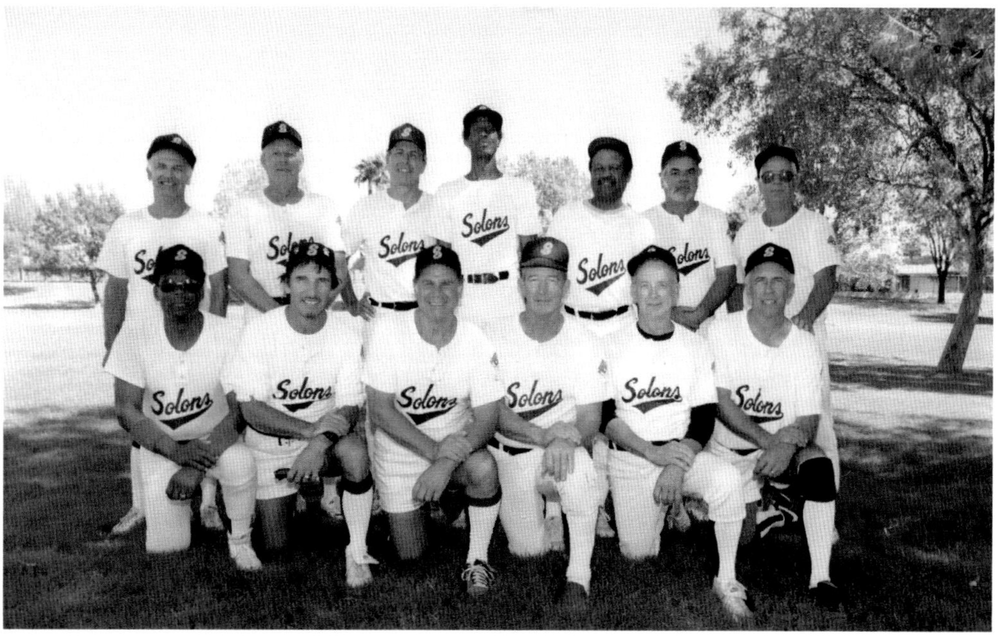

This 1990 Sacramento Golden Seniors World Series photograph pictures the senior league's Sacramento Solons as the winning team. From left to right are (first row) Norm Blackwell, Jules Morgenstern, Peter Norris, Jerry Hall, Thomas Tinney, and Ken Sturgion; (second row) Bob Jackson (manager), Irv Schafer, Don Holt, John Blackwell, Bill Venable, Bob Silva, and Marion Page. (Courtesy of Norman Blackwell Sr.)

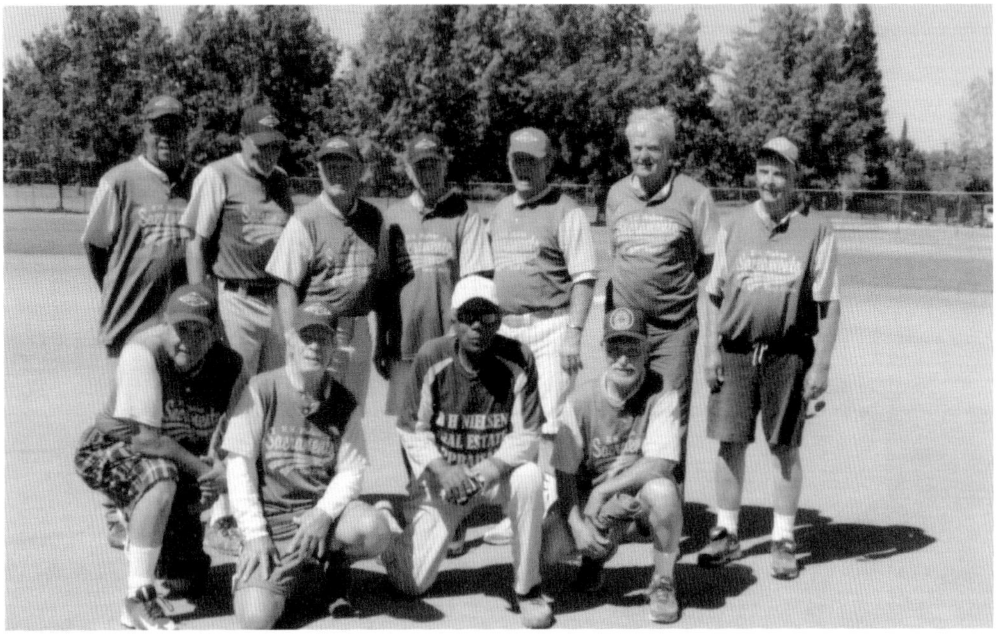

This photograph of the 2015 Sacramento Golden Seniors over 70 champions includes, from left to right, (first row) Doug Blue, Robert McBee, Norm Blackwell, and Al Tirapelli; (second row) Alphonso Wyndham, John Mains, John R. Meyer, Charles Gard, James Stinson, Bob Nielson (team sponsor), and Jack Jacinto. (Courtesy of Norman Blackwell Sr.)

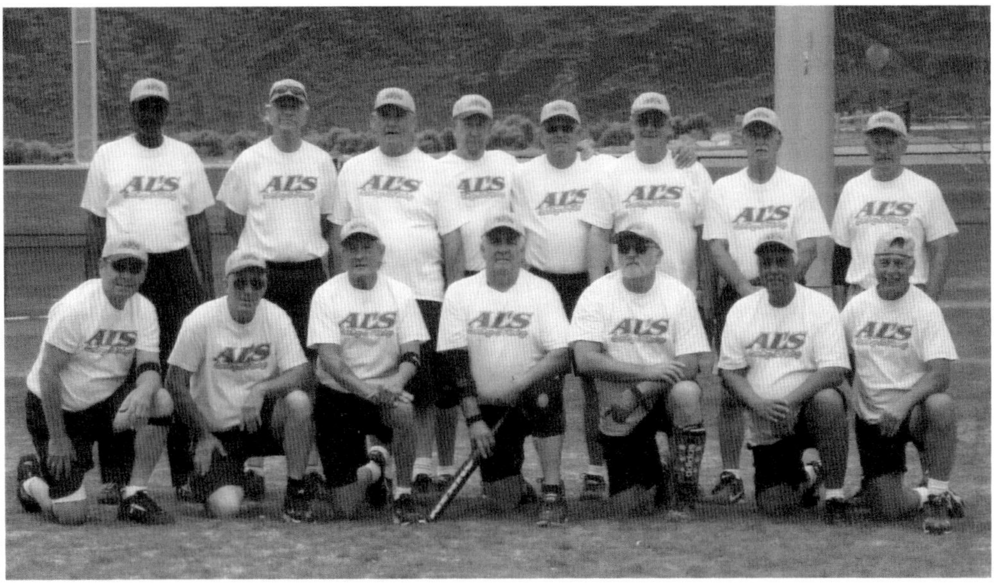

In 2007, a Sacramento Golden Seniors team, sponsored by Al's Grading and Paving, played in the Senior Games championship in Utah. Pictured are, from left to right, (first row) Norm Lusk, Ray Bivert, Vic Tafoya, Jaime Correa, Danny Kleier, Corlo Cordero, and Frank Seman; (second row) Willie Elder, Rick Knee, Bill Kanada, Marion Newton, Mert Horsman, Larry Yoder, Bill Drinnen, and Jerry Ford. (Courtesy of Marion and Gloria Newton.)

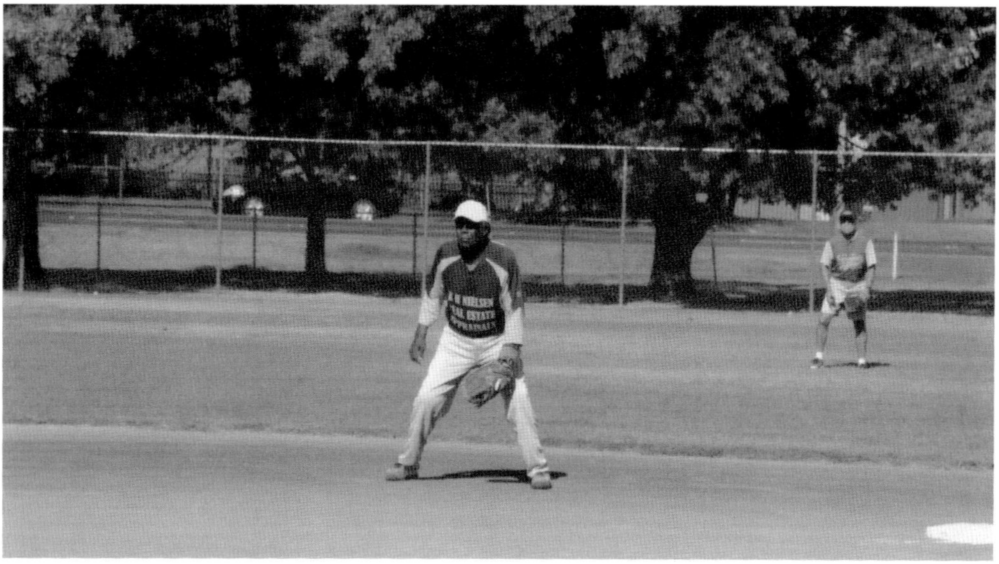

This photograph shows Norm Blackwell playing shortstop in the 2015 Golden Seniors over 70 championship series. (Courtesy of Norman Blackwell Sr.)

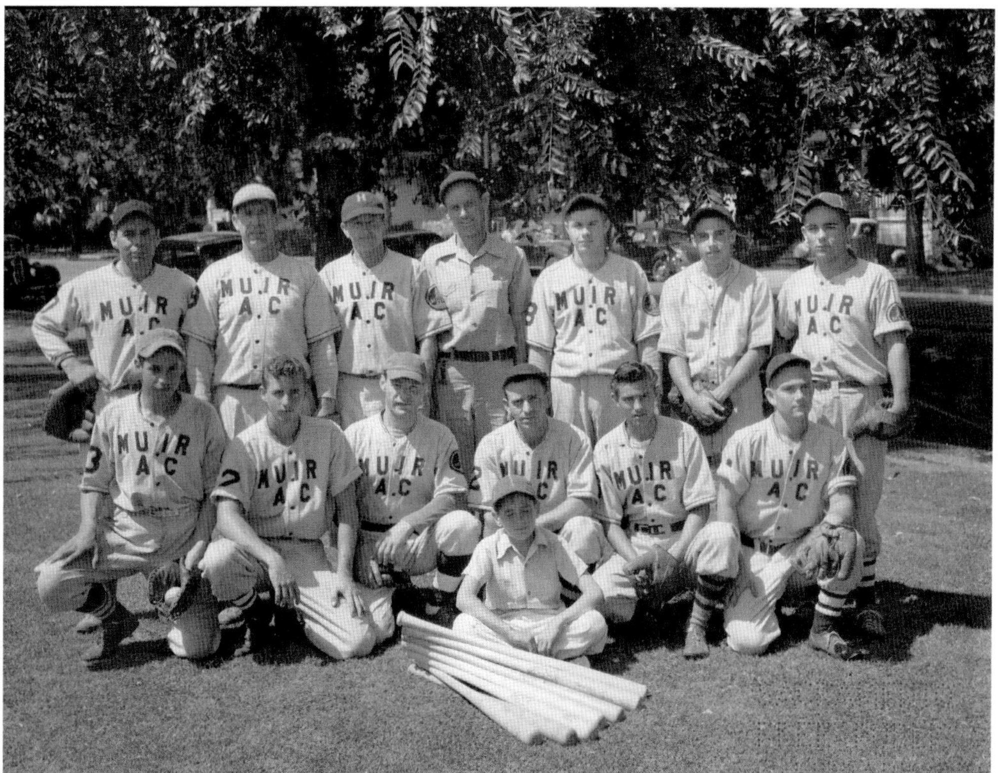

The Muir Athletic Club team, pictured above, was one of many teams formed during the mid-20th century that participated in city leagues. This photograph was taken at an unidentified location on July 18, 1943. (Courtesy of Sacramento Public Library, Sacramento Room Special Collections.)

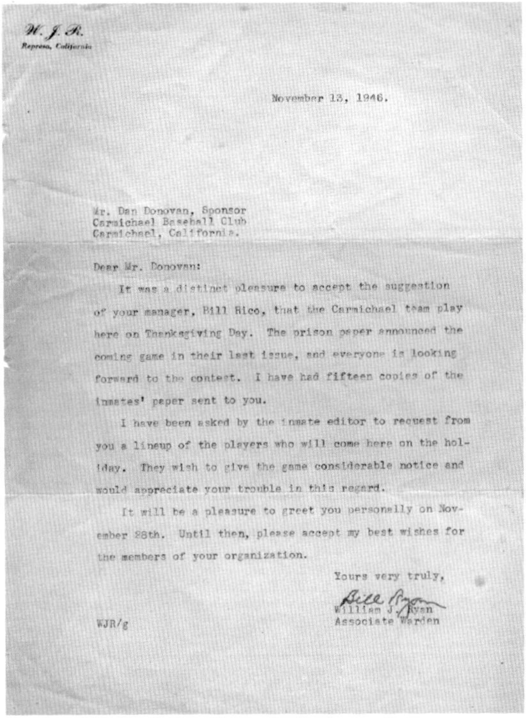

W. J. R.
Represa, California

November 13, 1946.

Mr. Dan Donovan, Sponsor
Carmichael Baseball Club
Carmichael, California.

Dear Mr. Donovan:

It was a distinct pleasure to accept the suggestion of your manager, Bill Rico, that the Carmichael team play here on Thanksgiving Day. The prison paper announced the coming game in their last issue, and everyone is looking forward to the contest. I have had fifteen copies of the inmates' paper sent to you.

I have been asked by the inmate editor to request from you a lineup of the players who will come here on the holiday. They wish to give the game considerable notice and would appreciate your trouble in this regard.

It will be a pleasure to greet you personally on November 28th. Until then, please accept my best wishes for the members of your organization.

Yours very truly,

Bill Ryan
William J. Ryan
Associate Warden

WJR/g

This letter, dated November 13, 1946, was sent to the Carmichael Baseball Club by the Folsom State Prison associate warden. In it, he confirms the club is playing on Thanksgiving Day and that it is being announced in the inmate newspaper. (Courtesy of Sacramento Public Library, Sacramento Room Special Collections.)

This photograph of the Sacramento Mexican Athletic Club at Folsom State Prison was taken around 1950, outside of what was probably the prison chapel. During this time period, whenever an outside team came to the prison, which was frequently, to play against the inmates or other teams, security included prison guards on horseback patrolling the game. (Courtesy of Juanita Evans and Bobby Ramirez.)

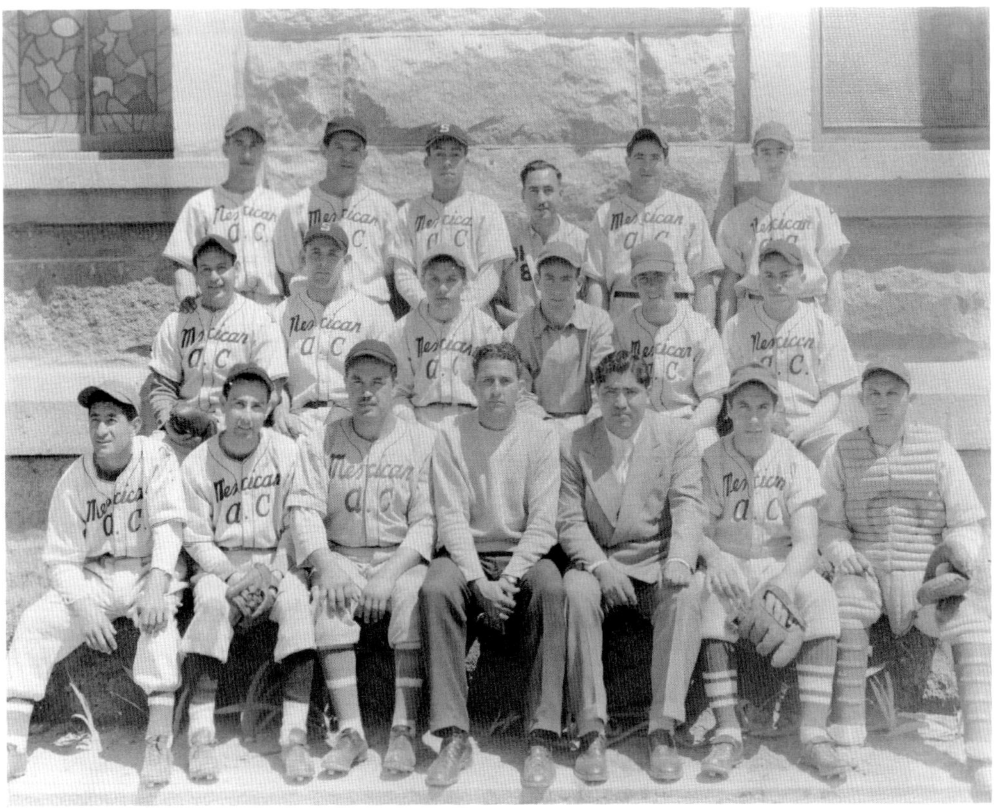

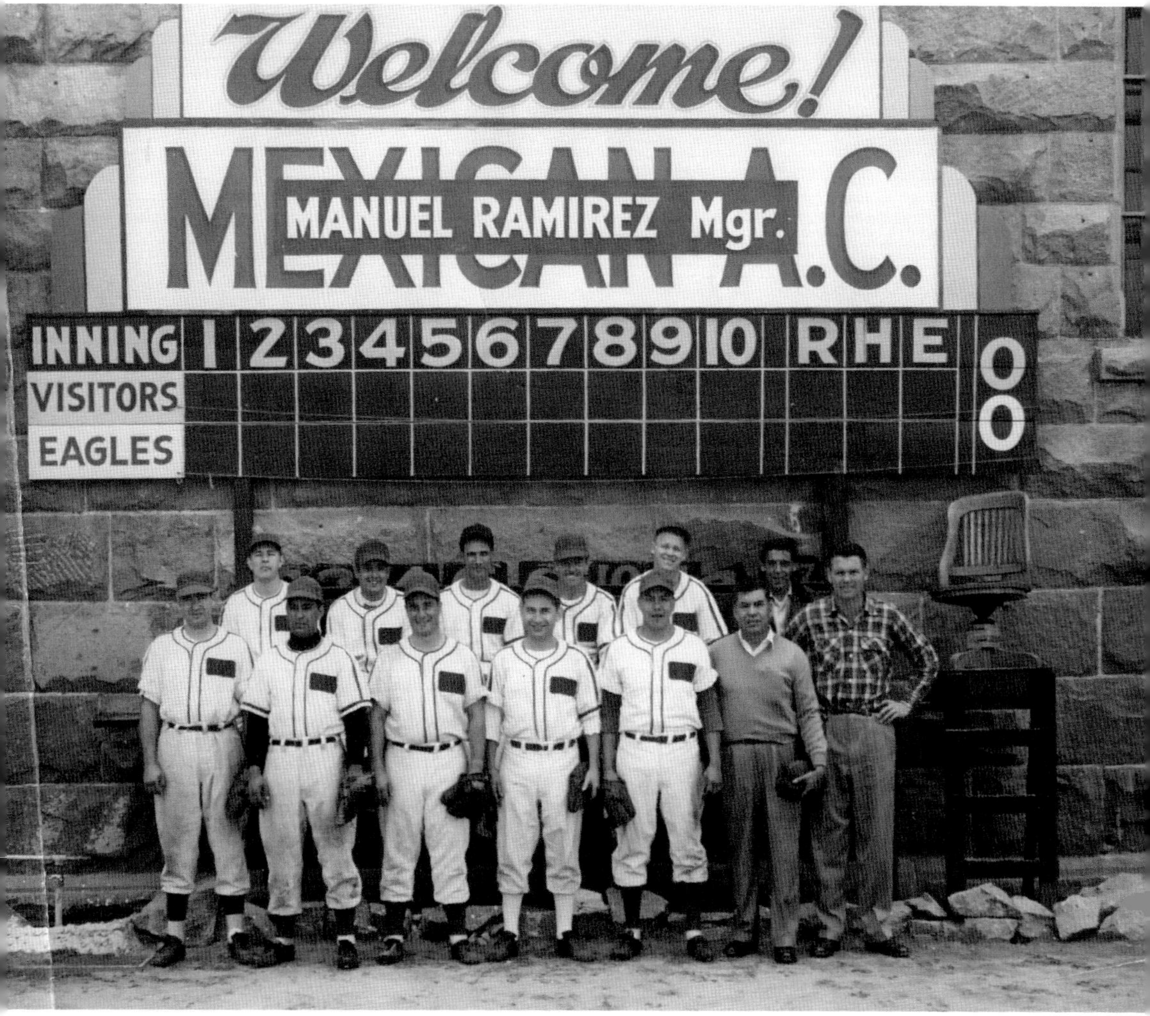

This photograph of the Sacramento Mexican Athletic Club at Folsom State Prison was taken on April 19, 1953. Although there is no score indicated on the scoreboard behind the team, a note on the reverse side of the image says the Sacramento Mexican Athletic Club beat the inmate team by a score of 6-4. (Courtesy of Juanita Evans and Bobby Ramirez.)

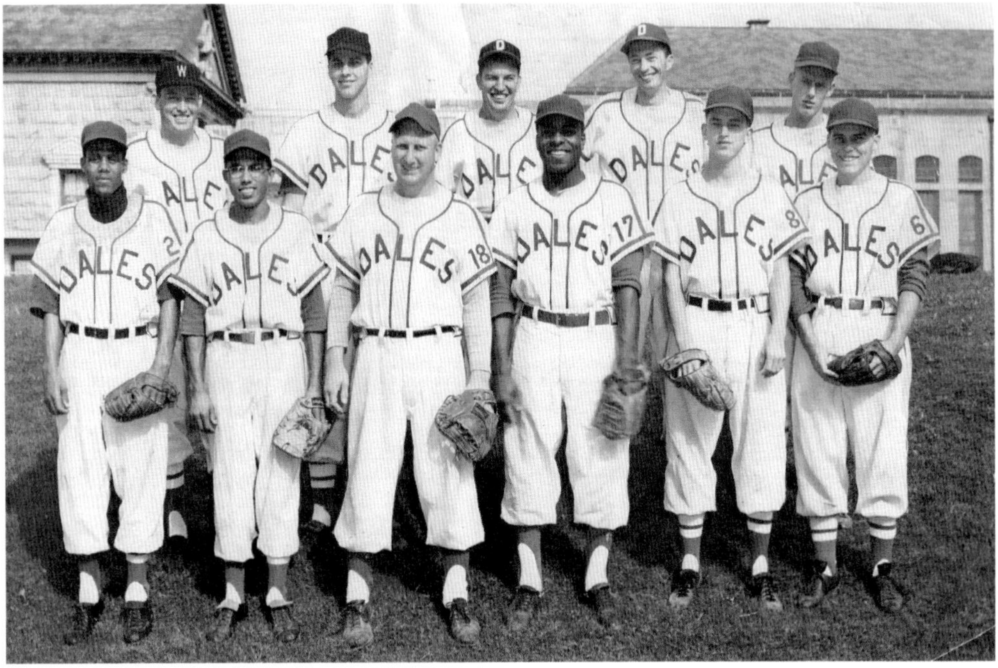

This c. 1950 photograph shows a Sacramento Winter League team sponsored by Dale's Tire Shop. The Dales was amateur hardball team that traveled throughout Northern California. Pictured here are, from left to right, (first row) Norm Blackwell, Peter Gonzales, Wally Rath, Leroy Molder, Larry Kelly, and George Dickett; (second row) two unidentified, Dale Millie (the sponsor), Al Dunlap and unidentified. (Courtesy of Norman Blackwell Sr.)

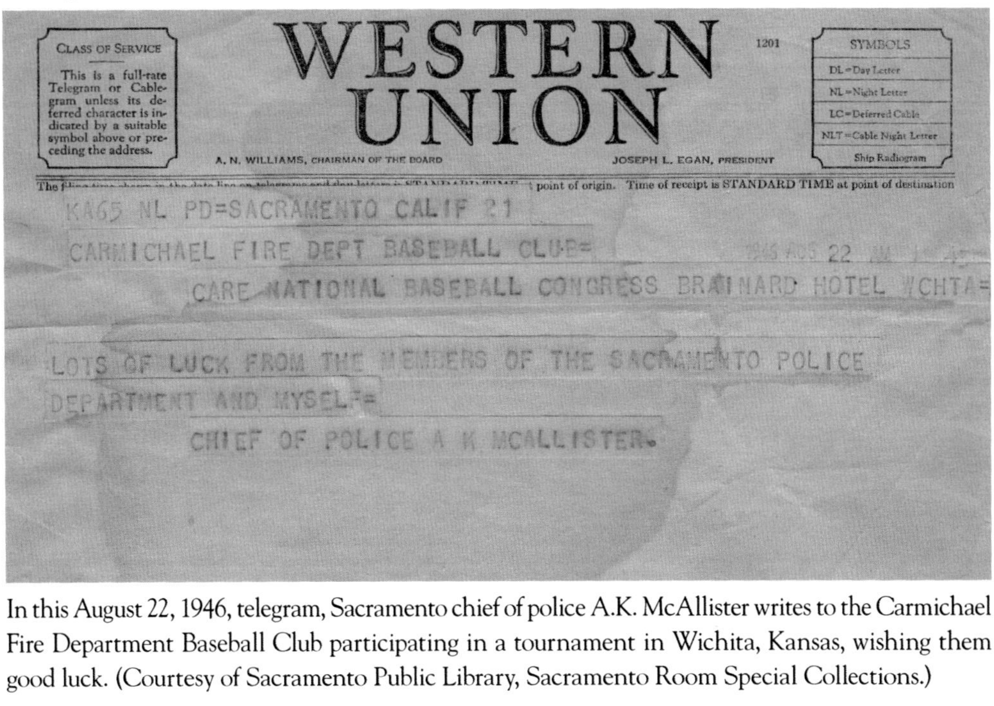

CLASS OF SERVICE

This is a full-rate Telegram or Cablegram unless its deferred character is indicated by a suitable symbol above or preceding the address.

WESTERN UNION

1201

SYMBOLS

DL = Day Letter

NL = Night Letter

LC = Deferred Cable

NLT = Cable Night Letter

Ship Radiogram

A. N. WILLIAMS, CHAIRMAN OF THE BOARD

JOSEPH L. EGAN, PRESIDENT

The ... point of origin. Time of receipt is STANDARD TIME at point of destination

KA65 NL PD=SACRAMENTO CALIF 21

CARMICHAEL FIRE DEPT BASEBALL CLUB=

1946 AUG 22

CARE NATIONAL BASEBALL CONGRESS BRAINARD HOTEL WCHTA=

LOTS OF LUCK FROM THE MEMBERS OF THE SACRAMENTO POLICE DEPARTMENT AND MYSELF=

CHIEF OF POLICE A K MCALLISTER.

In this August 22, 1946, telegram, Sacramento chief of police A.K. McAllister writes to the Carmichael Fire Department Baseball Club participating in a tournament in Wichita, Kansas, wishing them good luck. (Courtesy of Sacramento Public Library, Sacramento Room Special Collections.)

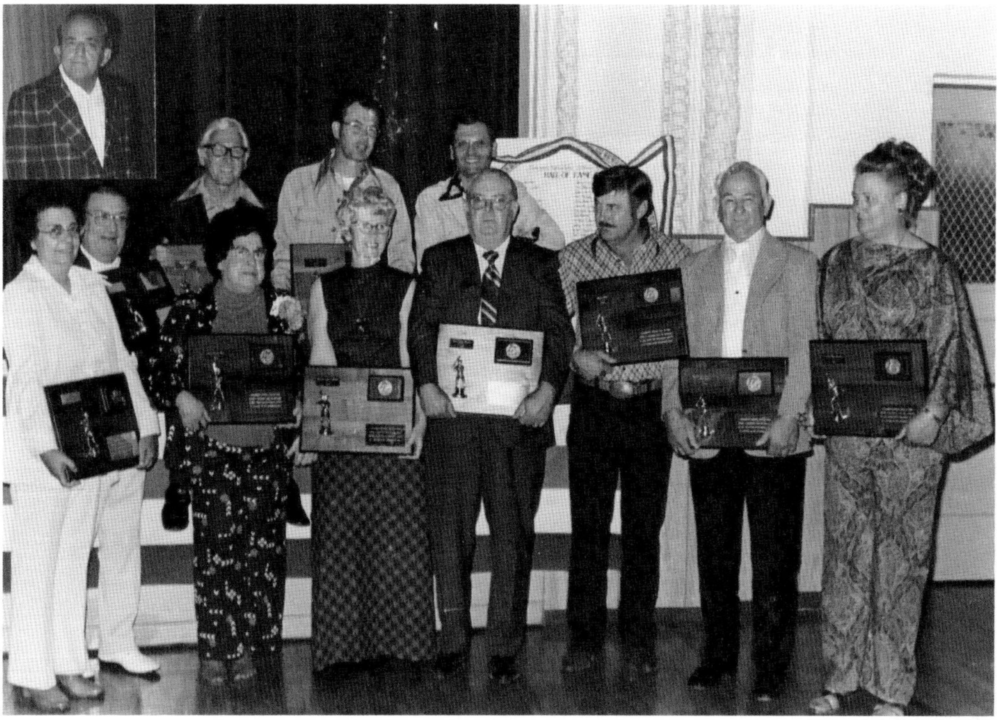

This c. 1970 photograph shows 12 new members inducted into the Sacramento Metropolitan Softball Association Hall of Fame. They are, from left to right, (first row) Lorraine Dutra, Dale Smith, Mary Guido, Genevieve Ward McPoil, Elton J. Rogers, Charlie Nash, Steve Zupan, and Mern Dom Shreeve; (second row) Izzy Smith, Bob Rodness, and Stan Priebe. The inset image shows Jack Androvich, who was not present at the function. (Courtesy of Carol McPoil Isom.)

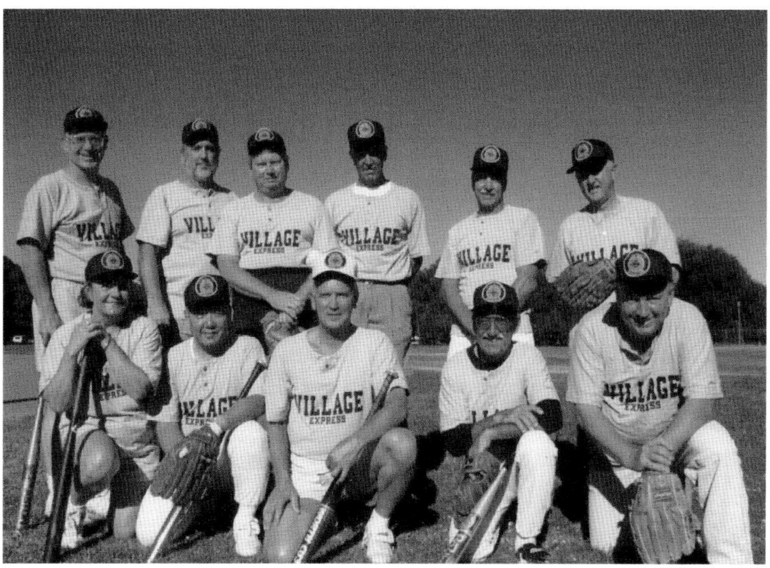

This 1996 photograph shows the Sacramento Golden Seniors Village Express team, which played in the over-60 league at Tahoe Park. (Courtesy of Marion and Gloria Newton.)

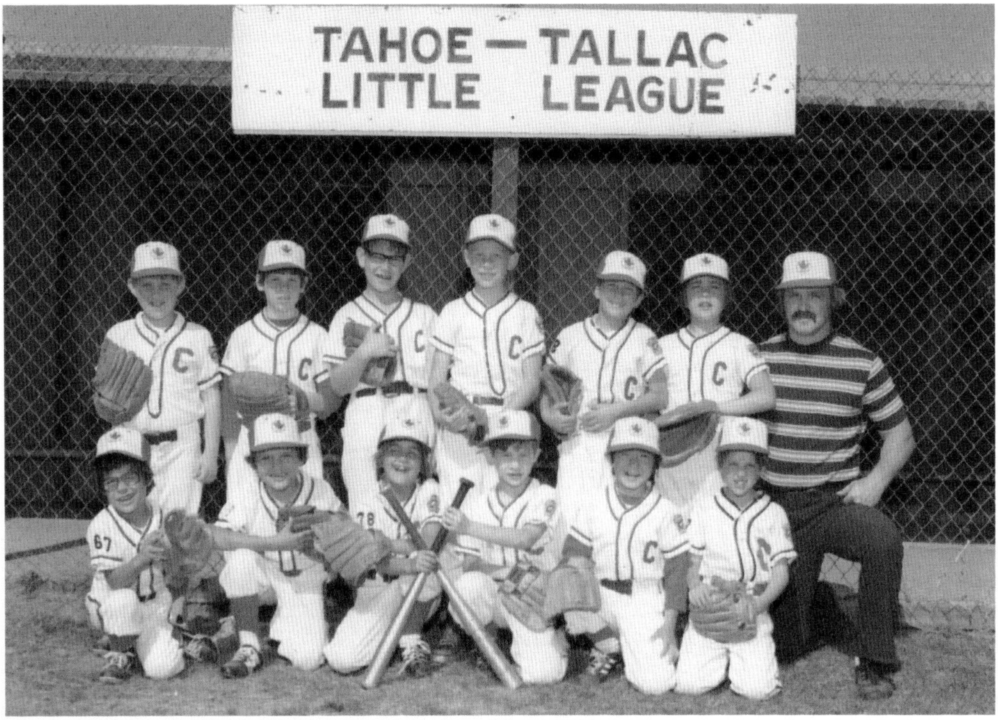

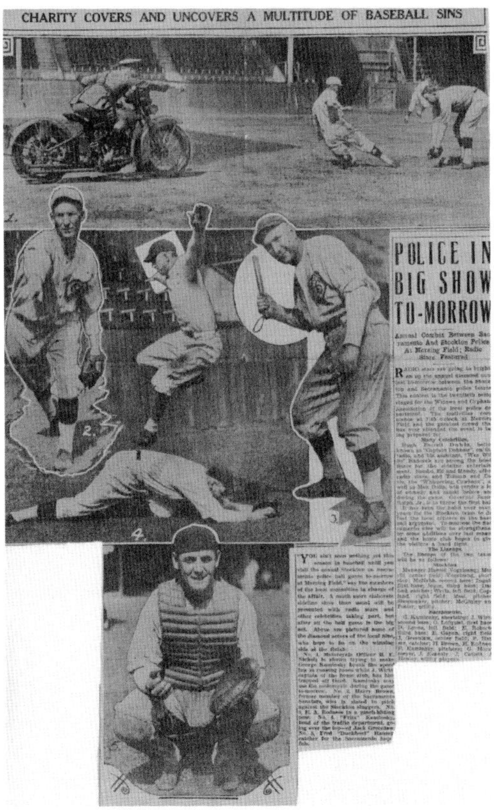

CHARITY COVERS AND UNCOVERS A MULTITUDE OF BASEBALL SINS

POLICE IN BIG SHOW TO-MORROW

Annual Combat Between Sacramento And Stockton Police At Moreing Field; Radio Stars Featured

This 1978 Little League photograph shows the Tahoe-Tallac Cardinals. When Tahoe-Tallac Little League was chartered in the early 1950s, the teams played at Tahoe Park, a park a few blocks away with a swimming pool, picnic areas, and ball diamonds. By the time this photograph was taken, the league played on fields used only for their practice and games at the east end of San Joaquin Street. (Courtesy of Gayle Maita.)

This newspaper clipping announces a charity game coming to Moreing Field between the Sacramento Police Department and the Stockton Police Department. The date is unknown but was probably around 1950. (Courtesy of Sacramento Police Officers Association.)

3

High School and College Baseball

As the Area Grew, So Did the High School and College Teams

In 1856, six years after Sacramento was incorporated, the first high school was built, making it the second-oldest American high school west of the Mississippi River. Sacramento High School remained the only public high school within the city limits for eight decades, when C.K. McClatchy High School was established. The population growth in the second half of the 20th century required still more schools, and between 1958 and 1967, three additional schools were built. Outside the city limits, numerous high schools were created as residents moved to more distant suburbs. The first private high school was founded in 1876 by the De La Salle Christian Brothers. In 1924, it reopened under a new name—Christian Brothers School. It finally became a formal boys high school for grades 9 through 12 in 1968 and became coeducational in 1990.

Most high schools began fielding baseball teams shortly after they came into existence, and as more schools were built in the city and unincorporated areas, schedules and rivalries grew. With the final regulations published in 1975 by the Department of Health, Education, and Welfare detailing how Title IX would be implemented, girls' softball programs throughout the Sacramento area proliferated. High school and college programs, along with private softball organizations, began to appear, including the Sacramento State Softball Program, which seven years later won the College World Series.

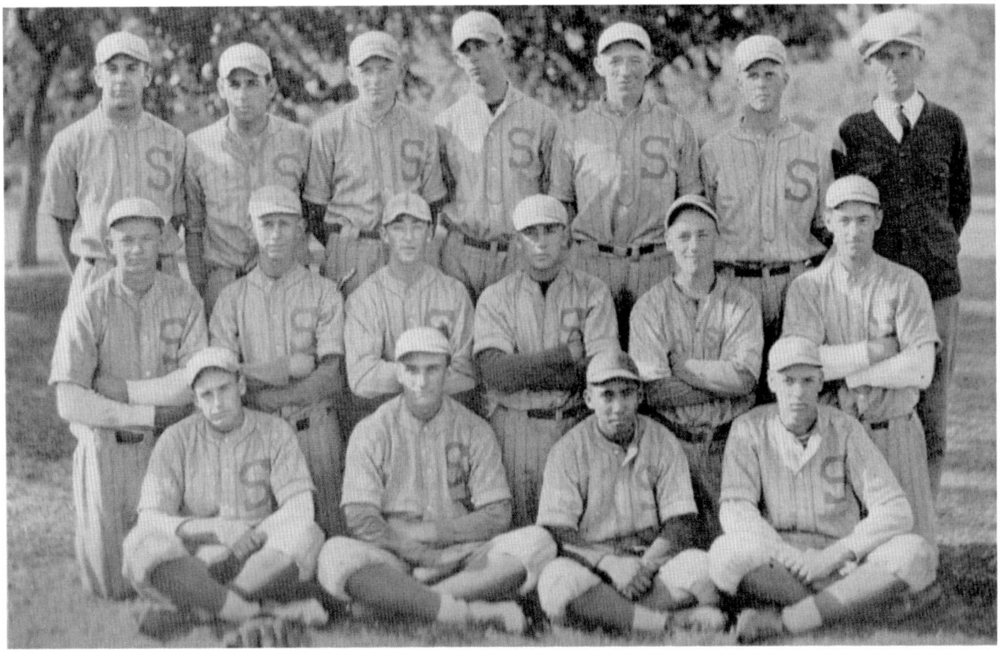

This 1923 photograph displays the Sacramento High School team, the winners of the league championship that year. Although the players are unidentified, it is known that Walter Mails, who pitched for the Sacramento Senators in 1919 and 1920 and was pitching for the Cleveland Indians at that time, coached the team in the weeks prior to him leaving for spring training. (Courtesy of Sacramento Public Library, Sacramento Room Special Collections.)

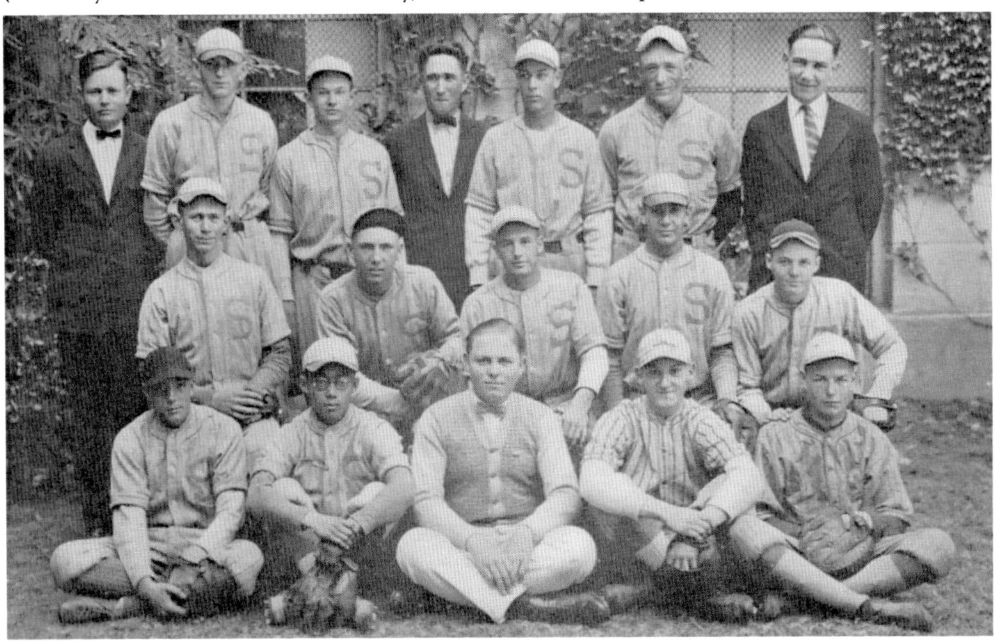

This photograph displays the 1924 Sacramento High School team. (Courtesy of Sacramento Public Library, Sacramento Room Special Collections.)

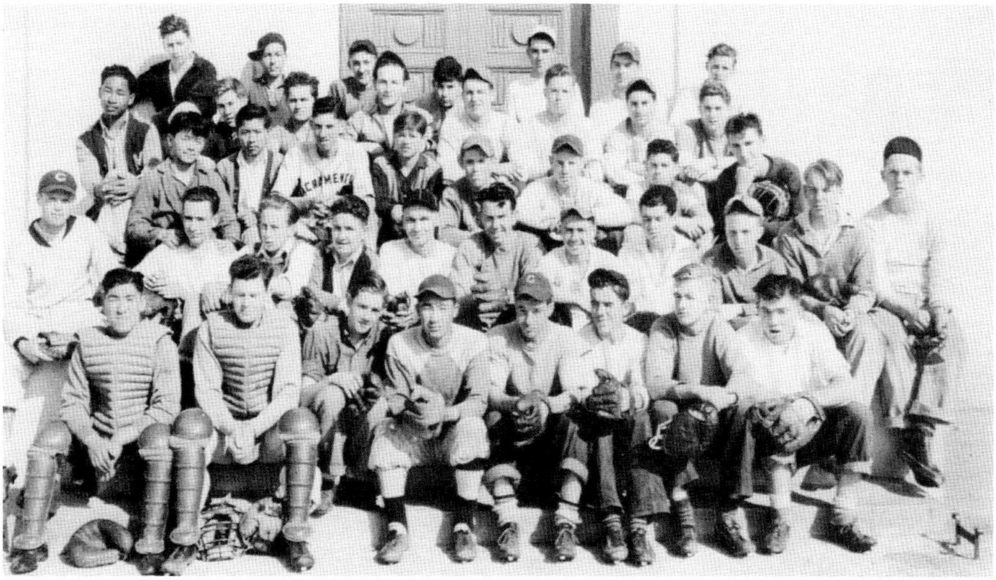

C.K. McClatchy High School was built in 1937. This portrait of the 1938 varsity team shows some 42 players. Their names are not identified anywhere, and it is not known if they had uniforms given that this was their first year of play. (Courtesy of Sacramento Public Library, Sacramento Room Special Collections.)

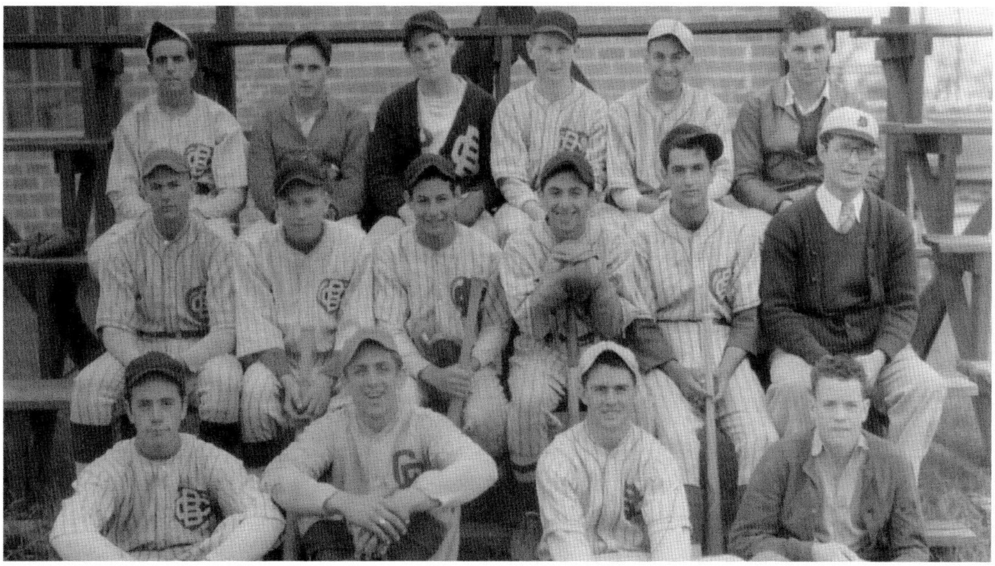

Christian Brothers High School (renamed from Christian Brothers School in 1968), founded by the De La Salle Christian Brothers, began fielding baseball teams in 1930. In this 1933 team picture are, from left to right, (first row) Alex Sweet, Joe Culjis, Frank Russell, and Jack Hartgrove (manager); (second row) Al Scott, Tony Separovich, Lupe Cisneros, Joe Valine, Leroy Nevis, and coach Steve Porcella; (third row) Tom Sugar, Leo Visintainer, Frank Nugent, Gene Sullivan, Jack Dark, and Ed Stetson. The only game the team lost that season was to the St. Mary's College freshmen. (Courtesy of Sacramento Public Library, Sacramento Room Special Collections.)

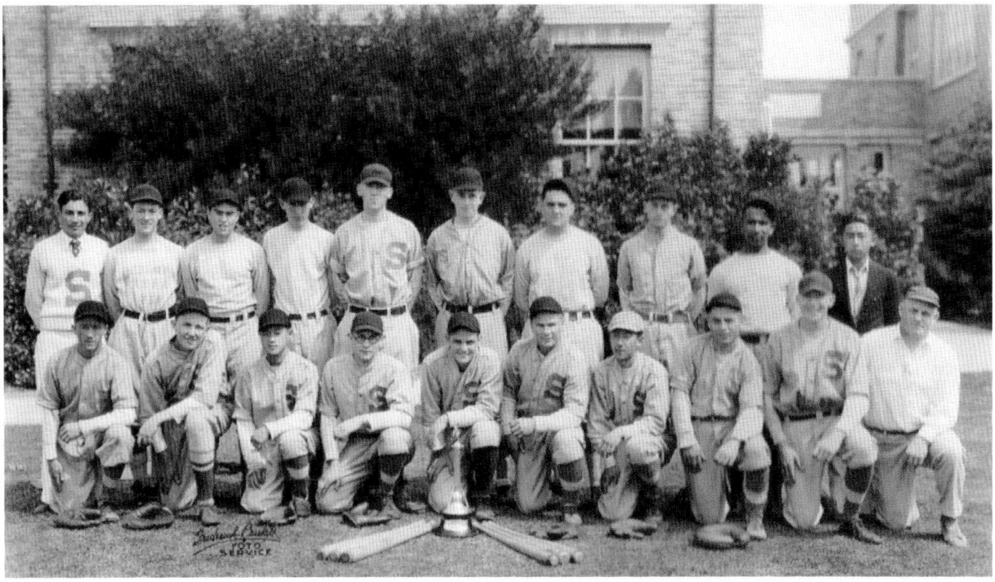

According to the *Sacramento High School Review*, the school's yearbook, the 1928 Sacramento High School baseball team was comprised almost entirely of former players who had previously lettered in baseball, making this one of the best prospective teams in the region. (Courtesy of Sacramento Public Library, Sacramento Room Special Collections.)

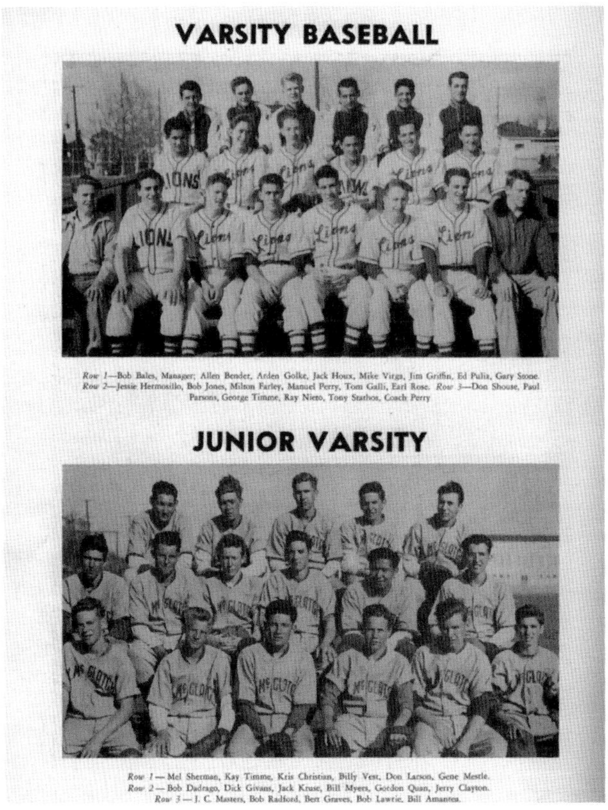

VARSITY BASEBALL

Row 1—Bob Bales, Manager; Allen Bender, Arden Golke, Jack Houx, Mike Virga, Jim Griffin, Ed Puliz, Gary Stone. *Row 2*—Jessie Hermosillo, Bob Jones, Milton Farley, Manuel Perry, Tom Galli, Earl Rose. *Row 3*—Don Shouse, Paul Parsons, George Timme, Ray Nieto, Tony Stathos, Coach Perry

JUNIOR VARSITY

Row 1—Mel Sherman, Kay Timme, Kris Christian, Billy Vest, Don Larson, Gene Mestle. *Row 2*—Bob Dadrago, Dick Givans, Jack Kruse, Bill Myers, Gordon Quan, Jerry Clayton. *Row 3*—J. C. Masters, Bob Radford, Bert Graves, Bob Lawrie, Bill Amantea.

The 1949 C.K. McClatchy High School varsity and junior varsity teams are shown here. The varsity team included, from left to right, (first row) Bob Bales (manager), Allen Bender, Jack Hough, Mike Virga, Jim Griffen, Ed Puliz, and Gary Stone; (second row) Jessie Hermosillo, Bob Jones, Milton Farley, Manuel Perry, Tom Galli, and Earl Rose; (third row) Don Shouse, Paul Parsons, George Timme, Pay Nieto, Tony Stathos, and Coach Perry. (Courtesy of Sacramento Public Library, Sacramento Room Special Collections.)

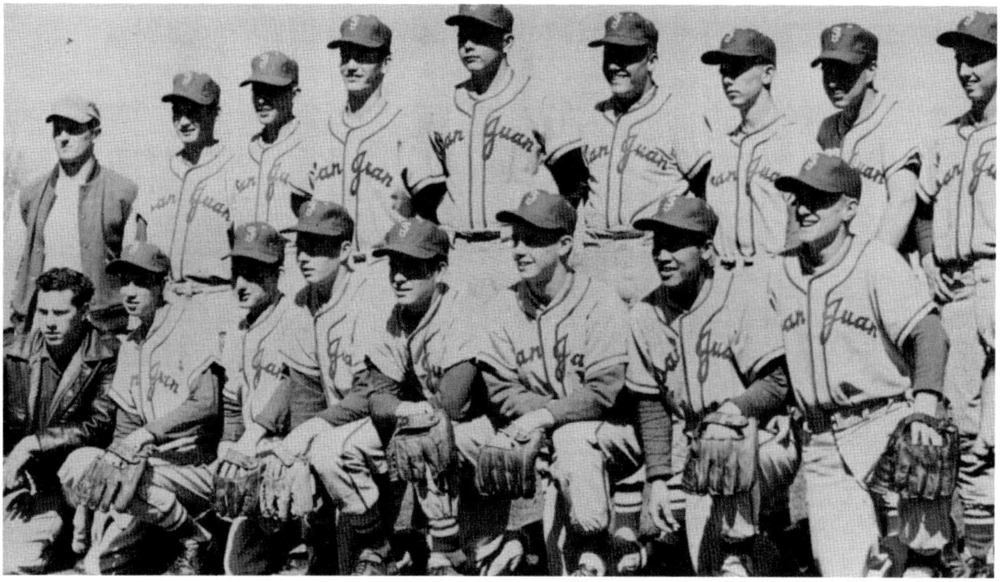

This photograph shows the 1956 Jan Juan High School varsity team. Pictured are, from left to right, (first row) K. Astill (manager), S. Violet, J. French, E. McDonell, B. Woods, T. Barnes, J. Yee, S. Harms, and A. Cupler (manager); (second row) coach Dick Pierucci, C. Agee, G. Schroeder, M. Ross, C. Lee, B. Trumbo, K. Burdock, P. Rees, R. Brinlee, and B. Edmonds. (Courtesy of Sacramento Public Library, Sacramento Room Special Collections.)

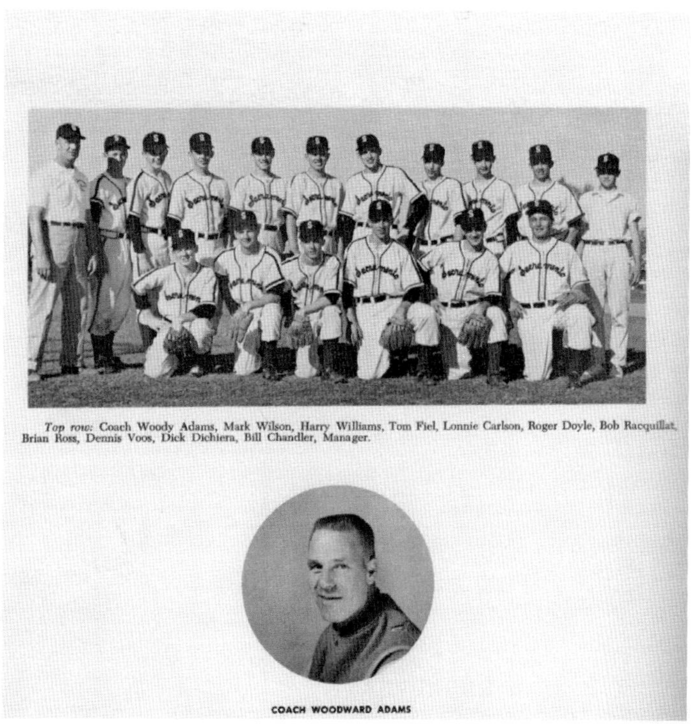

These 1959 portraits are of the varsity team and the coach, Woody Adams, of Sacramento High School. The players in the first row were not identified, but the second row includes, from left to right, Coach Adams, Mark Wilson, Harry Williams, Tom Fiel, Lonnie Carlson, Roger Doyle, Bob Racquillat, Brian Ross, Dennis Voos, Dick DiChiers, and Bill Chandler (team manager). (Courtesy of Sacramento Public Library, Sacramento Room Special Collections.)

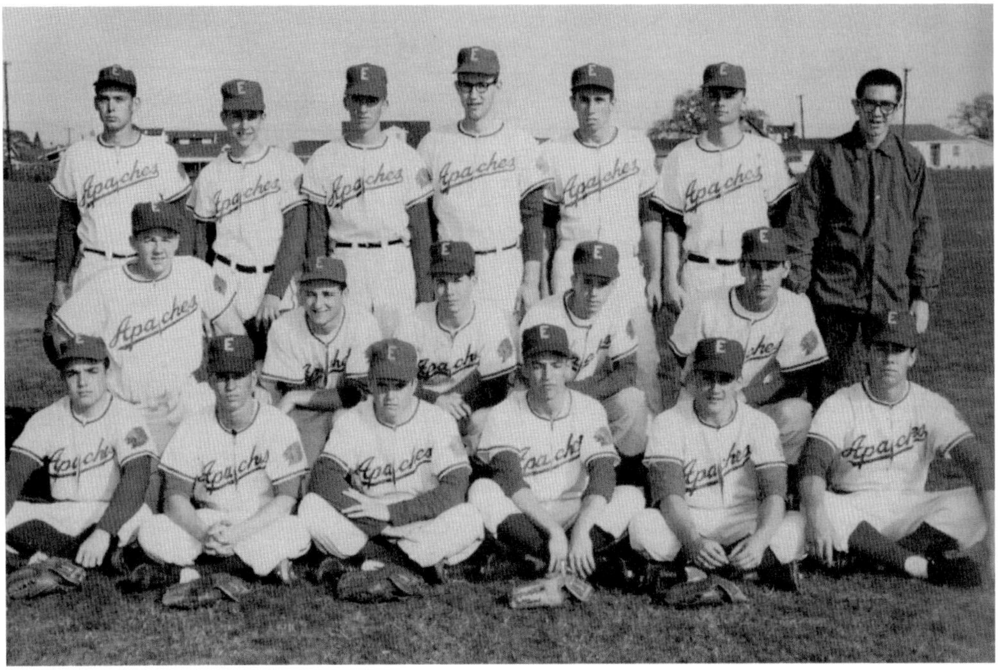

Encina High School graduated its first class in the spring of 1961. That year, the varsity baseball team pictured here included, from left to right, (first row) Stan Bechtold, James Dill, Neil Watson, Gary Hampton, Bob McDonald, and Tracy Spence; (second row) Henry Sims, Gary Kaestner, John Sacchetti, Terry Rhodes, and Dave Ledesma; (third row) Tom Rogers, Douge Dowms, Joe Hegesth, Charles Rosen, Rudy Minnic, Steve Downie, and Robert Witmore, the team manager. (Courtesy of Sacramento Public Library, Sacramento Room Special Collections.)

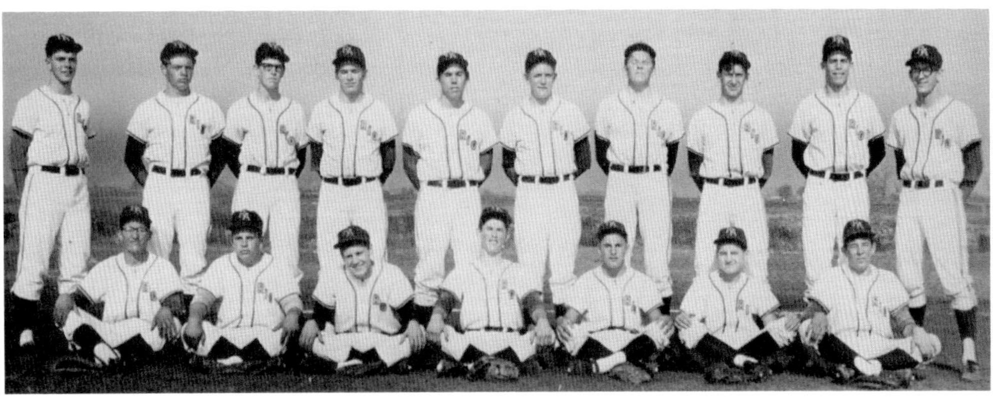

The 1966 Rio Americano High School junior varsity team was comprised of, from left to right, (first row) Bob Bleile, Kent Ward, Aaron Smith, Mike Prelly, Tom Keever, Dave Monzon, and Jim Elven; (second row) Randy Ronne, Don Sykes, Charles Winterberger, Russ Gould, Rick Bremmer, John Johnson, Dave Bartell, Mike Schmitz, Doug Holme, and Mike Garland. (Courtesy of Sacramento Public Library, Sacramento Room Special Collections.)

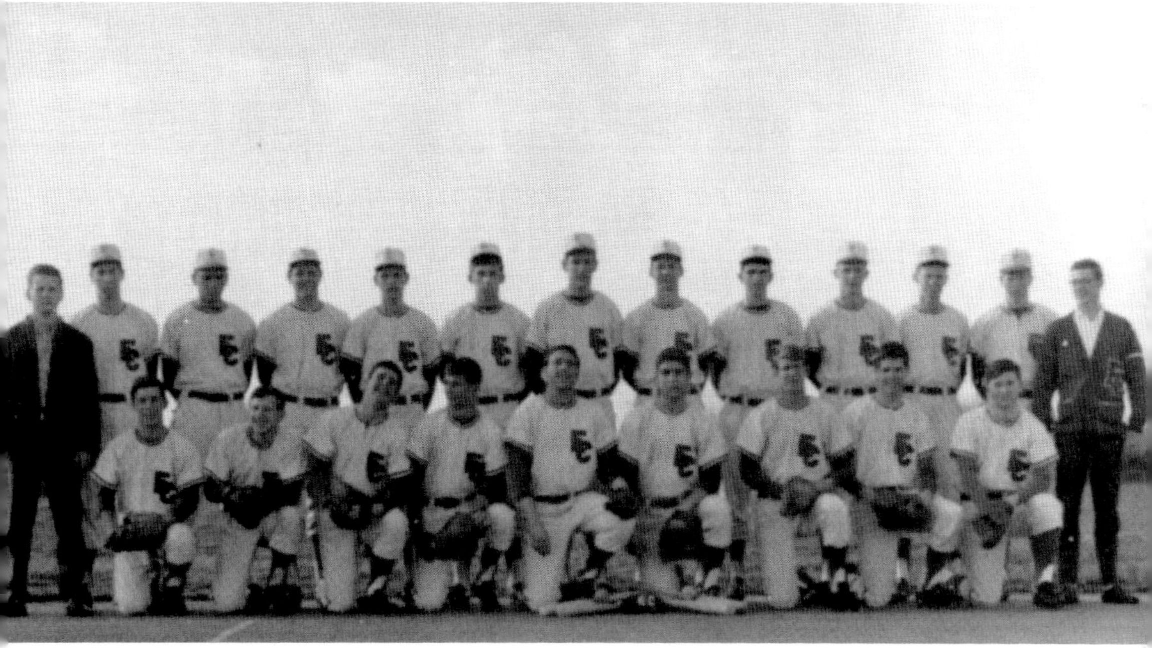

This 1967 photograph shows the El Camino High School varsity team. From left to right, are (kneeling) Bill Schlick, Mark Wiser, Jim Kaffen, John Subry, Roger Harris, Bill Schauer, John Mims, David Schnapp, and Jim Sullins; (standing) Jeff Brandt, Dick Bachman, Ron Haven, Geno Zaharie, Andy Crouch, Allen King, John Jackson, Andy Kafentzis, David Foster, Keith Bowman, and Bruce Machen. The two boys not in uniform are unidentified but are probably team managers. (Courtesy of Sacramento Public Library, Sacramento Room Special Collections.)

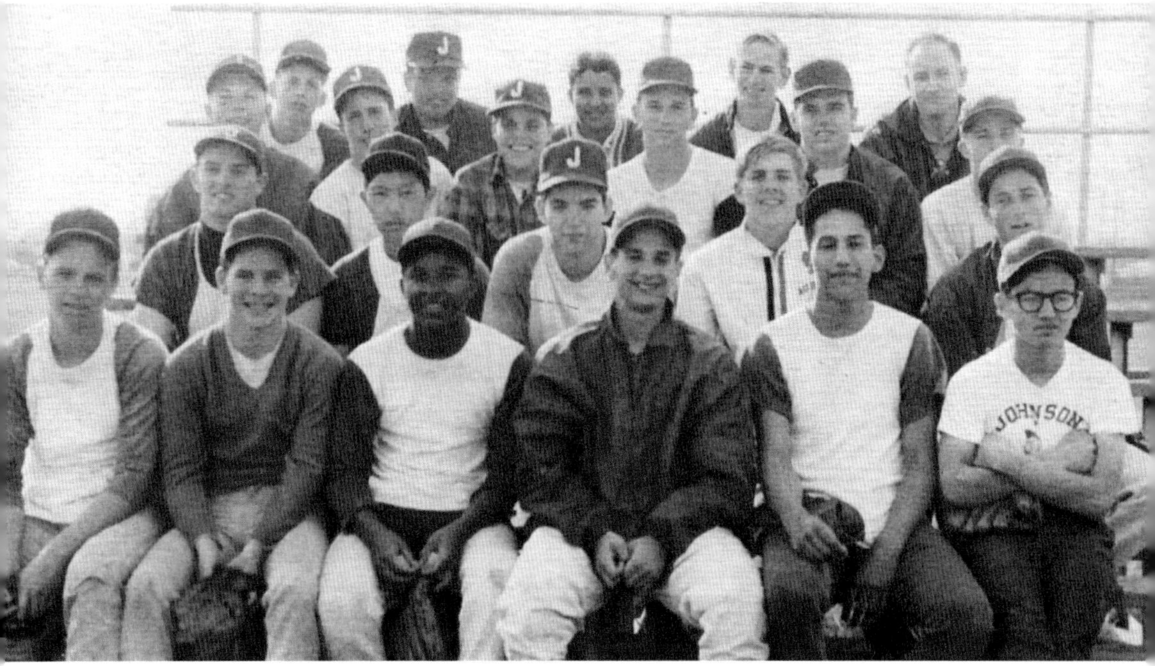

The 1966 Hiram Johnson junior varsity team is shown here. Since the team is not in uniform, this photograph was probably taken before or after a practice session. From left to right are (first row) Jay Brummer, Mark Lewis, Errol Moore, Danny Piacentini, Tony Ramirez, and Joe Ybarra; (second row) Frank Yates, Mike Morita, Jac Crase, Scott Lawson, Bob Del Chiaro; (third row) Bob Forsch (who went on to play professional baseball with the St. Louis Cardinals), Steve Cukovich, Brian Bush, Ed Wallace, and Rich O'Toole; fourth row, Aurther Claudiaiis, Dave Jackson, Gilbert Lagunas, Jerry Rosano, and Coach Haskell. (Courtesy of Sacramento Public Library, Sacramento Room Special Collections.)

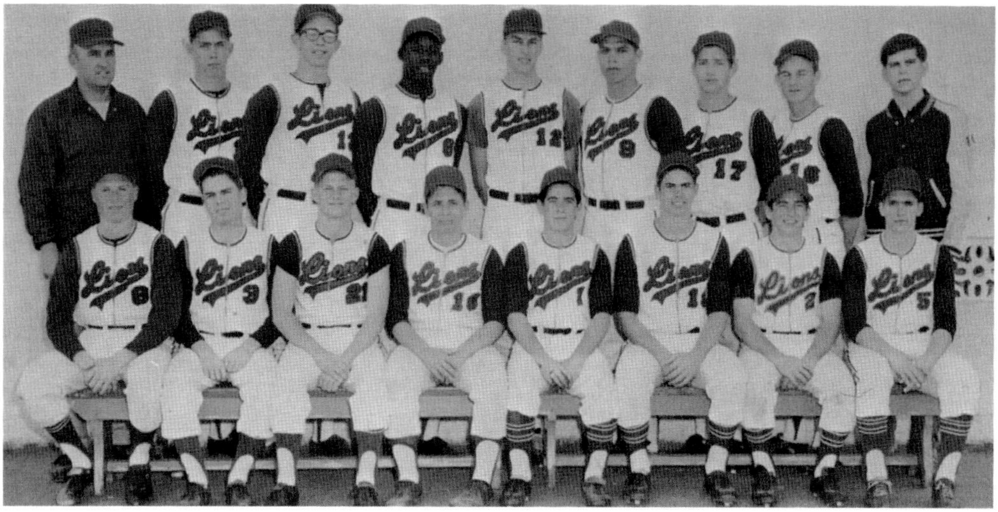

The 1967 varsity team from C.K. McClatchy High School included, from left to right, (first row) Kirt Digitale, Ron Stotz, Fritz Reynolds, Frank Carrass, Paul Muchetto, Mike Pesuit, John Muchetto, and Bruce Gilmore; (second row) coach Bill Whiteneck, Mike Bushing, Rick Schanz, Joe Kemp, Gordon Taylor, Charles Barr, Mark Honeycutt, Ray Russell, and Monty Stewart. (Courtesy of Sacramento Public Library, Sacramento Room Special Collections.)

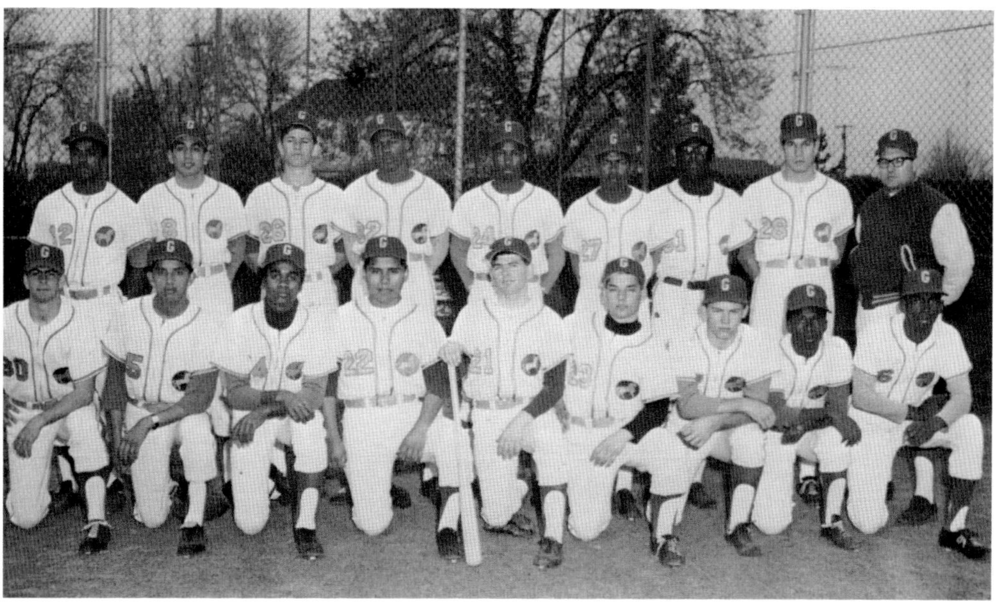

Grant Union High School sat in what was North Sacramento until it merged with Sacramento in a very contested election in 1964. This 17-member 1968 varsity team included, from left to right, (first row) Dave Rees, Tony Rodriguez, Fred Lyons, Carlos Contreras, LeRoy Hixon, Jack Maravilli, John Neely, Dwight Hogan, and Jerome Rogers; (second row) Nathaniel Harris, Henry Garcia, Ricky Harrison, David Fontain, Dave Thornton, James Pruit, Tommy Lee, Mike Willet, and coach Jim Ramey. (Courtesy of Sacramento Public Library, Sacramento Room Special Collections.)

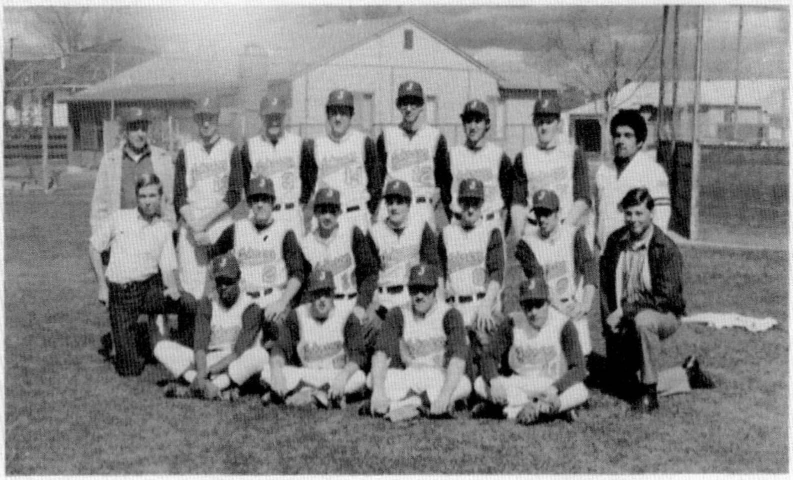

Left to right–Top row: Coach Perry, Tom Simas, Shane Scott, Joe Manos, Fred Maxon, Curtis Matos, Mike Keegan, Manager Frank Ramirez. Second row: Score keeper–Doug Bonham, Russ Wunderly, Dave Fox, Curtis Eid, Mike Stodghill, Larry Hale, Manager Tim Lloyd. Third row: Dave Johnson, Tom Nigro, Fred Turner, Rodney Clausen.

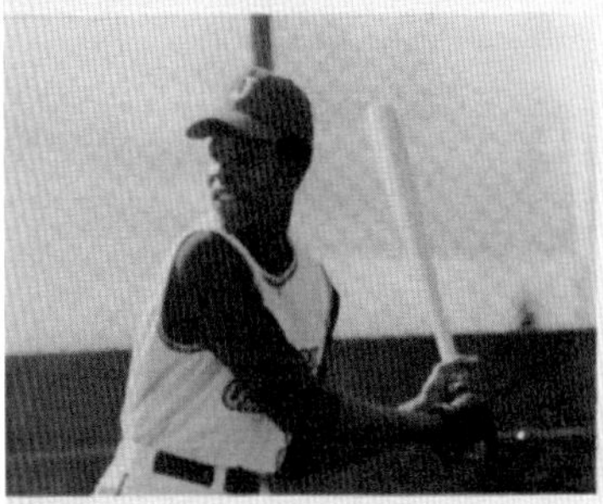

David Johnson prepares for grand slam.

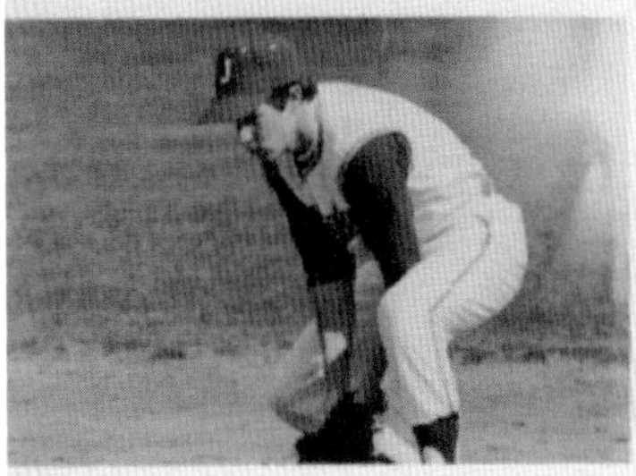

Curtis Eid picks up infield grounder.

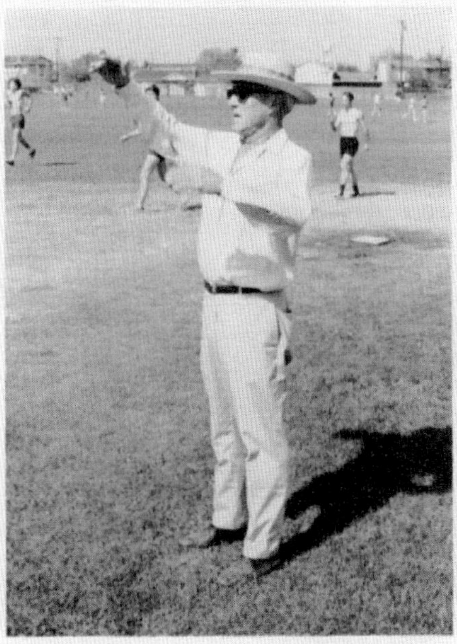

Coach Perry heads Varsity Baseball.

This 1971 photograph of the Hiram Johnson varsity team pictures, from left to right, (first row) Dave Johnson, Tom Nigro, Fred Turner, and Rodney Clausen; (second row) Doug Bonham, (scorekeeper), Russ Wunderley, Dave Fox, Kurtis Eid, Mike Stodghill, Larry Hale, and Tim Lloyd (manager); (third row) Coach Perry, Tom Simas, Shane Scott, Joe Manos, Fred Maxon, Curtis Mattos, Mike Keegan, and Frank Rameriz (manager). The bottom photographs show Dave Johnson with bat in hand, Kurtis Eid fielding a ball, and Coach Perry. (Courtesy of Sacramento Public Library, Sacramento Room Special Collections.)

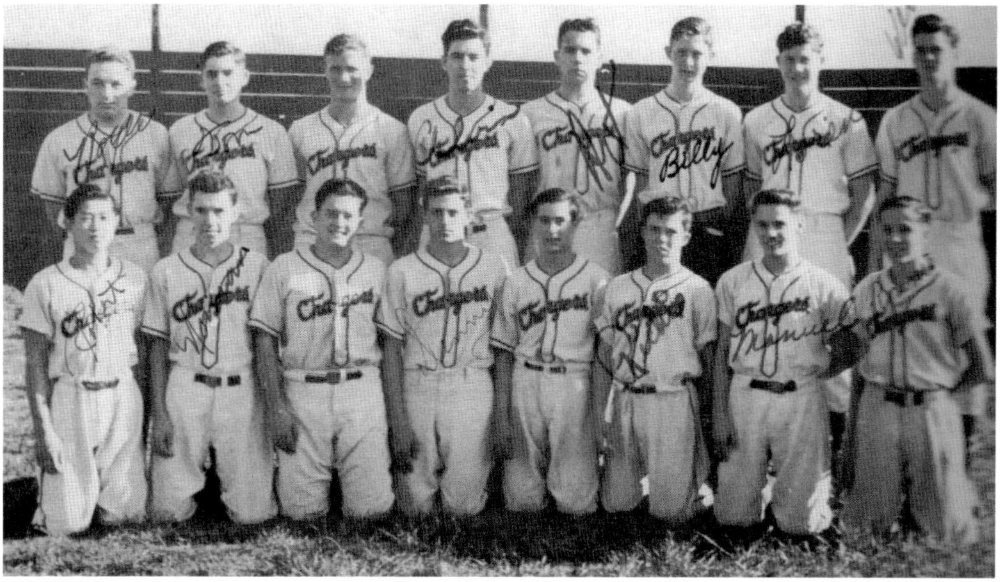

The 1947 Courtland Union High School team played a 17-game schedule that included 10 league and 7 non-league games. The players representing the school consisted of, from left to right, (first row) B. Jang, N. Zgraggen, E. Truman, D. Hill, N. Rose, R. Neves, M. Enos, and R. Reeve; (second row) R. Romani, T. Brown, R. Alspaw, A. Machado, A. Brown, B. Atkins, L. Harter, and V. Simoni. (Courtesy of Sacramento Public Library, Sacramento Room Special Collections.)

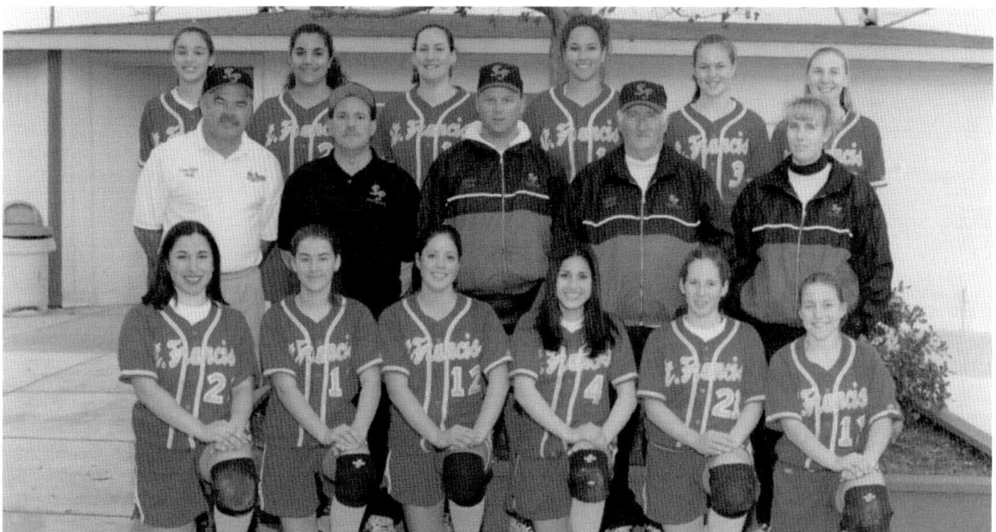

This photograph shows the 2001 St. Francis High School softball team. Pictured are, from left to right, (first row) Eleni Papailias, Michelle Padilla, Clairissa Rodriguez, Gina Firenze, Stephanie Williamson, and Michelle Vlahos-Lusi; (second row) coaches Ken McGuire, Al LoGiudice, Ken Van Meter, Don Deatherage, and Tera Carson; (third row) Hennessy Rodriguez, Melissa Valdez, Nikki Buchko, Karen Carmichael, Tara Van Meter, and Lindsey Krabbenhoft. (Courtesy of Bessie Papailias.)

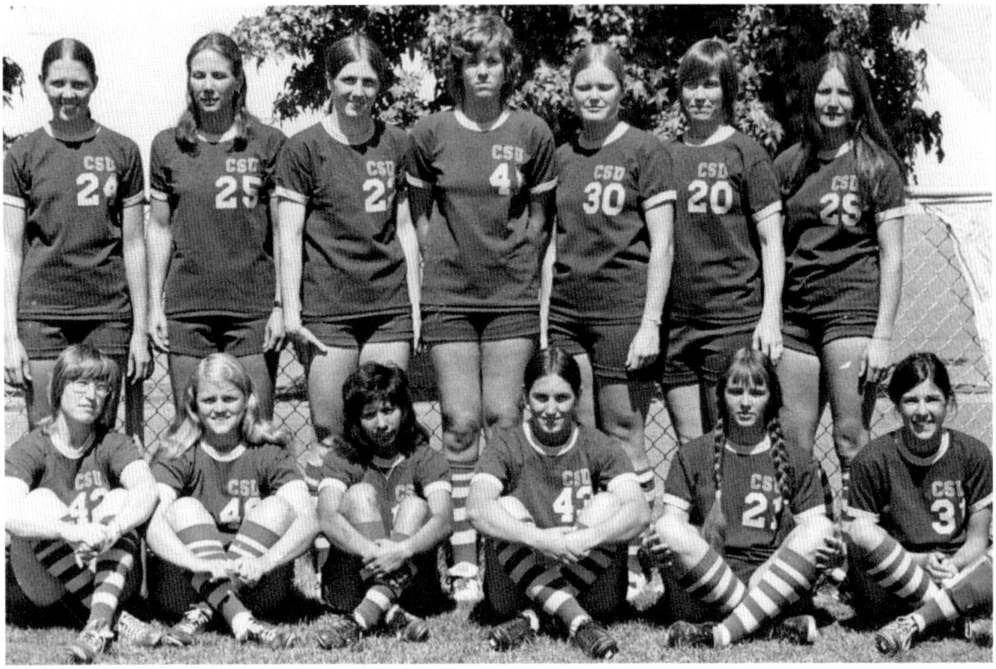

The year 1974 marked the first year Sacramento State College fielded a softball team. That same year, the school's name was changed to California State University, Sacramento. (Courtesy of California State University, Sacramento Library Archives.)

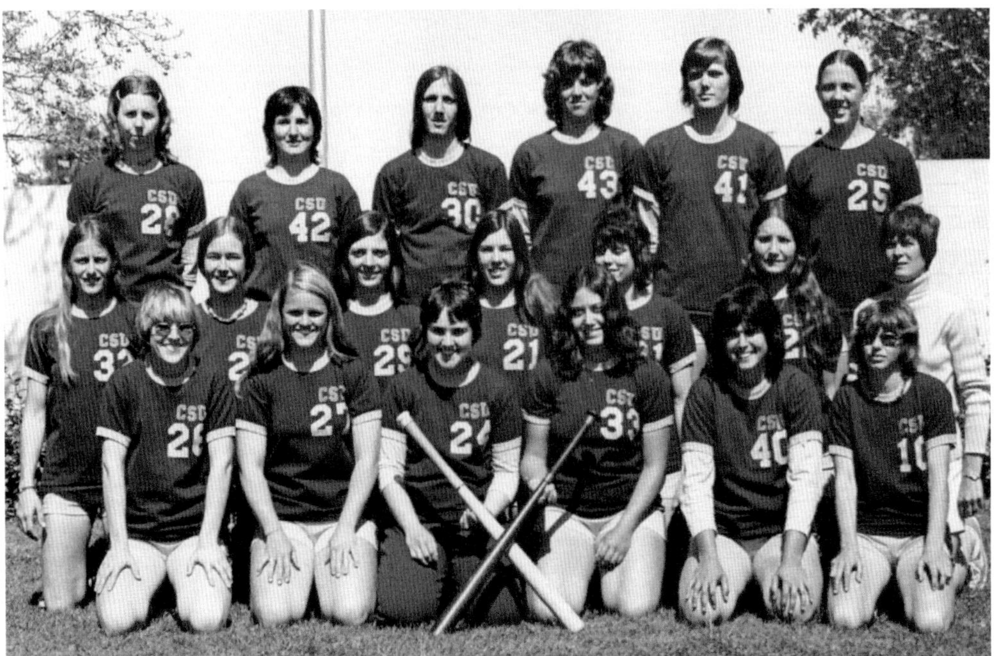

This photograph shows the 1975 Sacramento State College softball team. (Courtesy of California State University, Sacramento Library Archives.)

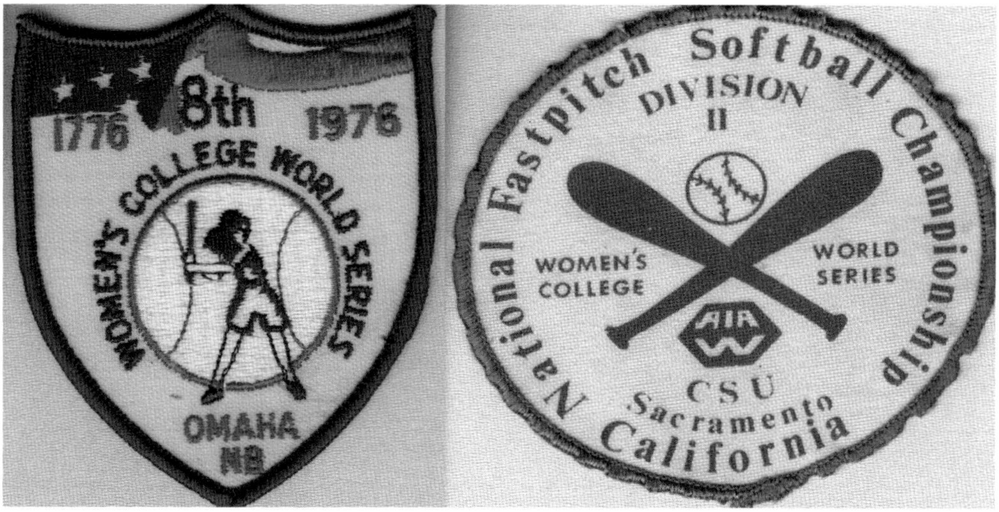

These two arm patches were worn by members of the CSU–Sacramento softball team when they played in the College World Series in Omaha, Nebraska. Although they did not win the championship in these years, they did win the regional championships to qualify for the series. (Courtesy of California State University, Sacramento Library Archives.)

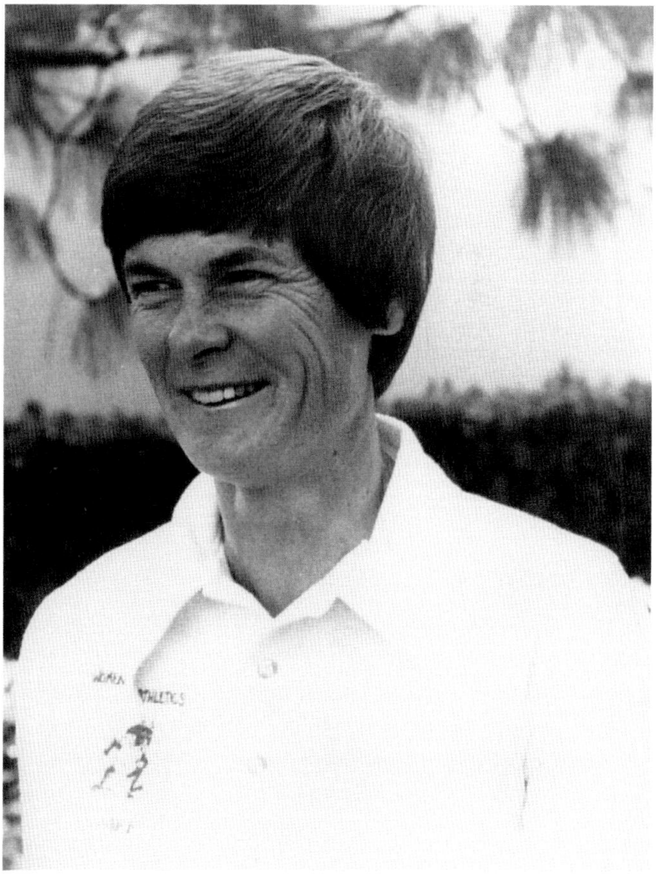

Emma McConkie (right), CSU–Sacramento softball coach from 1974 to 1986, recruited many of her best players from Sacramento area high schools and community colleges and took the teams through several successful years. They compiled a 45-4 regular season record from 1974 to 1976, the first two years of the program, and played in several national championships, including the College World Series in 1976, where they did well but finished ninth overall. The team made the College World Series again in 1981, this time clinching the national title. (Courtesy of California State University, Sacramento Library Archives.)

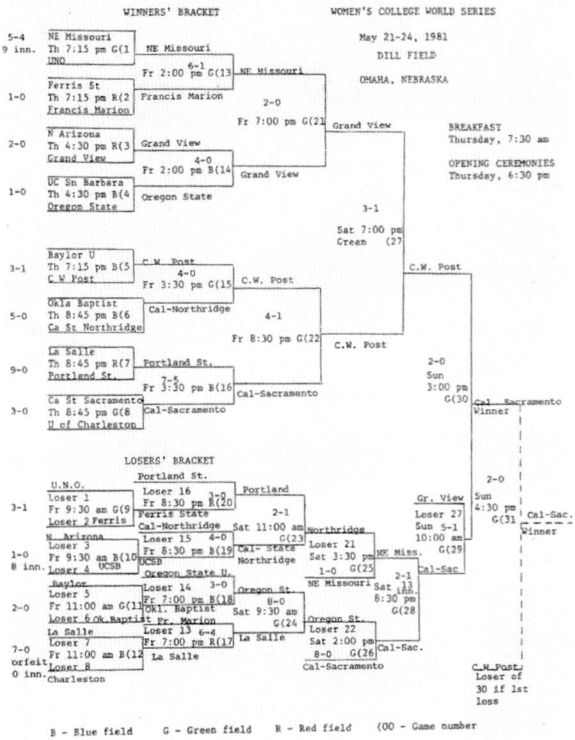

This 1981 photograph shows the Women's College World Series bracket with the CSU–Sacramento team as the winner of the College Softball World Series. The team had to first win the division series before advancing to the College World Series. Once they made it to Omaha, they had to play several more games in a double elimination format to win the championship. (Courtesy of California State University, Sacramento Library Archives.)

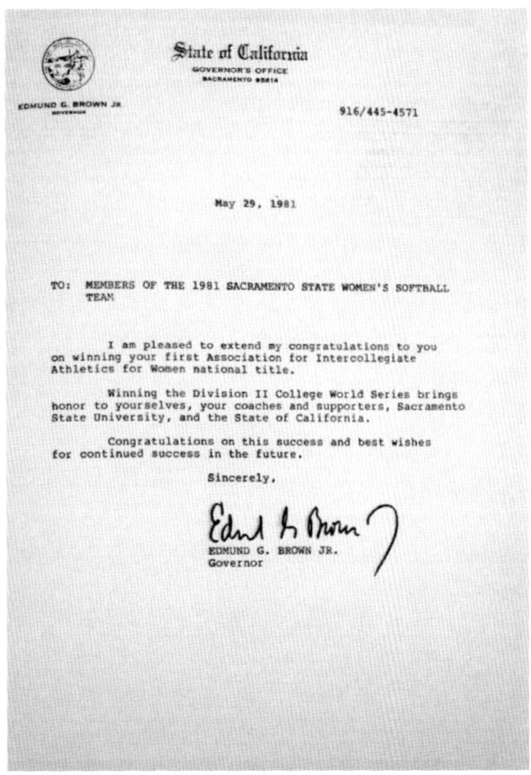

State of California
GOVERNOR'S OFFICE
SACRAMENTO 95814

EDMUND G. BROWN JR.
GOVERNOR

916/445-4571

May 29, 1981

TO: MEMBERS OF THE 1981 SACRAMENTO STATE WOMEN'S SOFTBALL TEAM

I am pleased to extend my congratulations to you on winning your first Association for Intercollegiate Athletics for Women national title.

Winning the Division II College World Series brings honor to yourselves, your coaches and supporters, Sacramento State University, and the State of California.

Congratulations on this success and best wishes for continued success in the future.

Sincerely,

Edmund G. Brown

EDMUND G. BROWN JR.
Governor

This 1981 letter from Gov. Jerry Brown during his second term (he served a total of four terms) congratulates the team for their College World Series championship. (Courtesy of California State University, Sacramento Library Archives.)

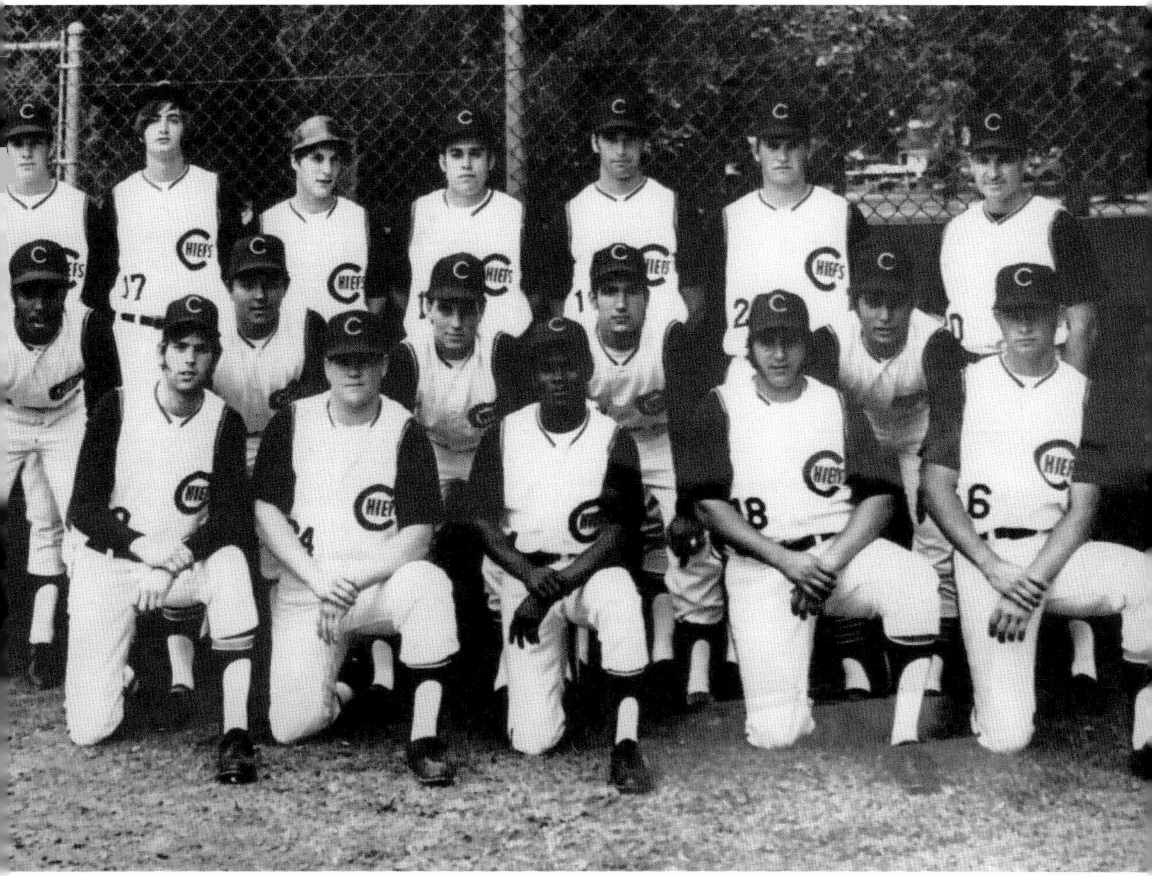

This 1971 photograph shows the Cosumnes River College Chiefs. The college opened on September 14, 1970, and fielded this baseball team, its first, in 1971. Pictured are, from left to right, (first row) Larry Fidler, Dan Sellers, Steve Pernell, Steve Brusha, and Randy Twilling; (second row) Duane Reed, Mario Villanueva, Gary Domingas, John Cimino, and Craig Lloyd; (third row) Joe Meyers, Jim Smith, Bob Boxley, Greg Kirtland, Dave Hubbard, Vince Lampman, and Del Bandy (coach). (Courtesy of Randy Twilling.)

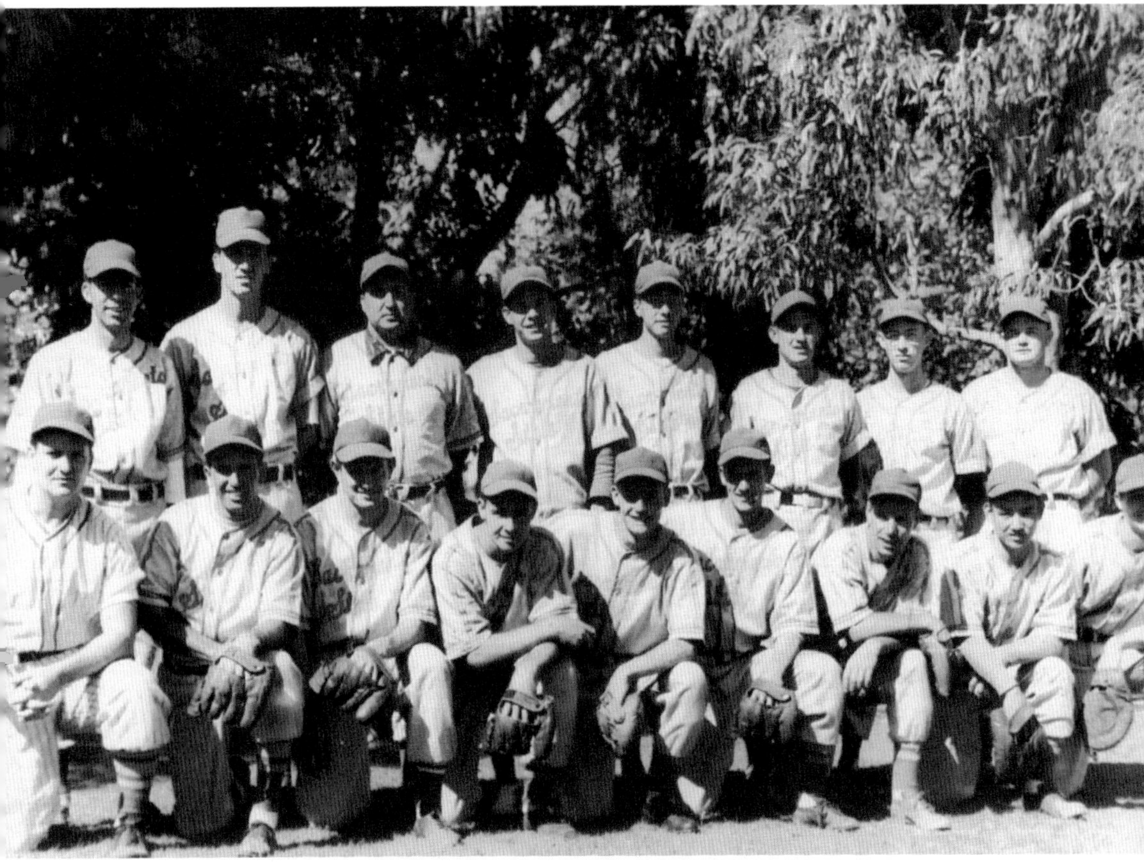

This photograph displays the 1949–1950 Sacramento State College baseball team. Team members are, from left to right, (first row) Dr. William Miller (coach), George Vernatchi, Marino Pierucci, Del Brandy, Don McKenzie, Bob Hanlon, Jim Tsukamoto, and Bob Osborn; (second row) Norm Silver, Jack Heron, John Valentino, Bob Rodness, Don Parsons, Dick Galvin, Jonh Runlet, and Larry Mann. This team played at Sacramento Junior (City) College as the campus at its current location in East Sacramento was not opened until 1952. (Courtesy of California State University, Sacramento Library Archives.)

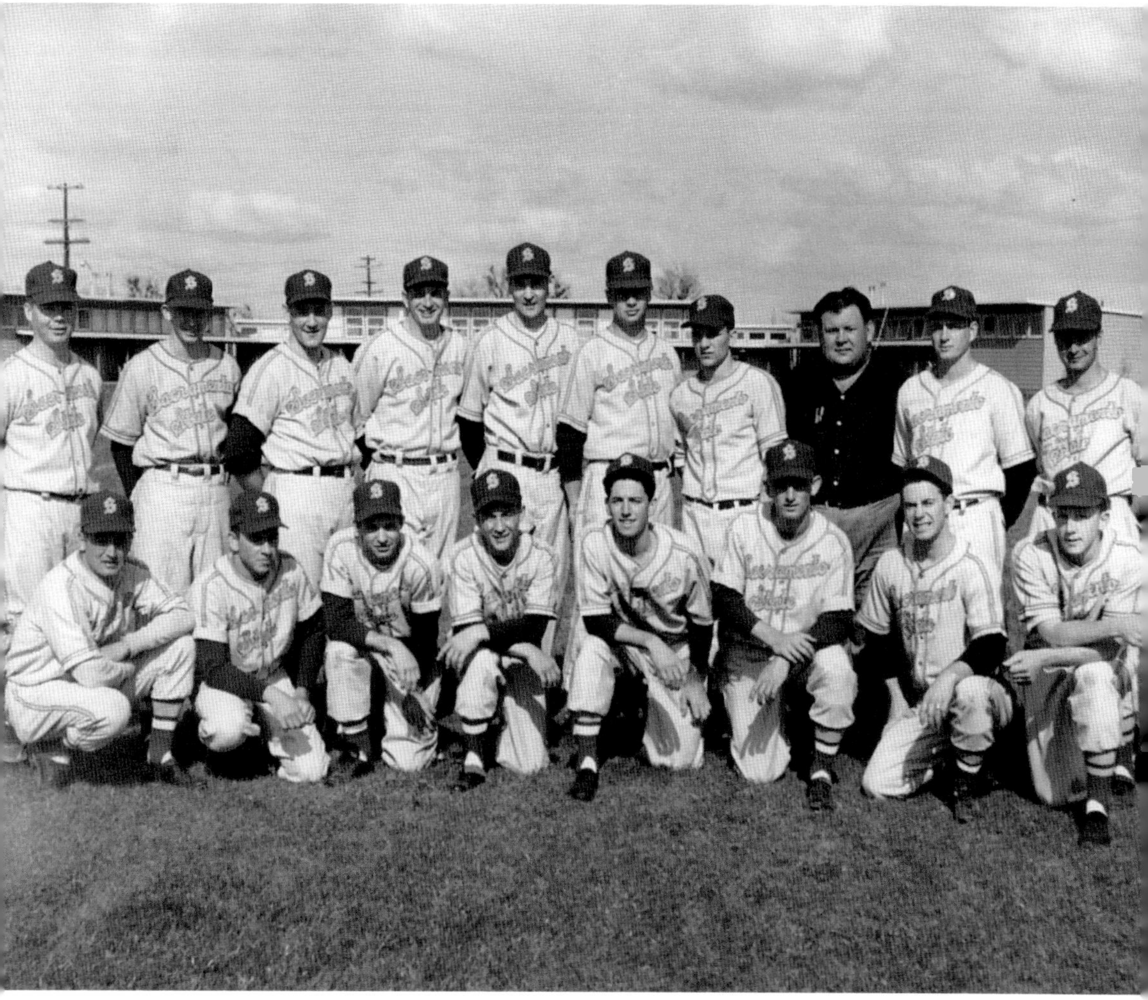

The 1952 Sacramento State College baseball team was the first team to play at the permanent campus. The members of the team included, from left to right, (first row) Hal Wolf (coach), John Mazzi, Atch Pedretti (team captain), San Pullaro, Mel Sherman, Tom Hocking, Dave Hotell, Dick Olson, Ron Hoy, Ed Pegram, and "Doc" Haskell; (second row) Akio Iwanaga (manager), Bob "Lefty" White, Tony Kosinski, Hank Wagner, Jim Casali, Fred Moeller, Dick Jacquier (assistant coach), Gordon Nixon, Bob Nelson, and Rolf Moeller (assistant coach). (Courtesy of California State University, Sacramento Library Archives.)

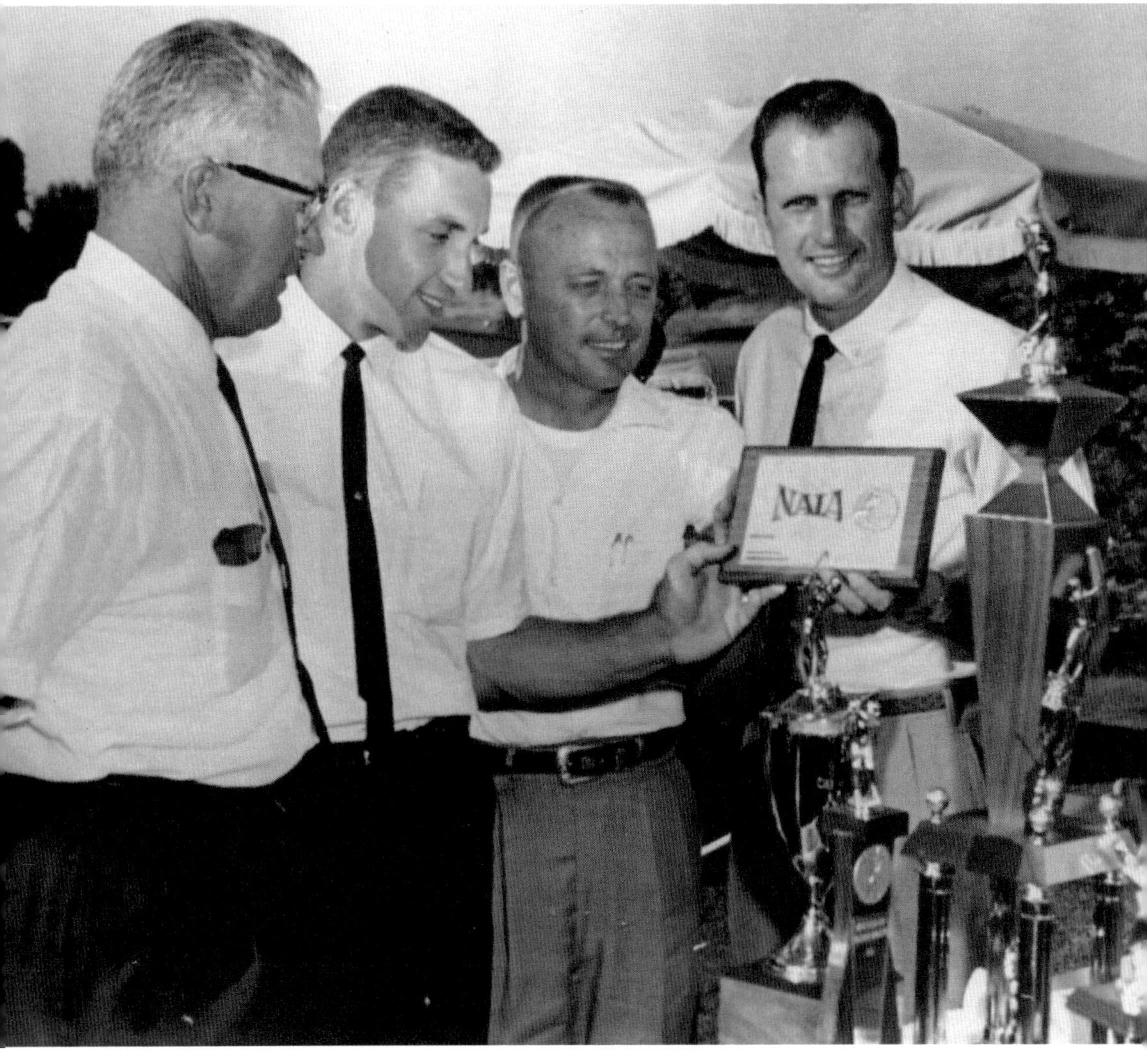

The year 1961 was the first time the Sacramento State baseball team played in a national championship. This photograph shows the National Association of Intercollegiate Athletics (NAIA) trophy being admired by, from left to right, John Baker, director of athletics; Dick Bach, All-American pitcher Bill Woods, of the Sacramento Chamber of Commerce; and Cal Boyes, Sacramento State baseball coach. (Courtesy of California State University, Sacramento Library Archives.)

4

Nisei Baseball in Sacramento

From the Florin Athletic Club to Internment Camps

Although Issei (first-generation Japanese immigrants) and Nisei (second-generation Japanese Americans) baseball was being played in Sacramento prior to 1914, in that year the first local Japanese American team in Florin, a small agricultural community nestled in the southern part of Sacramento County between the Sacramento city limits and what is now Elk Grove, was formed as the Florin Athletic Club. Although it was not the only Japanese American athletic club that had a competitive baseball team, it was recognized as one of the pioneer Japanese American teams in the Sacramento Valley and in all of America. In the 1920s and 1930s, the club achieved notoriety as a perennial powerhouse in the A division of the Northern California baseball circuit.

On April 14, 1923, in a short article, an all-Japanese baseball league was announced by the *Sacramento Bee* that consisted of teams from the San Francisco Bay Area and Sacramento. It noted that Stockton and Sacramento had their own ballparks.

Throughout the 1920s and 1930s, Sacramento area teams played each other and traveled the Sacramento and San Joaquin Valleys competing against other Japanese teams. The Florin Athletic Club gained statewide recognition during this period, earning several victories and championships.

Although Issei and Nisei played ball in and around Sacramento since the early 1900s, none of them played professionally. In 1932, that changed when Kenso Nushida became the first Japanese American to play professional baseball in the United States above the D level when he signed with the Sacramento Solons (Senators).

Following the declaration of war on Japan in December 1941, more than 120,000 Americans of Japanese descent were relocated to detention camps and detention centers, where they immediately formed baseball teams. Shortly after they were relocated to permanent camps, they built baseball diamonds and formed competitive teams. After the war's end in 1945, many new Japanese American teams and leagues were formed, including the Sacramento All-Stars.

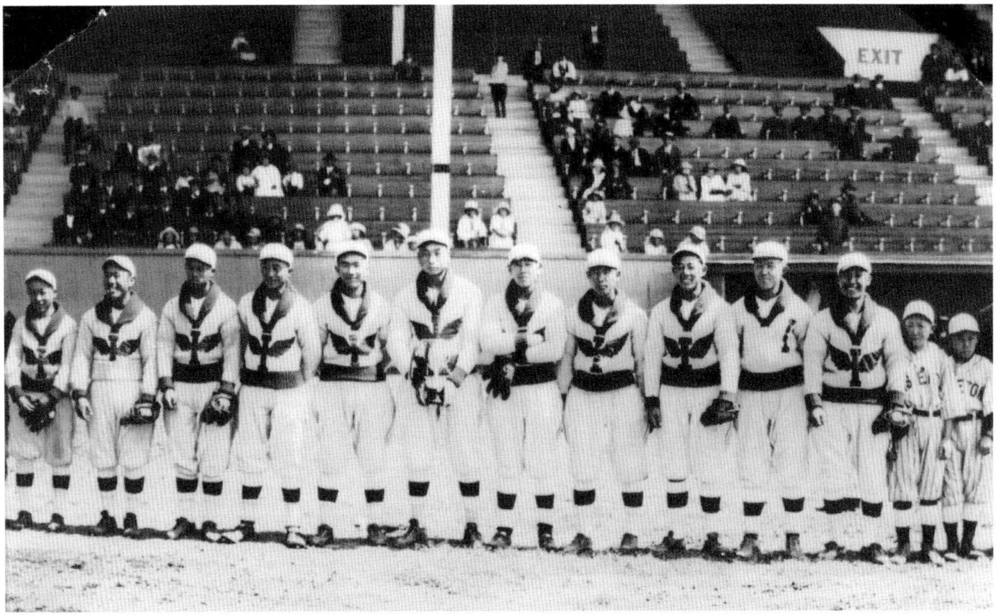

This photograph shows the 1923 Isleton Athletic Club's baseball team. Pictured are, from left to right, Laurence Nakano, Shu Sumi, Herbert H. Hoshiko, two unidentified, June Araki, unidentified, Kiyo Sumi, Terao "Tiger" Ogawa, Kitazumi, unidentified, Yukio Nakano, and Hiroki Hoshiko. (Courtesy of California State University, Sacramento Library Archives.)

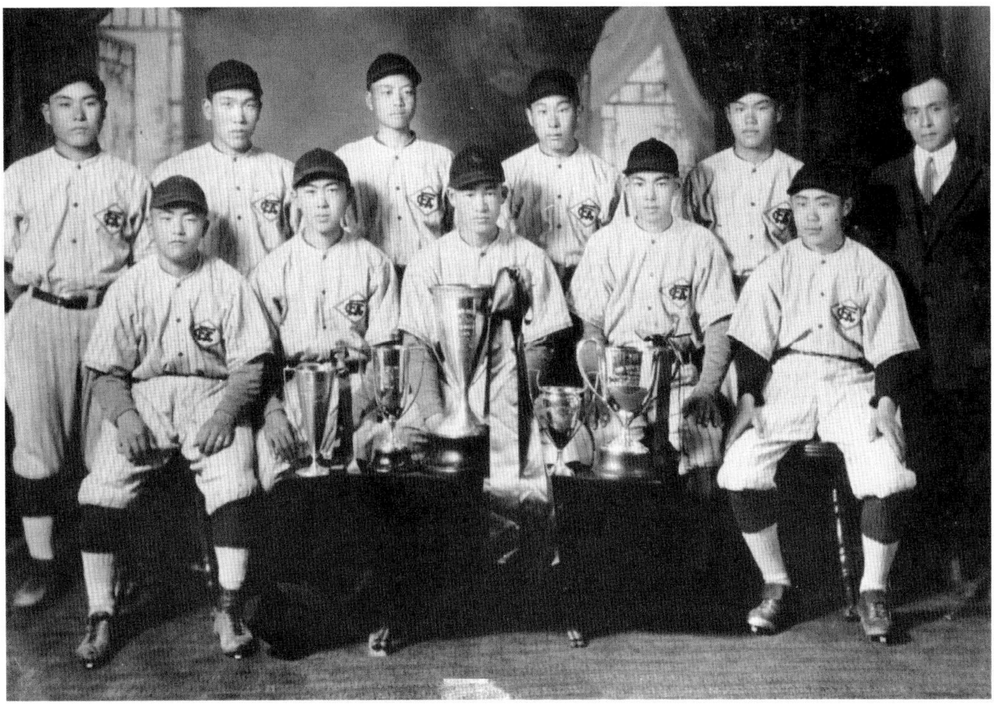

This photograph shows the 1922 or 1927 Florin Athletic Club baseball team with several of their trophies displayed. (Courtesy of California State University, Sacramento Library Archives.)

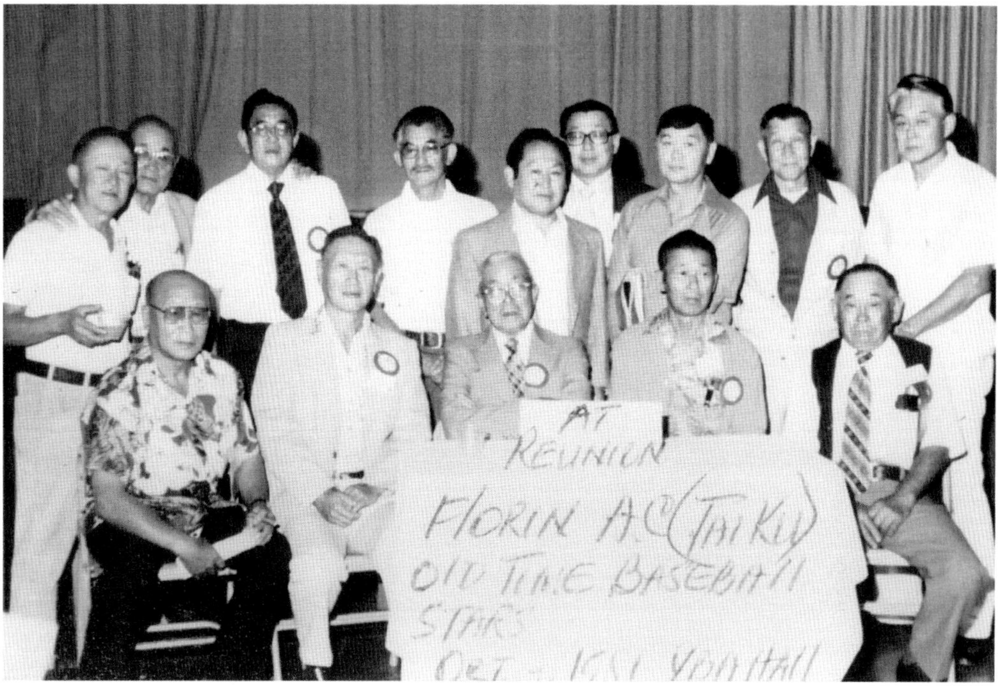

This October 9, 1981, photograph shows a reunion of many members of the pre–World War II Florin Athletic Club. (Courtesy of California State University, Sacramento Library Archives.)

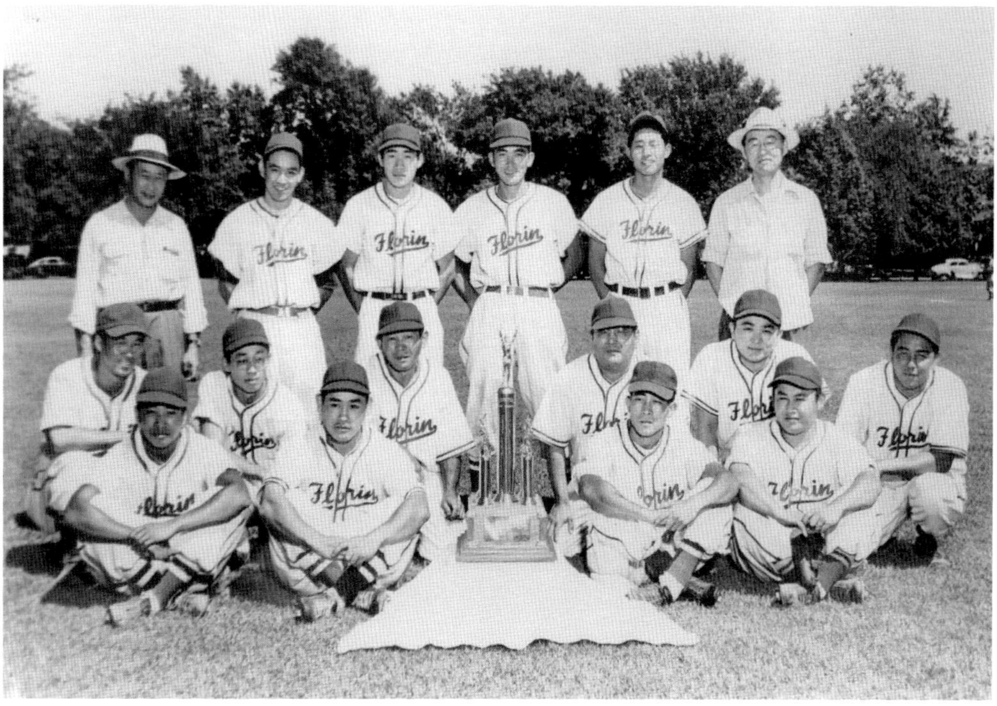

This photograph displays the Florin Athletic Club baseball team in 1949. (Courtesy of California State University, Sacramento Library Archives.)

ALL-STARS SHADE 442ND INFANTRY NINE, 3-2

A SOFTBALL LEAGUE SCHEDULE

(All games start at 6 p.m.)

• Today:
Bruins vs. Block 40
20th Century vs. Double Xs

• Tomorrow:
Islanders vs. Mustangs
Block 3 Sharks vs. Zorros

• Thursday:
LDQs vs. Block 40
Duration Knights vs. Co-op

• Friday:
Islanders vs. Bruins
Zorros vs. Double Xs

MEN'S SCHEDULE

(All games start at 6 p.m.)

• Today:
Block 17 vs. Block 35

• Tomorrow:
Block 14 vs. Block 46

• Thursday:
All-Stars Practice

• Friday:
All-Stars Practice

TRIBUNE SPORTS

September 7, 1943 Page 5

BILL TSUKAMOTO, TAK ABO LEAD A, B LOOP BATTING

A LEAGUE BATTING LEADERS

Name Team	AB	H	Ave.
Bill Tsukamoto (Florin)	41	19	.463
James Takigawa (Bowles)	33	14	.424
Shiro Tahara (Florin)	24	9	.375
Tsutomu Ishikawa (Long Beach)	24	9	.375
Yas Chono (Hanford)	36	13	.361
Kaz Shibata (Hanford)	42	14	.333
Yosh Tsukamoto (Florin)	45	15	.333
Yutaka Tokumoto (Bowles)	36	12	.333
Dick Kurima (Florin)	38	12	.316
Dick Kunishima (Hanford)	33	10	.303
Archie Yoshida (Florin)	20	6	.300

B LEAGUE BATTING LEADERS

Name Team	AB	H	Ave.
Takeshi Abe (Fresno)	52	21	.404
George Toyama (Fowler)	67	22	.328
William Odaka (Fresno)	47	15	.321
Hiroshi Uyehara (Hawaii)	53	17	.320
Ted Sekikawa (Elk Grove)	55	17	.309
Fumio Kusunoki (Hawaii)	46	14	.304
Ted Taniguchi (Elk Grove)	46	14	.304
James Renge (Fowler)	66	20	.303
Yosh Ushiro (Hanford)	50	15	.300
Tets Onishi (Elk Grove)	68	20	.294

BRILLIANT FIELDING, KURIMA COMBINE TO DOWN VISITORS

With the classy Denson infield displaying some brilliant defensive fielding and veteran Herbert "Moon" Kurima distributing six blows effectively, the Center All-Stars nipped the 442nd Infantry from Camp Shelby, 3-2, in the first and only fracas on the Block 21 diamond Saturday of a scheduled three-game series. The latter two slated for Sunday in a twin bill was rained out.

First baseman Hi Ikeda was credited with 20 putouts in the nine-inning battle.

Leading off in the first canto second baseman Bill Tsukamoto greeted Ikenaga with a sharp single to left. Shortstop Hiro Tahara laid the pill down sacrificing the runner to second. Yosh Tsukamoto came to bat and on the first pitch brother Bill made a dash for the hot corner, while catcher Duke Wataya scatter-armed the apple to third base and the base runner tallied from third with the first run.

The visitors tied it up in their half of the second. Wataya beat out an infield hit. Centerfielder Richard Imaoka moved his mate over to second on a sacrifice bunt. Goro Kashiwaeda who singled twice drove in Wataya.

Time Out with Nob Shino

BLAZING SPEED--The 442nd Infantry's diminutive Henry Kurihara, the fastest man on the squad who ran for Goro Kashiwaeda in the final stanza of the only contest, displayed some of his blazing speed by swiping second. Peppy Kurihara stands only 5 feet with no inches to spare and tips the "Fairbanks" at 120 pounds.

BUCKS--The visitors' starting lineup was formed of buck privates with the exception of first baseman Setsuo "Savage" Tanaka and Tsukasa Duke Wataya who are one and two stripers respectively.

A, B LOOP Pitching Records

A League

Name	W	L
Jim Tanigawa	5	0
Ernie Kurima	1	0
Herb Kurima	4	1
Kiyo Yemoto	2	1
Nob Sasaki	4	4
John Sakamoto	1	1
John Kobayashi	0	1
Tee Saisho	0	2
Cooper Sekikawa	0	2

The August 24 and September 7, 1943, relocation camp newspaper *Tribune* sports sections shown here highlight camp activities during World War II. On August 24, the Denson All-Stars shutout the Arkansas A&M College team 6-0. Herb "Moon" Kurima from the Florin Athletic Club pitched the shutout game. Then again, two weeks later, as the September 7 paper reads, Kurima pitched against the 442nd Infantry Regiment, an all-Nisei regiment, leading them to a 3-2 win. (Both, courtesy of Kerry Yo Nakagawa, Nisei Baseball Research Project.)

DENSON ALL-STARS DOWN ARKANSAS A. AND M.

'MOON' KURIMA SHUTS OUT MONTICELLO OUTFIT, 6-0

Marking the largest crowd ever to assemble on the local diamond, a throng of 4500 baseball enthusiasts watched Denson's "classy" Class A All-Star nine down the Arkansas A. and M. squad, 6-0, behind cool Herb "Moon" Kurima's deceptive six-hit twirling Sunday evening on the Block 21 field.

The winners clinched the tussle in the first three frames by tallying two unearned runs. Towering 6 feet 4, hurler Smokey Carden with three years of college baseball at Texas A. and M. and two years of semi-professional ball to his credit retired the side on strikes in the fourth inning and whiffed nine Densonians.

He had the 4500 on the end of their seats with his blazing fast ball with only veteran Dick Kunishima and Yas Chono both from the lowly Hanford nine tagging Carden for two hits each which accounted for four of the seven Denson hits.

Carden deliveries were so fast that the catcher, Tom Chandler took off his catching togs to move out in centerfield in favor of Chuck Lively who relieved him in the sixth panel.

The visitors had five batters hitting on the opposite side of the platter. Two of them, Bill Agee who played at Paschal High in Fort Worth,

Class B Nine Nips Camp Robinson, 5-4

NISEI SOLDIERS LOSE THIRD STRAIGHT TILT TO LOCALS

Denson made it three in a row as the local Class B All-Stars shaded Camp Robinson's Headquarter Detachment 1861st Unit nine, 5-4, under a sweltering sun on the Block 21 diamond Sunday afternoon.

Tak Abo of the locals mastered the visitors for the full nine-inning tilt, giving up six blows and fanning seven.

Second baseman Yosh Tachino's looping single to center which centerfielder Mits Sato booted checked in George Toyama and Ted Taniguchi which proved to be the tying and winning runs for the victors in the fifth inning.

Camp Robinson grabbed a two-run lead in the first half of the second stanza, but the All-Stars came zooming

TRIBUNE SPORTS

August 24, 1943 Page 7

Top Men's Loop Hitters

Name Team	AB	H	Ave.
Matsuo Sasaki (Block 9)	19	10	.526
Harold Ouchida (Block 9)	17	8	.470
Barry Tsuda (Block 35)	12	5	.416
John Taniguchi (Block 16)	22	9	.409
Kiyoto Ushijima (Block 19)	15	6	.400
Hideo Kadokawa (Block 9)	15	6	.400
Fred Kamioka (Block 19)	10	4	.400
Toshie Sanwo (Block 14)	20	7	.350
Joe Kitano (Block 14)	15	5	.333
Don Arata (Block 14)	19	6	.316

Leading Girls' B Hitters

Name Team	AB	H	Ave.
Eleanor Sekikawa (11-neers)	14	8	.572
Yoshiko Nii (Coronets)	21	11	.524
Shizu Kobashi (Ninerettes)	22	11	.500
Alice Okimura (11-neers)	16	8	.500
Miwako Hatashita (Coronets)	18	9	.500
Sumi Iwatsuru (Ninerettes)	23	11	.478
Rosie Tsukamoto (Ninerettes)	23	11	.478
Sajiko Mibu (Block 18)	17	8	.467
Sally Aoki (Coronets)	12	5	.417
Muriel Nishimura (11-neers)	17	7	.412
Shigeko Masuda (Coronets)	17	7	.412

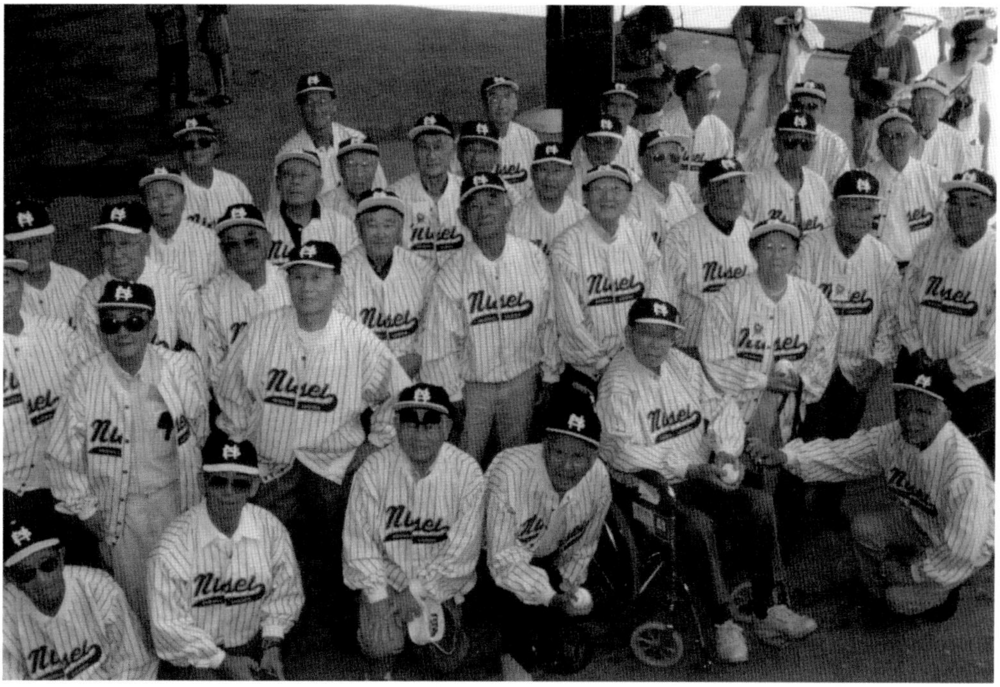

This 1996 photograph shows Northern California Neisi players, including many from the Sacramento area clubs, being honored at Candlestick Park in San Francisco. (Courtesy of Kerry Yo Nakagawa, Nisei Baseball Research Project.)

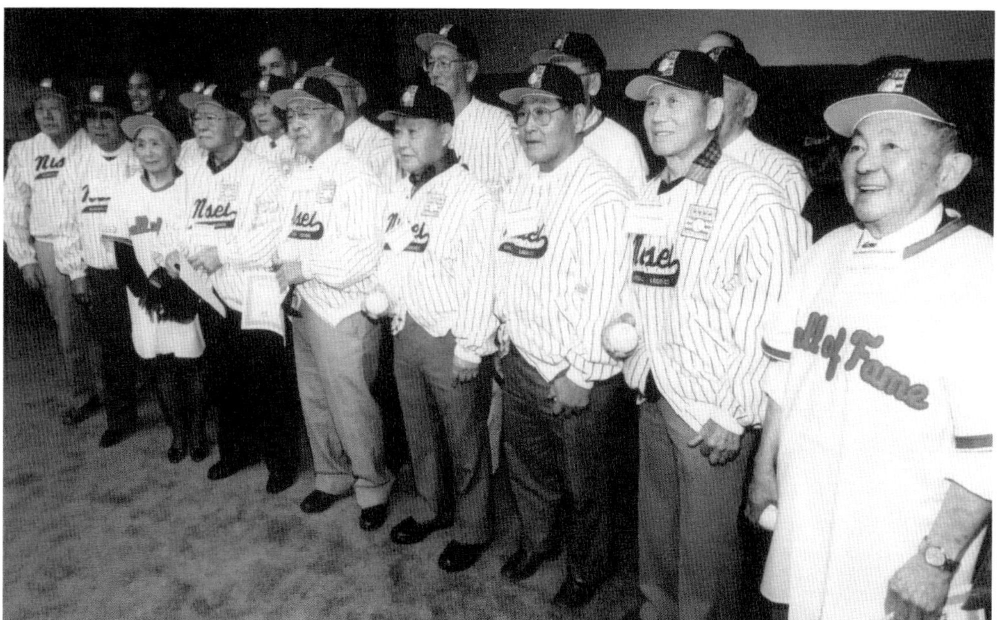

On February 17, 1998, Neisi players were honored at the Baseball Hall of Fame in Cooperstown, New York. Those recognized included several players from Sacramento area teams in 1930s and 1940s. (Courtesy of Kerry Yo Nakagawa, Nisei Baseball Research Project.)

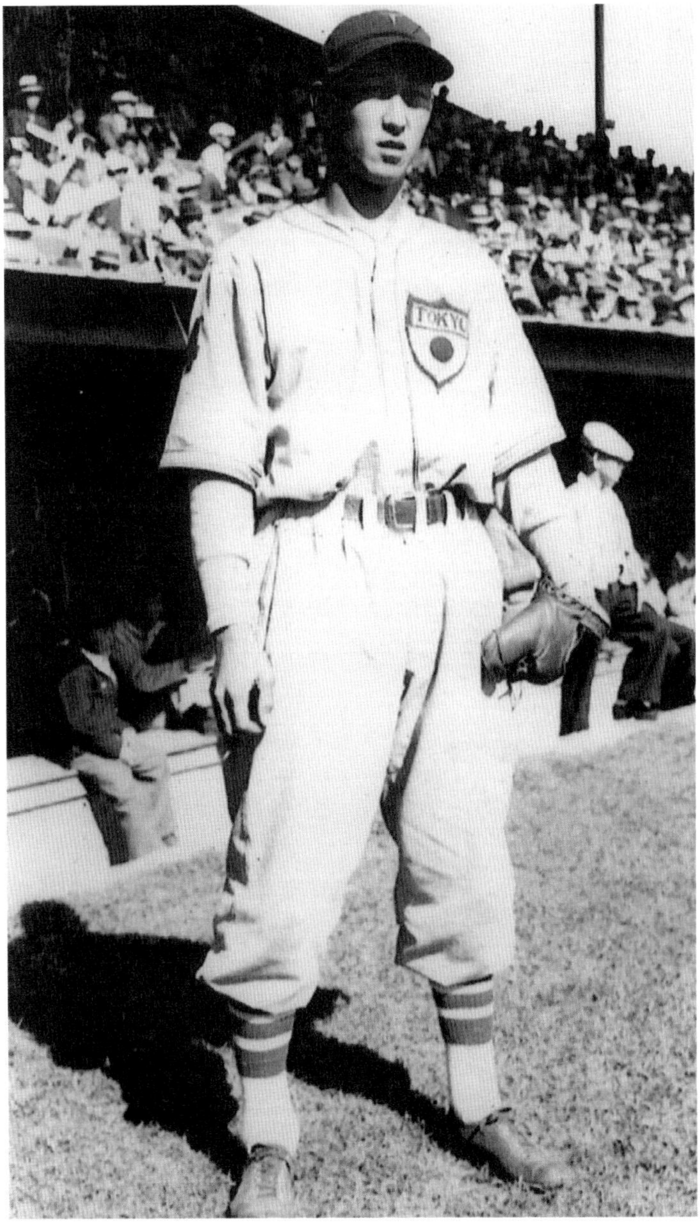

After playing for several minor league teams in the early 1930s, Jimmy Horio, a Hawaiian native, moved to Japan to play for the Tokyo Giants, which played against the Major League All-Star team that included Babe Ruth, Lou Gehrig, Jimmy Fox, and Charlie Gehiniger that toured Japan in 1934. While the Tokyo team was playing in the United States in 1935, Horio's play was impressive enough to win a contract with the Sacramento Solons. He was hitting .291 in late July when his wife was killed in an automobile accident, causing him to suspend his play, and when he returned, he went into a slump, batting .250 but with error-free defense in the remaining 20 games. He only played for the Solons for one season. (Courtesy of Kerry Yo Nakagawa, Nisei Baseball Research Project.)

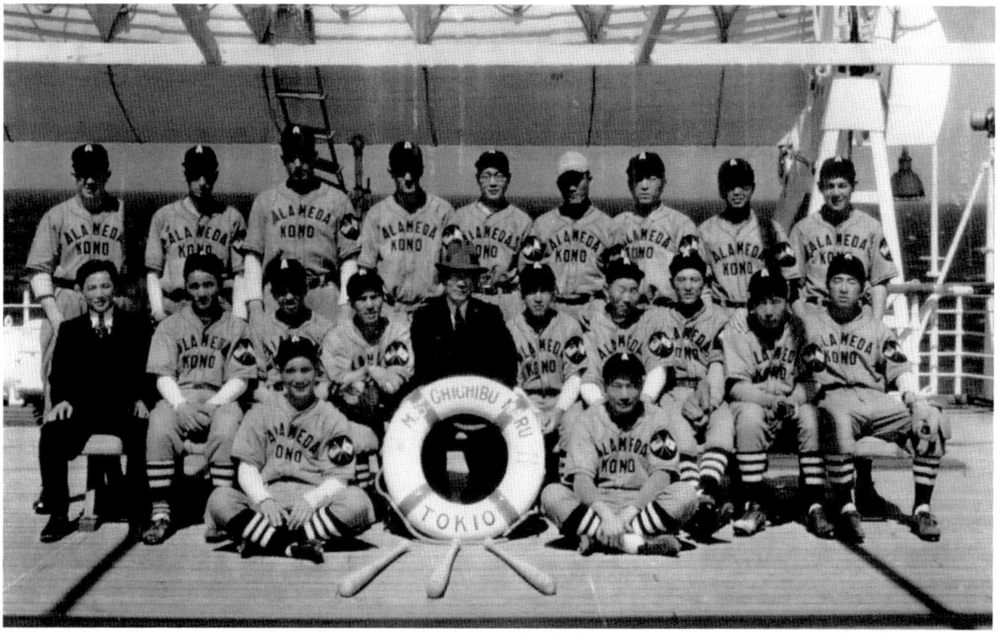

This 1937 photograph shows the Alameda Kono team aboard a ship either en route to or returning from their tour of Japan. Kenso Nushida, who played for the Sacramento Solons, is seated at left in the suit and coached the team. In addition to Nushida, there were four players from Sacramento Valley on the team. (Courtesy of Kerry Yo Nakagawa, Nisei Baseball Research Project.)

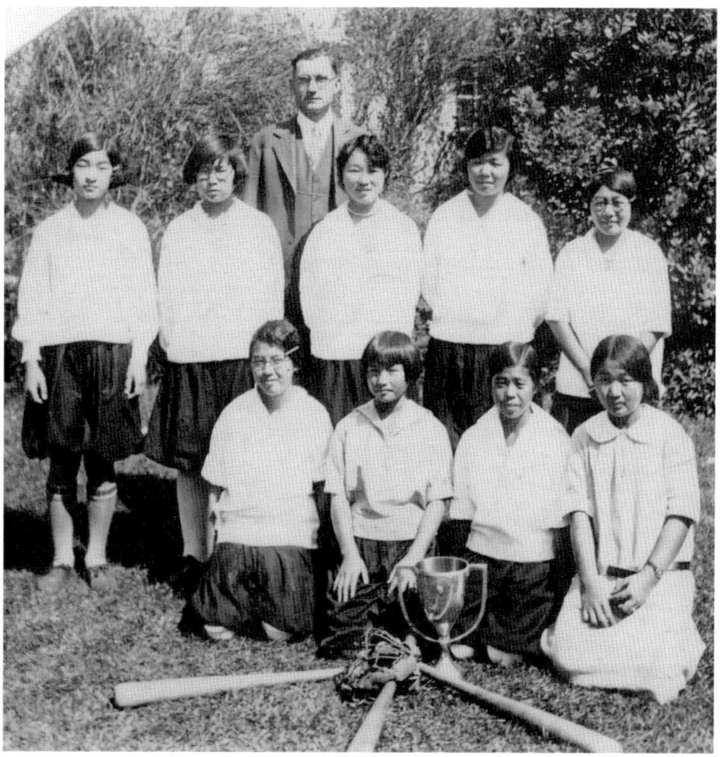

This 1926 photograph shows a Japanese girls' school softball team. Pictured are, from left to right, (first row) May Maruki, Amy Murakami, Frances Seno, and Shizue Kadokawa; (second row) Ruth Dakuzaku, Bernice Fukushima, Alice Yamada, Mary Tanihara, and Ruby Uchida; (third row) principal J.E. Kaler. (Courtesy of California State University, Sacramento Library Archives.)

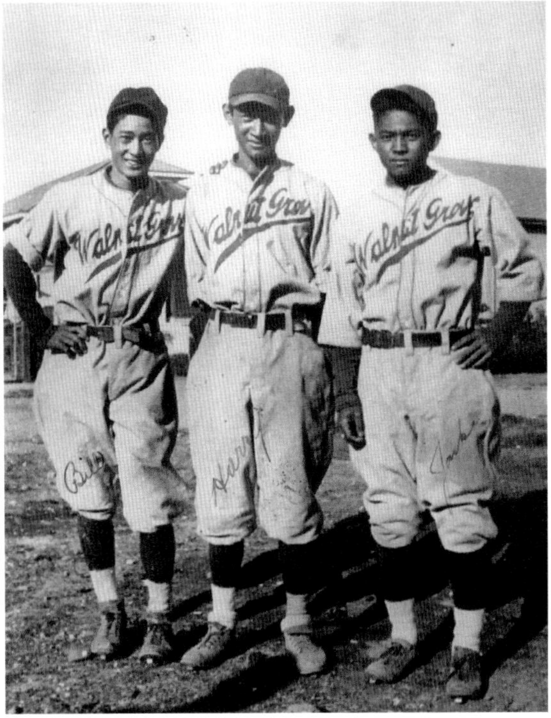

This c. 1930 photograph shows Bill Nikaido at left, Harry Shairo Naka at center, and an unidentified player of the Walnut Grove All-Stars, longtime rivals of the Florin Athletic Club, at right. (Courtesy of Kerry Yo Nakagawa, Nisei Baseball Research Project.)

This 1938 action shot shows Tokyo Giants player Hisanori Karita playing in Sacramento. It was presented to a Mr. Kiki on March 19, 1938, while Karita was in Marysville. (Courtesy of Kerry Yo Nakagawa, Nisei Baseball Research Project.)

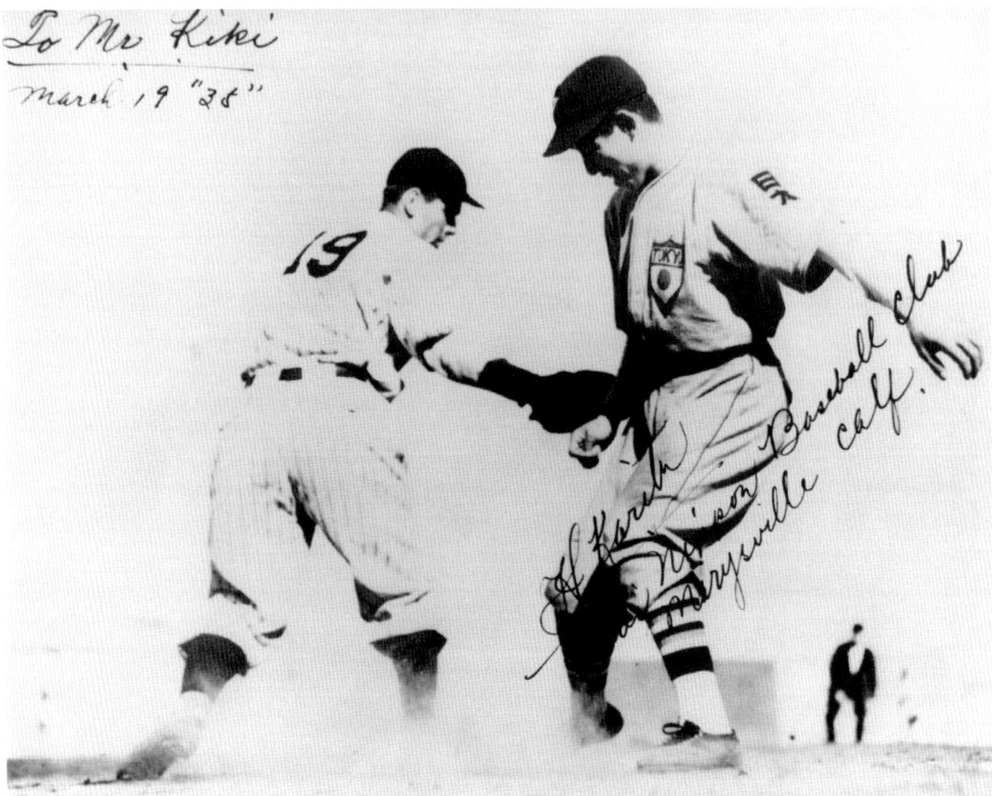

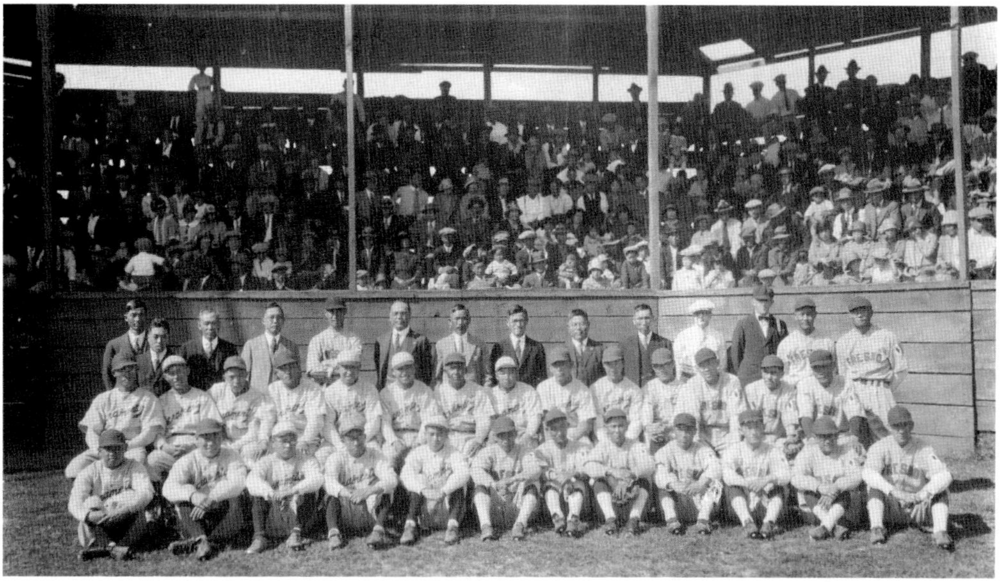

Although this photograph was taken in Fresno, the Tokyo Giants played against the Sacramento Nisei team on several occasions in the decades prior to World War II. (Courtesy of Kerry Yo Nakagawa, Nisei Baseball Research Project.)

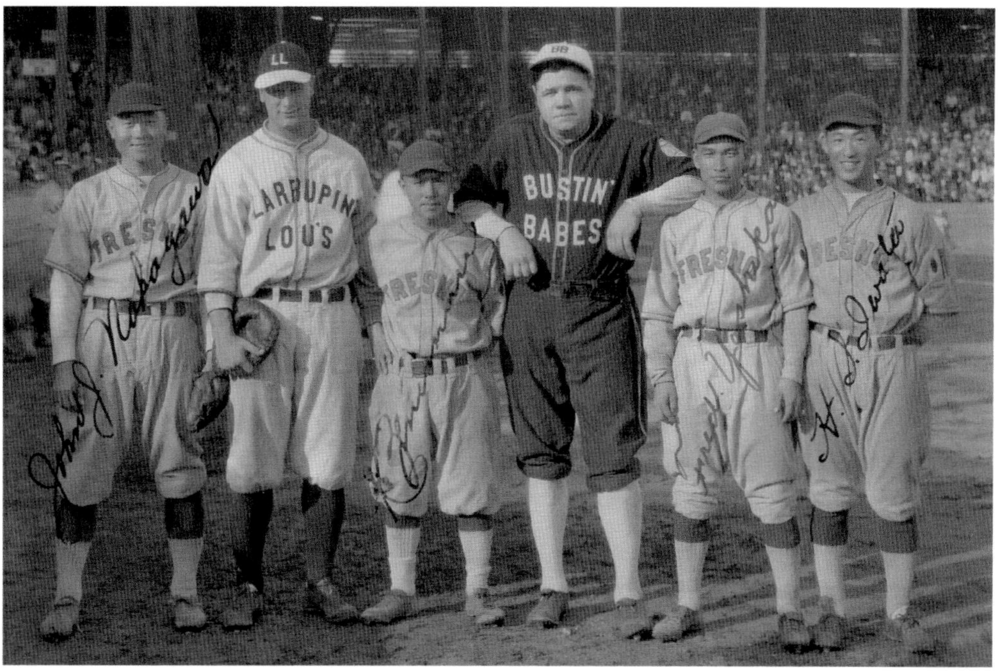

In the late 1920s, New York Yankees stars Babe Ruth and Lou Gehrig formed a touring company in the off-season that traveled from the East Coast to the West Coast performing baseball games against each other in as many as 20 or 30 games over the course of the tour. In this 1927 photograph, Ruth and Gehrig appear with four Nisei players who were part of teams that played in Fresno and Sacramento. (Courtesy of Kerry Yo Nakagawa, Nisei Baseball Research Project.)

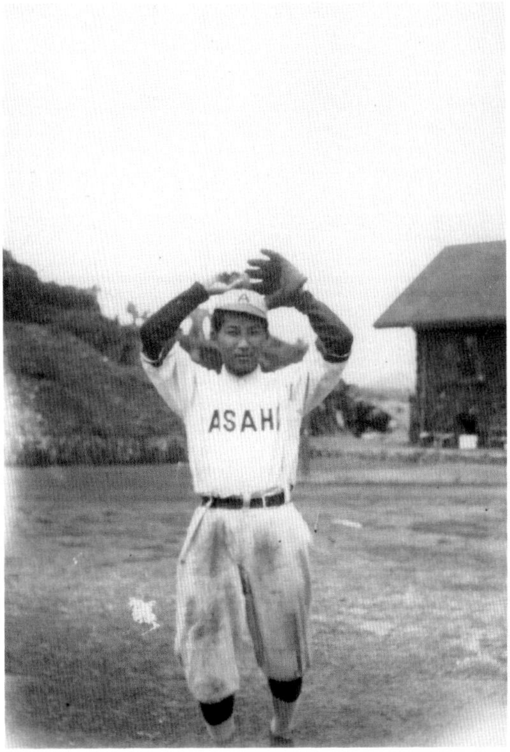

Kenso Nushida became one of the first Japanese American baseball players to play with the Sacramento Senators of the Pacific Coast League in 1932. In 1937, he was a player and coach for the Alameda Kono All-Stars when they toured Japan, Korea, Manchuria, and Harbin, Russia. (Courtesy of Kerry Yo Nakagawa, Nisei Baseball Research Project.)

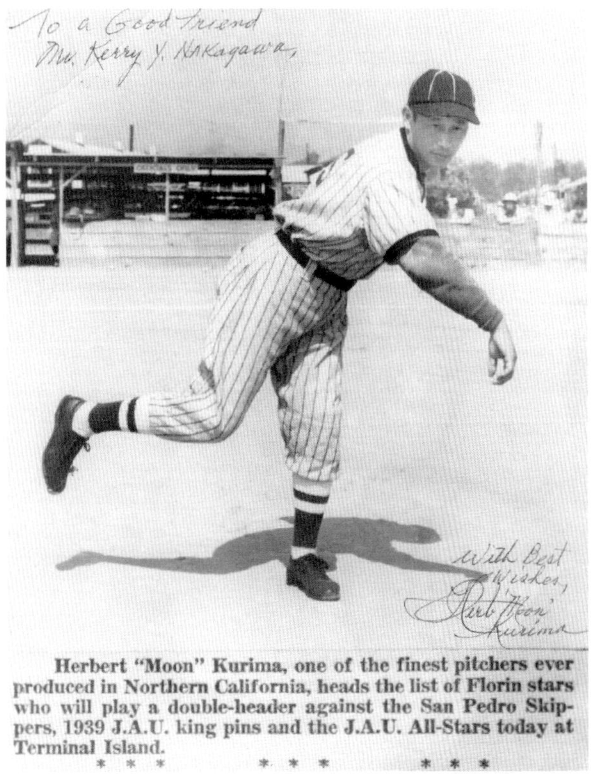

This photograph shows Herb "Moon" Kurima as he appeared with the 1939 Florin All-Stars. The Florin team, like other Nisei teams, were unable to join any official leagues because league competition began in June and the Nisei players had to harvest their strawberry fields, which took place in June, before they could play. (Courtesy of Kerry Yo Nakagawa, Nisei Baseball Research Project.)

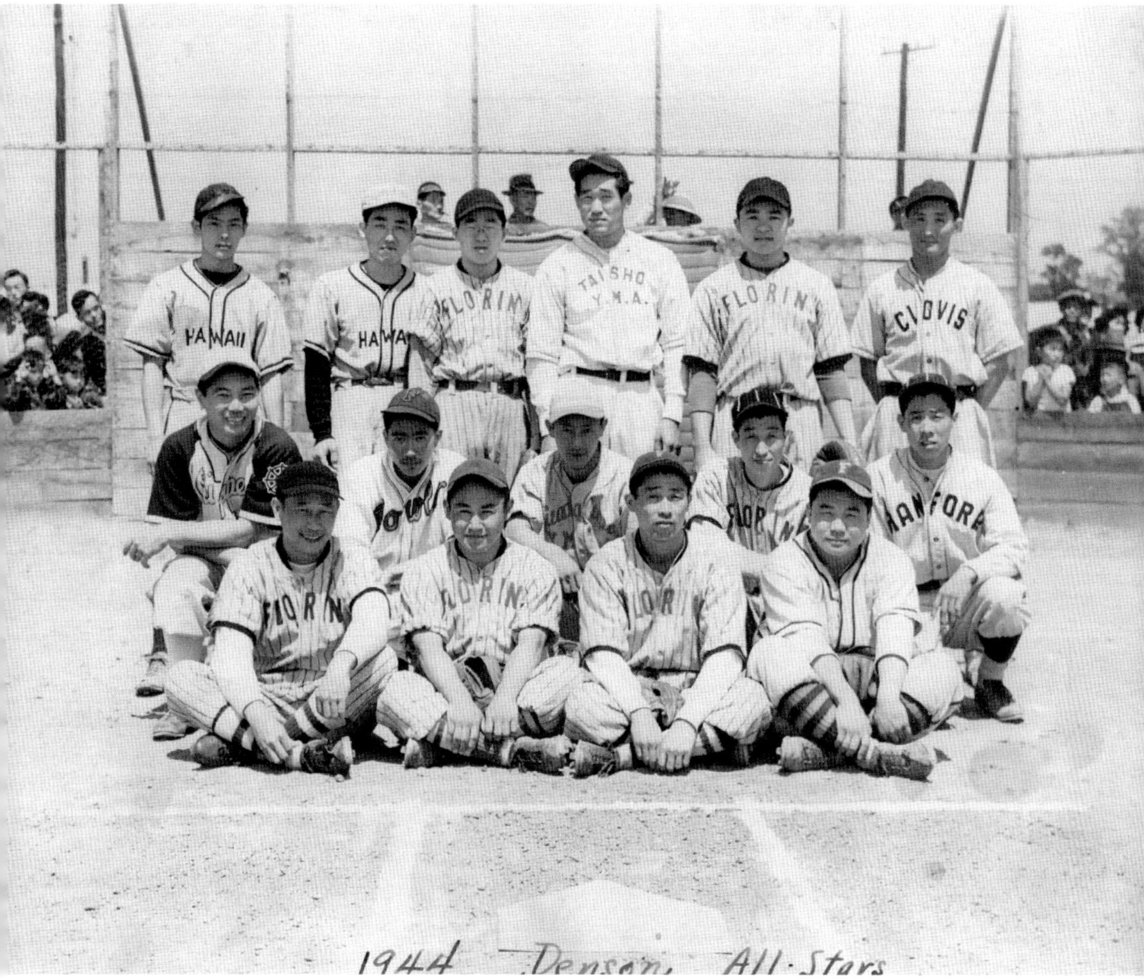

This team photograph shows the Jerome Arkansas Relocation Camp All Stars in 1944. The team features players from the Fresno and Florin Athletic Clubs. (Courtesy of Kerry Yo Nakagawa, Nisei Baseball Research Project.)

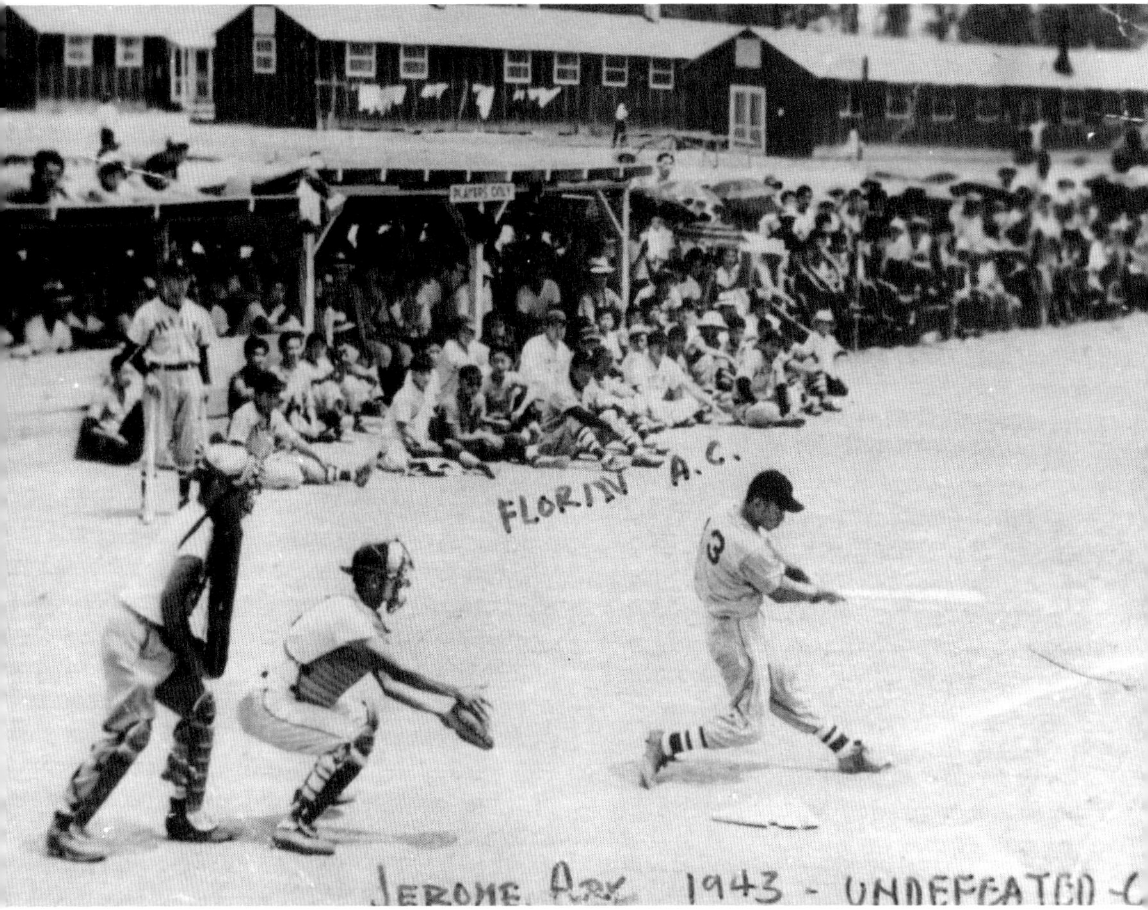

The Florin Athletic Club baseball team was comprised of Nisei players from the Florin area south of Sacramento, including Herb "Moon" Kurima, one of the best pitchers in California. The club, founded in 1914, is recognized as one of the pioneer Japanese American baseball teams. As a result of Executive Order 9066 authorizing the relocation of West Coast Americans of Japanese ancestry, the Florin team was broken up and sent to camps as far away as Jerome, Arkansas. In this photograph, the Jerome, Arkansas, internment camp team is playing against an unidentified team. Kurima, the coach of the Jerome camp team, is seen standing to the left of the seated players. One of the teams they played was the Arkansas A&M college team, which they won 6-0. (Courtesy of Kerry Yo Nakagawa, Nisei Baseball Research Project.)

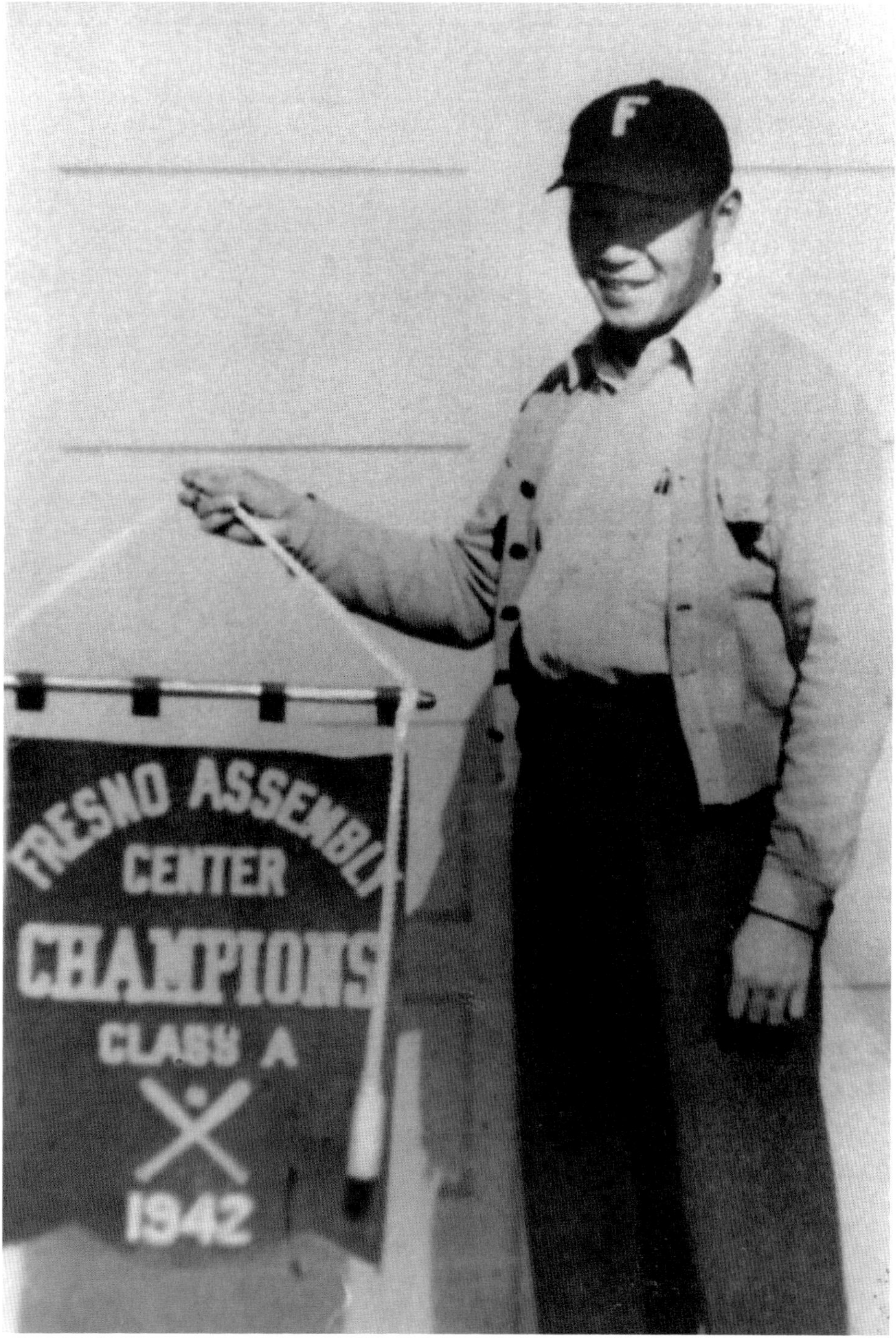

This 1943 photograph shows the 1942 Fresno Assembly Center champions flag being held by Herb "Moon" Kurima. Kurima's nickname came from the fact that his father made moonshine when Herb was a child. Before being relocated to Fresno, California, he played for the Florin Athletic Club. (Courtesy of California State University, Sacramento Library Archives.)

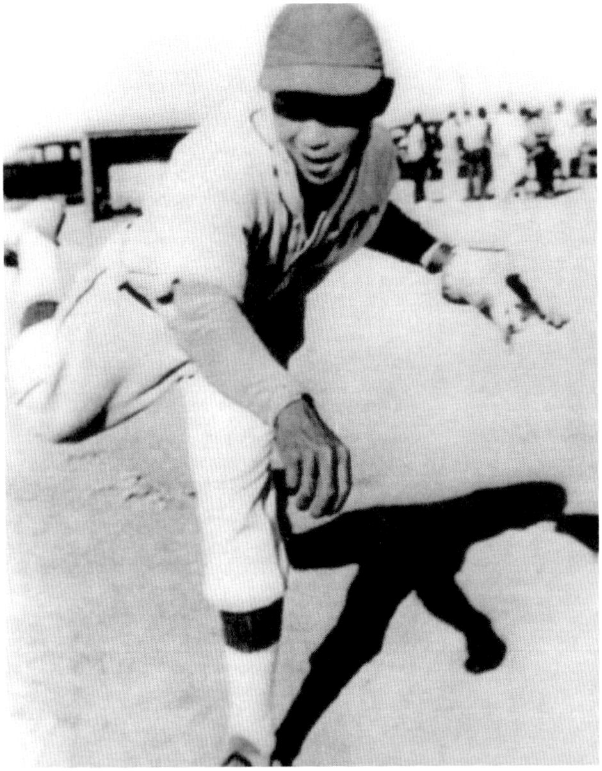

Herb "Moon" Kurima of the Florin Athletic Club recalled that the Nisei players were unable to join any leagues in the 1920s and 1930s because they always began competition in June—the same time the strawberry harvest began.

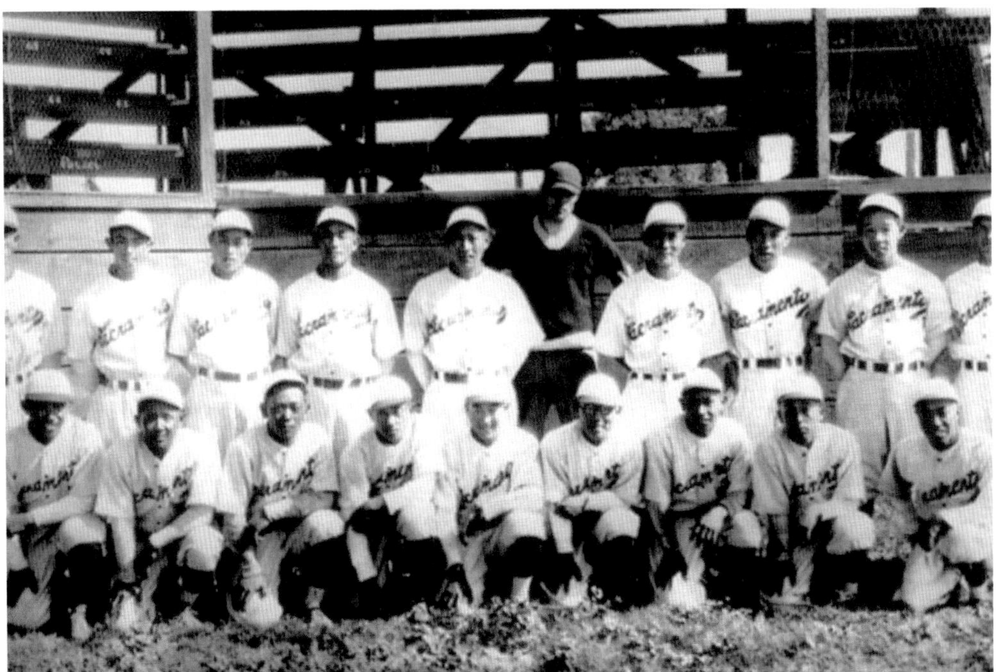

This photograph shows the 1925 Sacramento Nisei baseball team. Standing fourth from left is Henry Soichi Nomura. (Courtesy of Henry Soichi Nomura collection.)

5

The Sacramento Solons

1935–1960 and 1974–1976

Although professional baseball had been played in Sacramento for decades, Sacramento Solons officially became the team's name in 1935 when Branch Rickey, the owner of the St. Louis Cardinals, purchased the team. At the same time, Moreing Field, the home park for the club, was renamed Cardinal Field. While playing as the Sacramento Senators since 1901, the team was occasionally referred to as the Solons, making reference to the legislators in the California capital; the term "solons" was often used by journalists as a synonym for "senators." The team finished first in the regular season in 1937 for the first time since 1900; however, the actual league championship was determined by a playoff of the top four teams in the Governor's Cup tournament, and the Solons were eliminated in the first round. In 1938 and 1939, the Solons won the Governor's Cup, but as luck would have it, in those years, the championship was awarded to the season's actual first-place team.

The Solons' affiliation with the Cardinals ended in 1944 when the team was sold to a group of local businessmen. *Sacramento Union* sports editor Dick Edmonds was instrumental in forming the group, which saved the Solons and kept them in Sacramento. In 1944, following a newspaper contest, Cardinal Field was renamed Doubleday Field, a reference to Abner Doubleday, the Civil War general and mythical founder of American baseball. When Edmonds died in 1945, the field was renamed in his honor. Edmonds Field burned to the ground in 1948, was rebuilt in 1949, and remained at Riverside Boulevard and Broadway until 1960. In 1960, games began to be broadcast on television, attendance plummeted, and the team was sold, becoming the Hawaiian Islanders. While at Edmonds Field, the Solons broke the color barrier by signing infielder Marvin Williams and pitcher Walter McCoy. The Solons returned to Sacramento in 1974 as a minor league affiliate of the Milwaukee Brewers, but that arrangement lasted only until 1975. A short agreement with the Texas Rangers followed, but that ended in 1976.

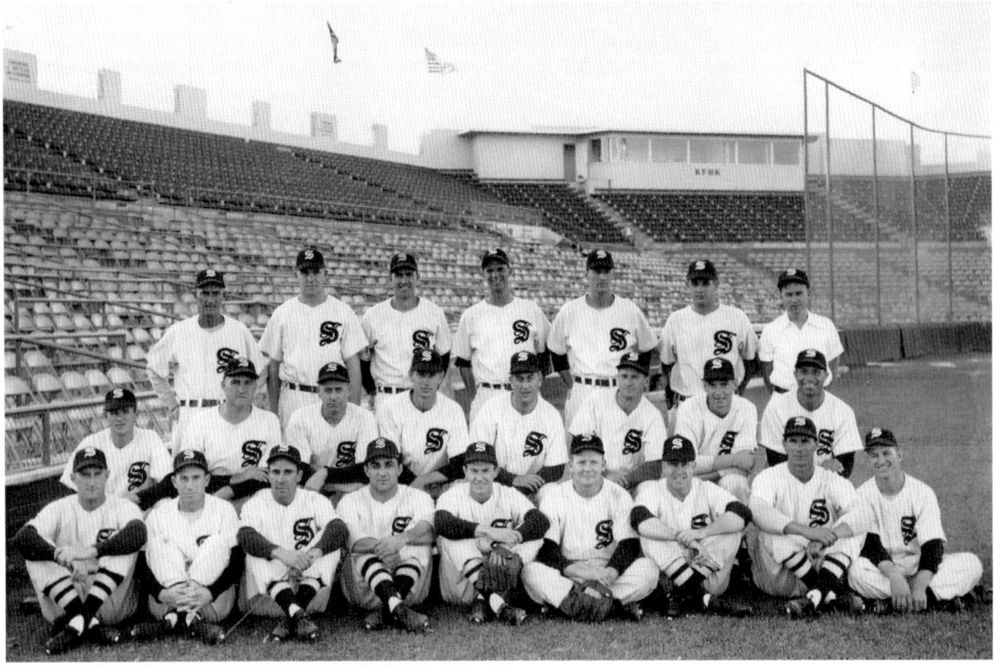

The Sacramento Solons posed for this photograph at Edmonds Field in 1949. After finishing in last place in the Pacific Coast League in 1948, the team returned in 1949 to finish third. They year 1949 was the first year the Solons played at their new ballpark following the July 1948 fire. (Courtesy of Sacramento Public Library, Sacramento Room Special Collections.)

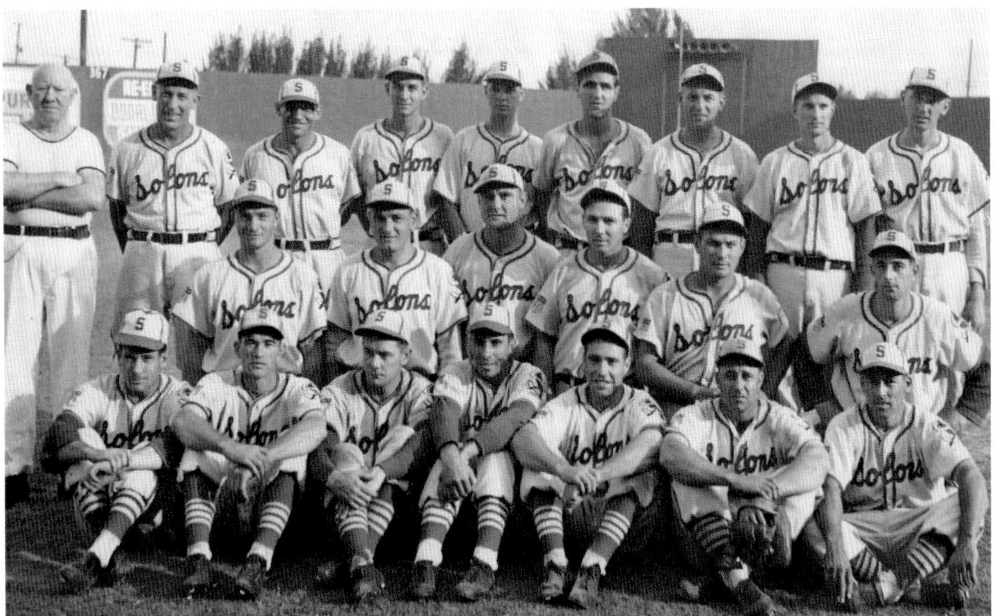

Although the Solons had some good years, the only year they won the Pacific Coast League championship was 1942. (Courtesy of Alan O'Connor.)

This 1951 photograph shows the Sacramento Solons at Edmonds Field. In 1951, the Solons got off to a great start and were in first place halfway through the season with the record of 44-33. They lost two-thirds of their remaining games to sink out of contention and finished eighth in the Pacific Coast League. (Courtesy of Sacramento Public Library, Sacramento Room Special Collections.)

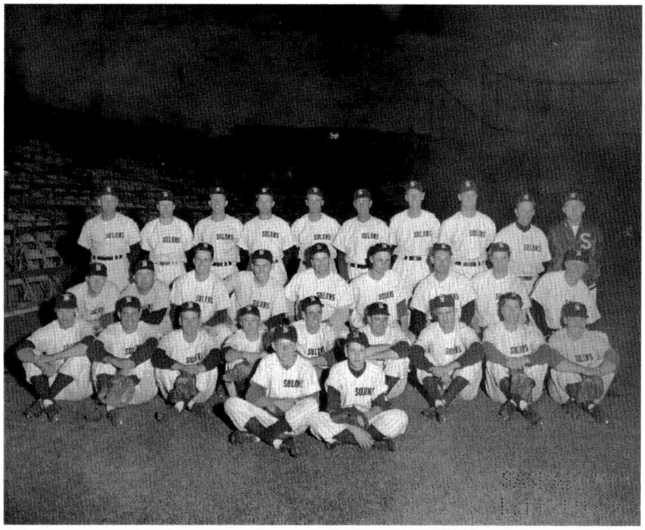

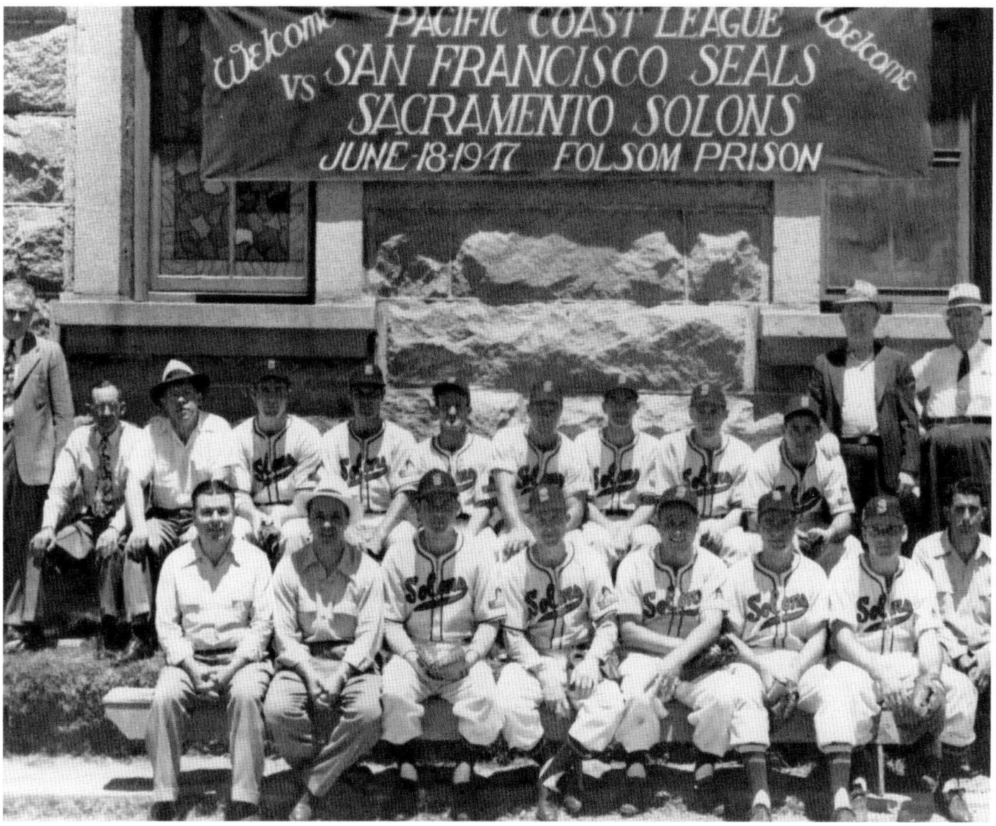

This June 1947 photograph shows a partial Sacramento Solons team seated at Folsom State Prison during an exhibition game with the San Francisco Seals, another team in the Pacific Coast League. (Courtesy of California State Archives.)

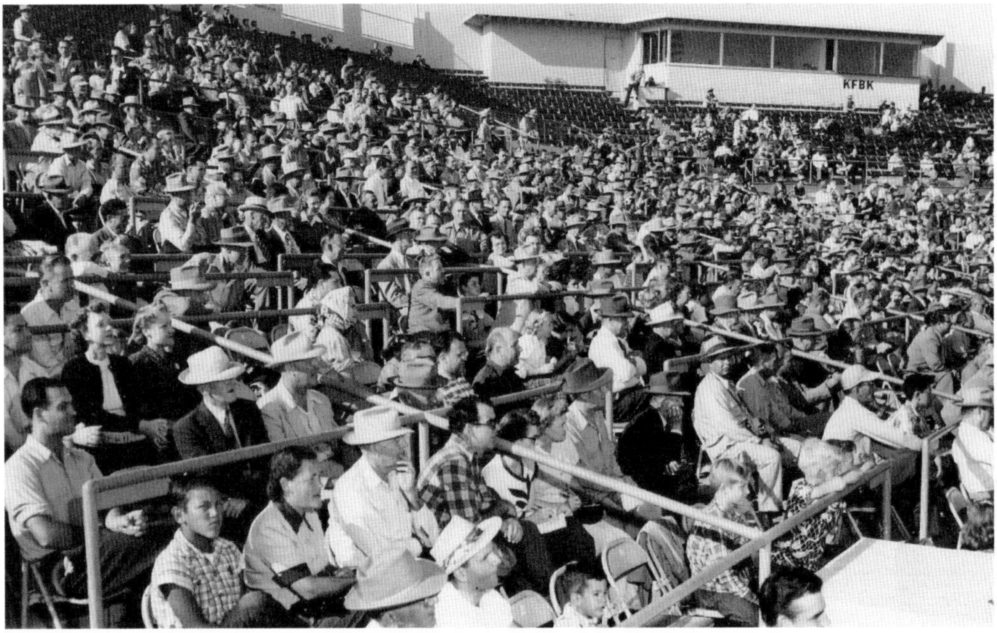

This shot of the crowd in 1950 was taken at Edmonds Field. Bill Avila, a scout for the Philadelphia Phillies who also wrote the Bushers column for the *Sacramento Union*, sits in the foreground in a white shirt. (Courtesy of Sacramento Public Library, Sacramento Room Special Collections.)

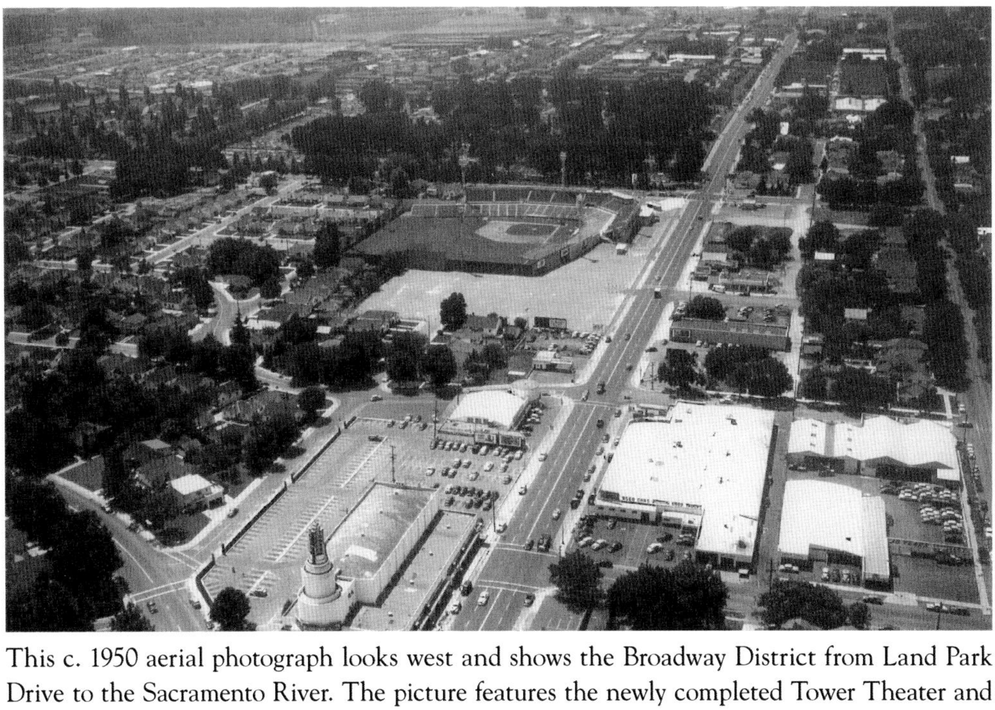

This c. 1950 aerial photograph looks west and shows the Broadway District from Land Park Drive to the Sacramento River. The picture features the newly completed Tower Theater and the Cardinal Grocery Store between the theater and Edmonds Field. (Courtesy of Sacramento Public Library, Sacramento Room Special Collections.)

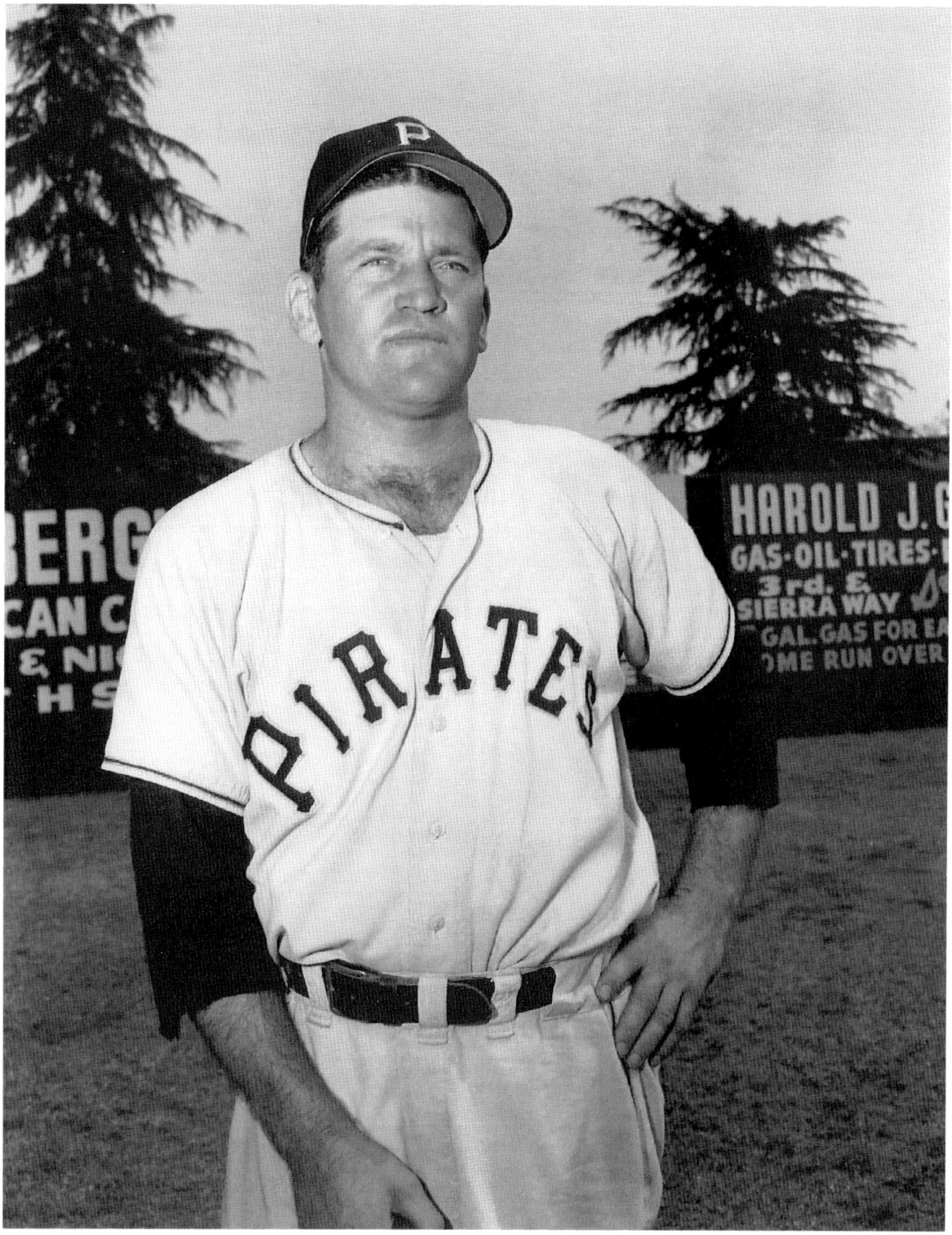

Wally Westlake, with a lifetime batting average of .280, is pictured here. He played for several minor league clubs, including the Solons, and had a 10-year major league career, which included four seasons with the Cleveland Indians and a trip to the 1954 World Series. (Courtesy of Tim and Cathleen Corr.)

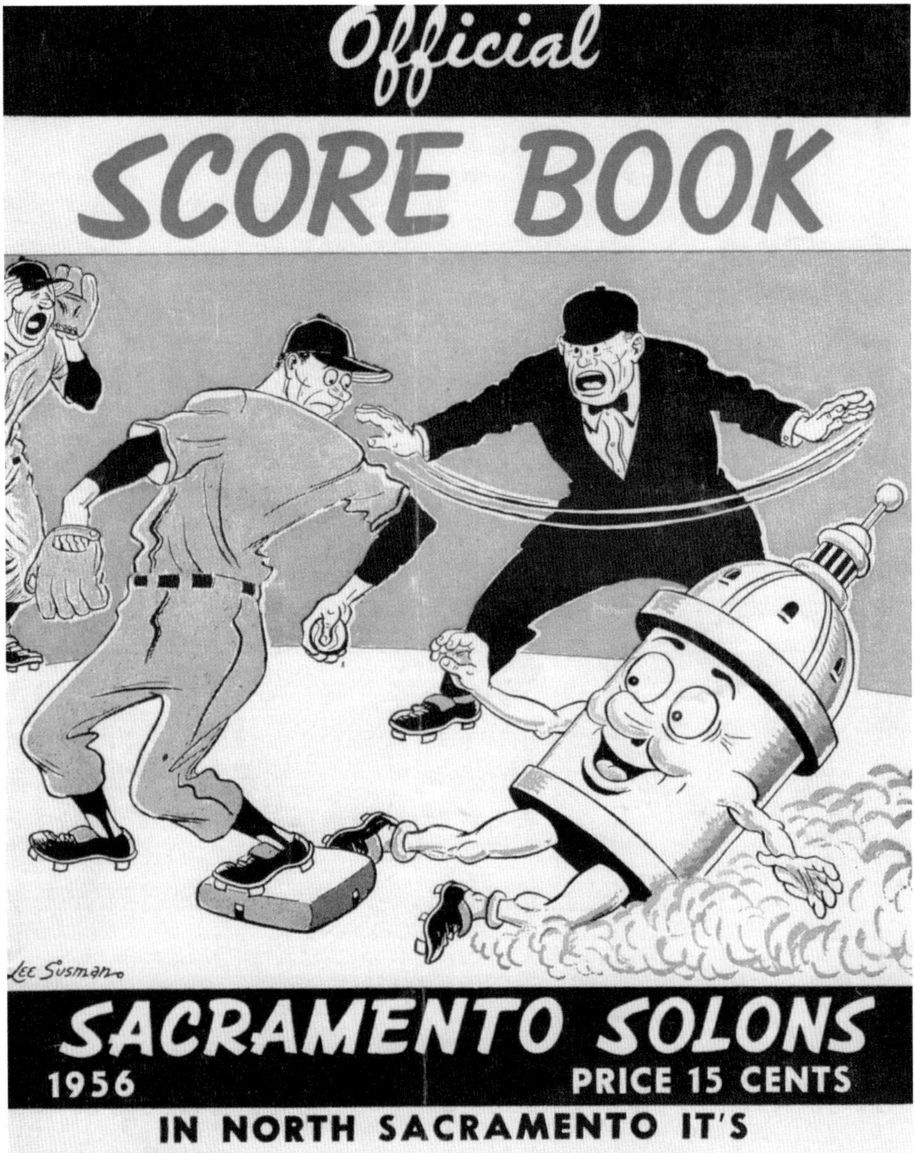

By the 1950s, the price of the official scorecard had tripled in price from 5¢ to 15¢. It also changed in format to resemble a glossy magazine more than a card. Although there was still a place to keep score, the scorecard contained many more advertisements and information about the league. (Courtesy of Sacramento Public Library, Sacramento Room Special Collections.)

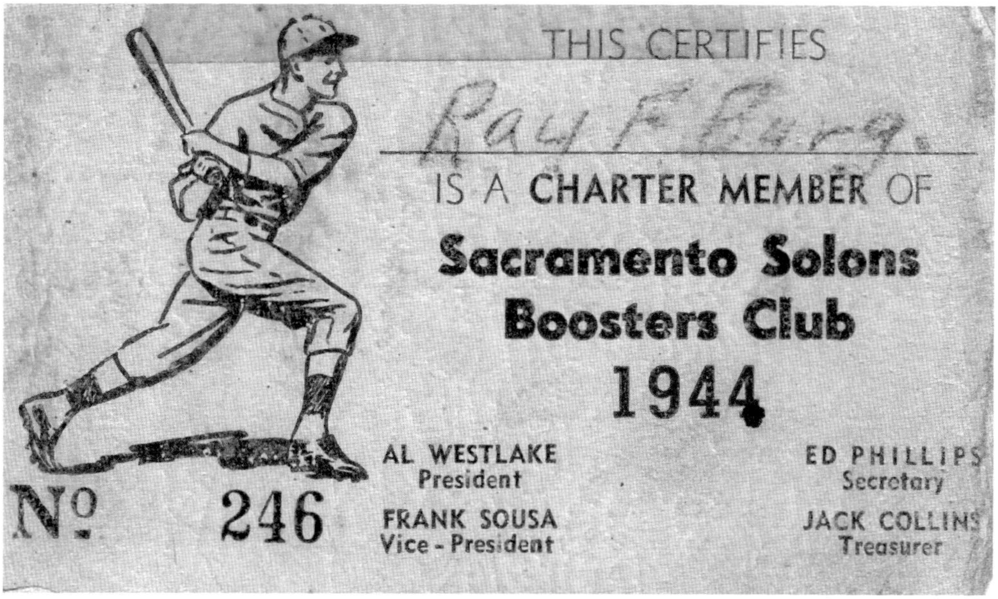

Booster clubs for professional teams were very popular in the 20th century and remain so today. They exist as independent, not-for-profit organizations that work with the approval and cooperation of team management to provide support of the team and enjoyable, healthy, safe environments for the fans; encourage courtesy at all club activities and events; and be involved with charitable organizations in the community. (Courtesy of Sacramento Public Library, Sacramento Room Special Collections.)

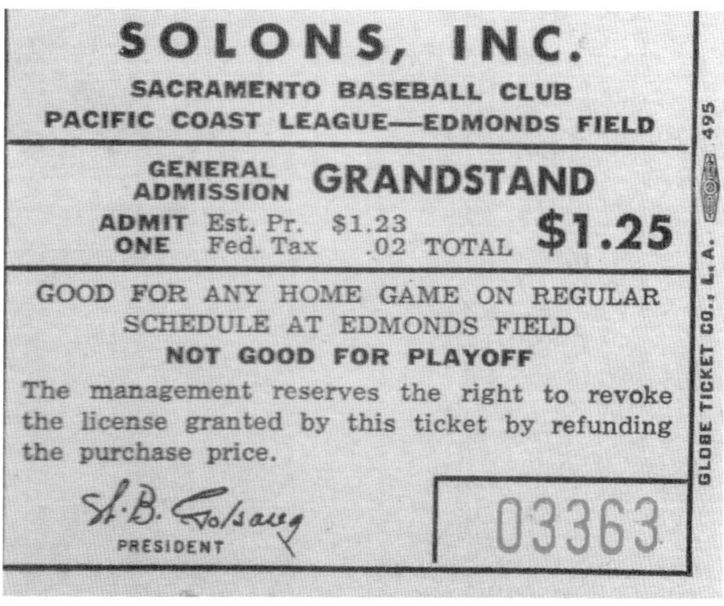

General admission tickets, such as this one seen around 1955, admitted a fan to the park, allowing them to sit anywhere not designated as a box seat. Typically, box seats were closer to the field on the first and third base lines and were more comfortable. (Courtesy of Sacramento Public Library, Sacramento Room Special Collections.)

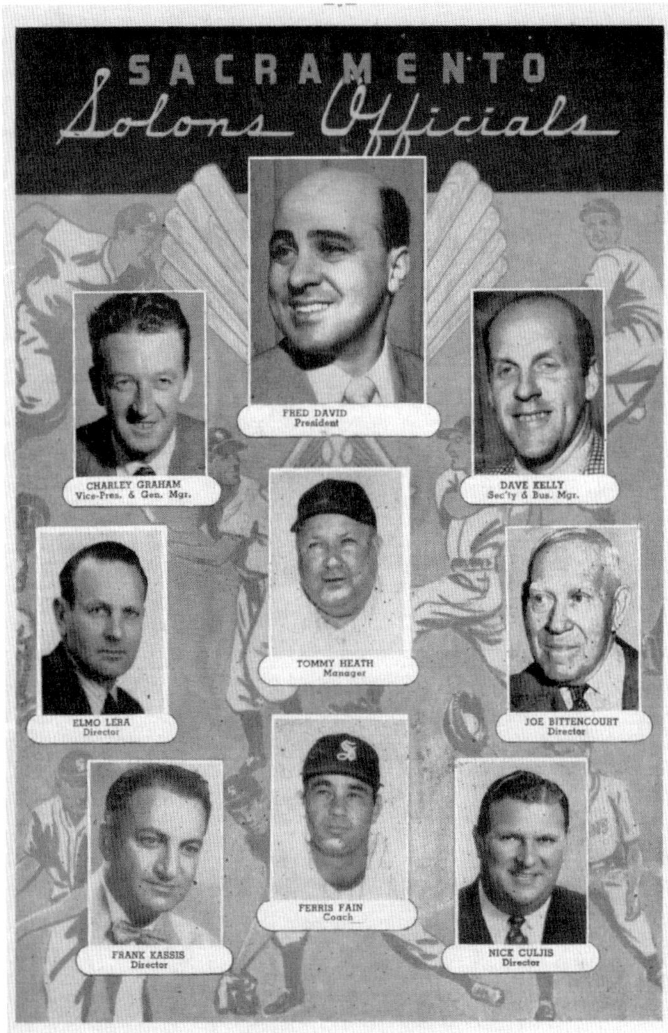

This 1956 collage shows the board of directors for the Solons. Some of them were local notables of the day, including Fred David, president and team owner, who according to Graham Womack, creator of the blog *Baseball: Past and Present*, first worked in the concession stand for the Solons at the age of 15 and became a stockholder in the team in 1944. David bought stock in the team 10 years later at a time of uncertainty for the club, starting with $1,000 "to keep baseball in Sacramento." David owned the Solons from 1954 to 1960, when they moved to Honolulu. Also pictured are Frank Kassis, whose family founded Stop-n-Shop markets in Sacramento; Nick Culjis, who was an original board member of the Babe Ruth League program established locally in 1953, city councilman from 1952 until 1960, and vice mayor in 1959 and 1960 (William Land Park Diamond No. 2 is named Nick Culjis field); and Tommy Heath, who managed the San Francisco Seals in the Pacific Coast League from 1952 to 1955. The Seals never finished better than 15 games out of first place under his leadership. When he managed the Solons, they finished fifth in 1956 and seventh in 1957, which were 23 and 38 games back of first place, respectively. (Courtesy of Sacramento Public Library, Sacramento Room Special Collections.)

In 1950, the Sacramento Solons broke the color line by hiring infielder Marvin Williams, pictured here at left, and pitcher Walter McCoy away from the Negro Leagues. Despite their talent, they never made it to the major league, in large part due to the unwritten "quota system" applied to the major league teams by the team owners. (Courtesy of Alan O'Connor.)

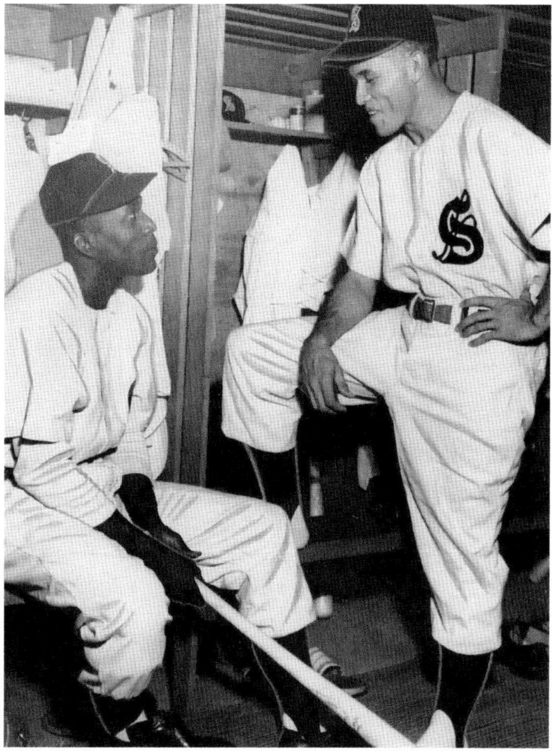

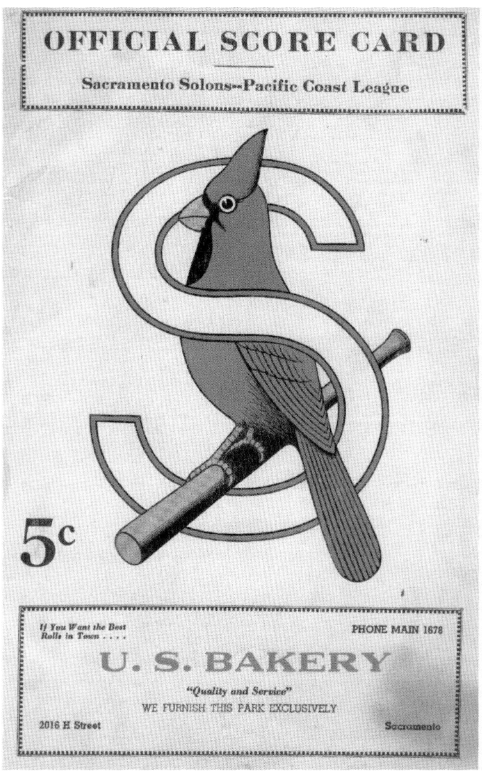

The "S" in this photograph stands for Sacramento. The bird perched on the bat running through the S is a cardinal, signifying the Solons' parent club in 1938, the St. Louis Cardinals. As was the case with scorecards and programs during this period, there is an advertisement for a local merchant. (Courtesy of Sacramento Public Library, Sacramento Room Special Collections.)

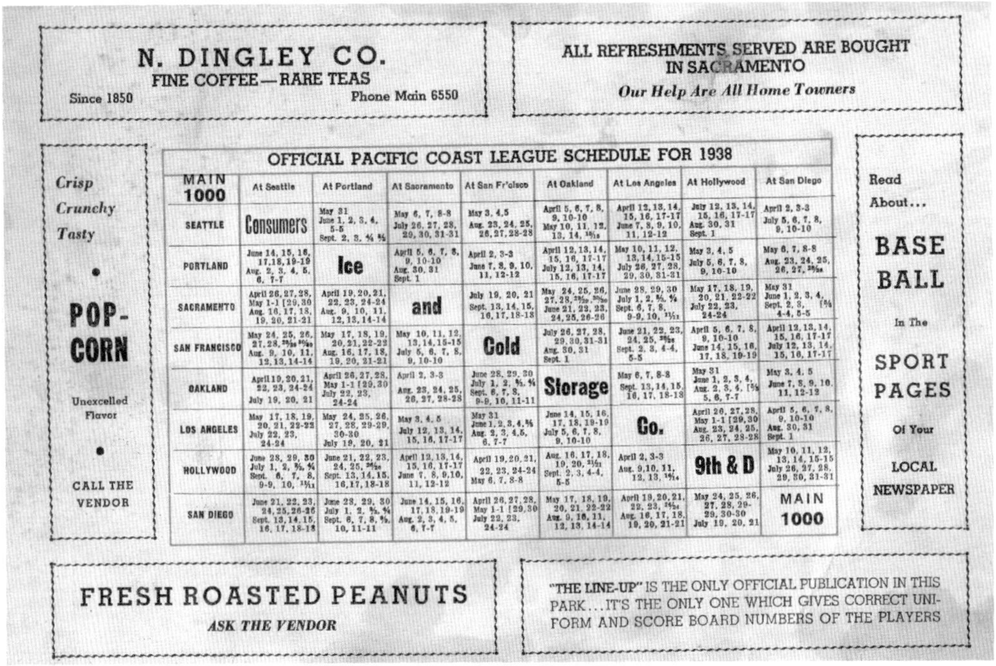

N. DINGLEY CO.
FINE COFFEE—RARE TEAS
Since 1850 Phone Main 6550

ALL REFRESHMENTS SERVED ARE BOUGHT IN SACRAMENTO
Our Help Are All Home Towners

Crisp
Crunchy
Tasty
POP-CORN
Unexcelled Flavor
CALL THE VENDOR

OFFICIAL PACIFIC COAST LEAGUE SCHEDULE FOR 1938

MAIN 1000	At Seattle	At Portland	At Sacramento	At San Fr'cisco	At Oakland	At Los Angeles	At Hollywood	At San Diego
SEATTLE	Consumers	May 31 June 1, 2, 3, 4, 5-5 Sept. 2, 3, 4/4 5/5	May 6, 7, 8-8 July 26, 27, 28, 29, 30, 31-31	May 3, 4,5 Aug. 23, 24, 25, 26, 27, 28-28	April 5, 6, 7, 8, 9, 10-10 May 10, 11, 12, 13, 14, 15/15	April 12, 13, 14, 15, 16, 17-17 June 7, 8, 9, 10, 11, 12-12	July 12, 13, 14, 15, 16, 17-17 Aug. 30, 31 Sept. 1	April 2, 3-3 July 5, 6, 7, 8, 9, 10-10
PORTLAND	June 14, 15, 16, 17, 18, 19-19 Aug. 2, 3, 4, 5, 6, 7-7	Ice	April 5, 6, 7, 8, 9, 10-10 Aug. 30, 31 Sept. 1	April 2, 3-3 June 7, 8, 9, 10, 11, 12-12	April 12, 13, 14, 15, 16, 17-17 July 12, 13, 14, 15, 16, 17-17	May 10, 11, 12, 13, 14, 15-15 July 26, 27, 28, 29, 30, 31-31	May 3, 4, 5 July 5, 6, 7, 8, 9, 10-10	May 6, 7, 8-8 Aug. 23, 24, 25, 26, 27, 28/28
SACRAMENTO	April 26, 27, 28, May 1-1 [29, 30 Aug. 16, 17, 18, 19, 20, 21-21	April 19, 20, 21, 22, 23, 24-24 Aug. 9, 10, 11, 12, 13, 14-14	and	July 19, 20, 21 Sept. 13, 14, 15, 16, 17, 18-18	May 24, 25, 26, 27, 28, 29/29, 30/30 June 21, 22, 23, 24, 25, 26-26	June 28, 29, 30 July 1, 2, 3/3, 4/4 Sept. 6, 7, 8, 9-9, 10, 11/11	May 17, 18, 19, 20, 21, 22-22 July 22, 23, 24-24	May 31 June 1, 2, 3, 4, Sept. 2, 3, [5/5 4-4, 5-5
SAN FRANCISCO	May 24, 25, 26, 27, 28, 29/29 30/30 Aug. 9, 10, 11, 12, 13, 14-14	May 17, 18, 19, 20, 21, 22-22 Aug. 16, 17, 18, 19, 20, 21-21	May 10, 11, 12, 13, 14, 15-15 July 5, 6, 7, 8, 9, 10-10	Cold	July 26, 27, 28, 29, 30, 31-31 Aug. 30, 31 Sept. 1	June 21, 22, 23, 24, 25, 26/26 Sept. 2, 3, 4-4, 5-5	April 5, 6, 7, 8, 9, 10-10 June 14, 15, 16, 17, 18, 19-19	April 12, 13, 14, 15, 16, 17-17 July 12, 13, 14, 15, 16, 17-17
OAKLAND	April 19, 20, 21, 22, 23, 24-24 July 19, 20, 21	April 26, 27, 28, May 1-1 [29, 30 July 22, 23, 24-24	April 2, 3-3 Aug. 23, 24, 25, 26, 27, 28-28	June 28, 29, 30 July 1, 2, 3/3, 4/4 Sept. 6, 7, 8, 9-9, 10, 11-11	Storage	May 6, 7, 8-8 Sept. 13, 14, 15, 16, 17, 18-18	May 31 June 1, 2, 3, 4, Aug. 2, 3, 4, [5/5 5, 6, 7-7	May 3, 4, 5 June 7, 8, 9, 10, 11, 12-12
LOS ANGELES	May 17, 18, 19, 20, 21, 22-22 July 22, 23, 24-24	May 24, 25, 26, 27, 28, 29-29, 30-30 July 19, 20, 21	May 3, 4, 5 July 12, 13, 14, 15, 16, 17-17	May 31 June 1, 2, 3, 4, 5/5 Aug. 2, 3, 4, 5, 6, 7-7	June 14, 15, 16, 17, 18, 19-19 July 5, 6, 7, 8, 9, 10-10	Co.	April 26, 27, 28, May 1-1 [29, 30 Aug. 23, 24, 25, 26, 27, 28-28	April 5, 6, 7, 8, 9, 10-10 Aug. 30, 31 Sept. 1
HOLLYWOOD	June 28, 29, 30 July 1, 2, 3/3, 4/4 Sept. 6, 7, 8, 9-9, 10, 11/11	June 21, 22, 23, 24, 25, 26/26 Sept. 13, 14, 15, 16, 17, 18-18	April 12, 13, 14, 15, 16, 17-17 June 7, 8, 9, 10, 11, 12-12	April 19, 20, 21, 22, 23, 24-24 May 6, 7, 8-8	Aug. 16, 17, 18, 19, 20, 21/21 Sept. 2, 3, 4-4, 5-5	April 2, 3-3 Aug. 9, 10, 11, 12, 13, 14/14	9th & D	May 10, 11, 12, 13, 14, 15-15 July 26, 27, 28, 29, 30, 31-31
SAN DIEGO	June 21, 22, 23, 24, 25, 26-26 Sept. 13, 14, 15, 16, 17, 18-18	June 28, 29, 30 July 1, 2, 3/3, 4/4 Sept. 6, 7, 8, 9/9, 10, 11-11	June 14, 15, 16, 17, 18, 19-19 Aug. 2, 3, 4, 5, 6, 7-7	April 26, 27, 28, May 1-1 [29, 30 July 22, 23, 24-24	May 17, 18, 19, 20, 21, 22-22 Aug. 9, 10, 11, 12, 13, 14-14	April 19, 20, 21, 22, 23, 24/24 Aug. 16, 17, 18, 19, 20, 21-21	May 24, 25, 26, 27, 28, 29-29, 30-30 July 19, 20, 21	MAIN 1000

Read About...
BASE BALL
In The
SPORT PAGES
Of Your
LOCAL NEWSPAPER

FRESH ROASTED PEANUTS
ASK THE VENDOR

"THE LINE-UP" IS THE ONLY OFFICIAL PUBLICATION IN THIS PARK...IT'S THE ONLY ONE WHICH GIVES CORRECT UNIFORM AND SCORE BOARD NUMBERS OF THE PLAYERS

The back page of this scorecard shows the schedule for all the teams in the Pacific Coast League for the 1938 season, as well as advertisements for some local businesses. (Courtesy of Sacramento Public Library, Sacramento Room Special Collections.)

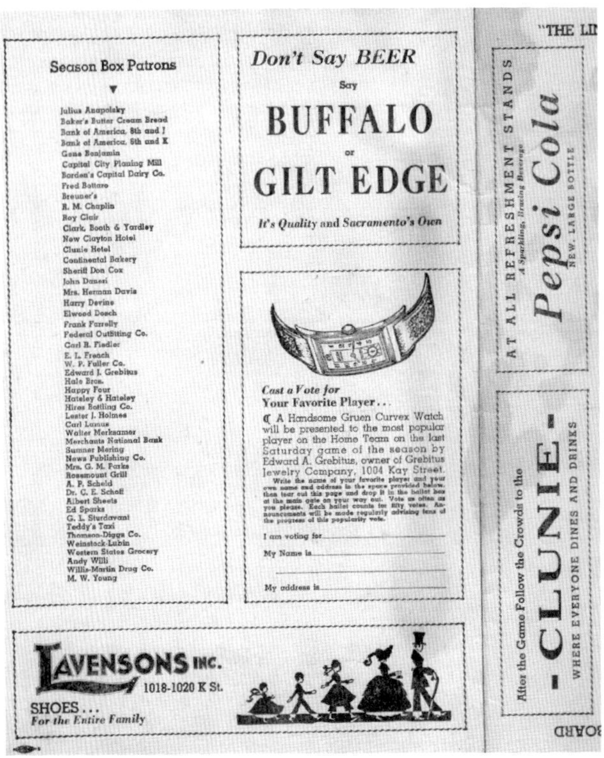

Season Box Patrons

Julius Anapolsky
Baker's Butter Cream Bread
Bank of America, 8th and J
Bank of America, 8th and K
Gene Benjamin
Capital City Planing Mill
Borden's Capital Dairy Co.
Fred Bottaro
Breuner's
R. M. Chaplin
Roy Clair
Clark, Booth & Yardley
New Clayton Hotel
Clunie Hotel
Continental Bakery
Sheriff Don Cox
John Danesi
Mrs. Herman Davis
Harry Devine
Elwood Dosch
Frank Farrelly
Federal Outfitting Co.
Carl R. Fiedler
E. L. French
W. P. Fuller Co.
Edward J. Grebitus
Hale Bros.
Happy Four
Hateley & Hateley
Hires Bottling Co.
Lester J. Holmes
Carl Lamus
Walter Merksamer
Merchants National Bank
Sumner Mering
News Publishing Co.
Mrs. G. M. Parks
Rosemount Grill
A. P. Scheld
Dr. C. E. Schoff
Albert Sheets
Ed Sparks
G. L. Sturdavant
Teddy's Taxi
Thomson-Diggs Co.
Weinstock-Lubin
Western States Grocery
Andy Willi
Willis-Martin Drug Co.
M. W. Young

Don't Say BEER
Say
BUFFALO
or
GILT EDGE
It's Quality and Sacramento's Own

Cast a Vote for
Your Favorite Player...
A Handsome Gruen Curvex Watch will be presented to the most popular player on the Home Team on the last Saturday game of the season by Edward A. Grebitus, owner of Grebitus Jewelry Company, 1004 Kay Street.
Write the name of your favorite player and your own name and address in the space provided below, then tear out this page and drop it in the ballot box at the main gate on your way out. Vote as often as you please. Each ballot counts for fifty votes. Announcements will be made regularly advising fans of the progress of this popularity vote.
I am voting for ____________
My Name is ____________
My address is ____________

AT ALL REFRESHMENT STANDS
Pepsi Cola
A Sparkling, Bracing Beverage
NEW, LARGE BOTTLE

After the Game Follow the Crowds to the
-CLUNIE-
WHERE EVERYONE DINES AND DRINKS

LAVENSONS INC.
1018-1020 K St.
SHOES...
For the Entire Family

"THE LI

This inside cover of a 1938 Solons program features the ubiquitous advertisements, but it also lists the box seat season ticket holders. (Courtesy of Sacramento Public Library, Sacramento Room Special Collections.)

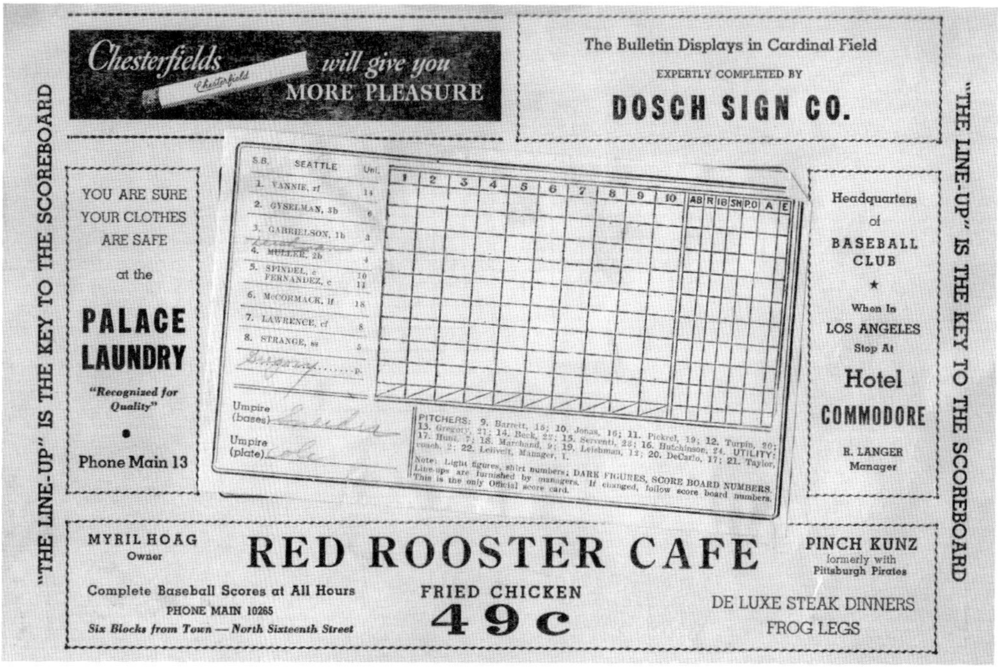

Pictured here is the center of an official scorecard, which shows a grid where fans could keep score during the game. (Courtesy of Sacramento Public Library, Sacramento Room Special Collections.)

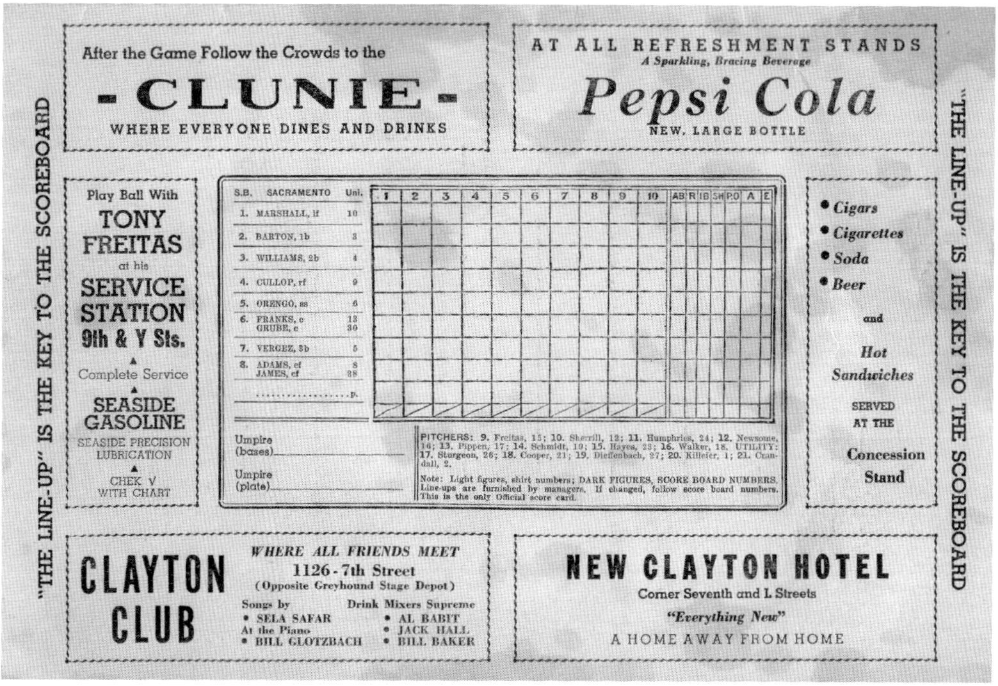

This 1938 scorecard is made of a heavy stock paper that was sold to fans at a 1938 game between the Solons and the Seattle Rainiers. Pictured on this page is the Sacramento line up for the game. (Courtesy of Sacramento Public Library, Sacramento Room Special Collections.)

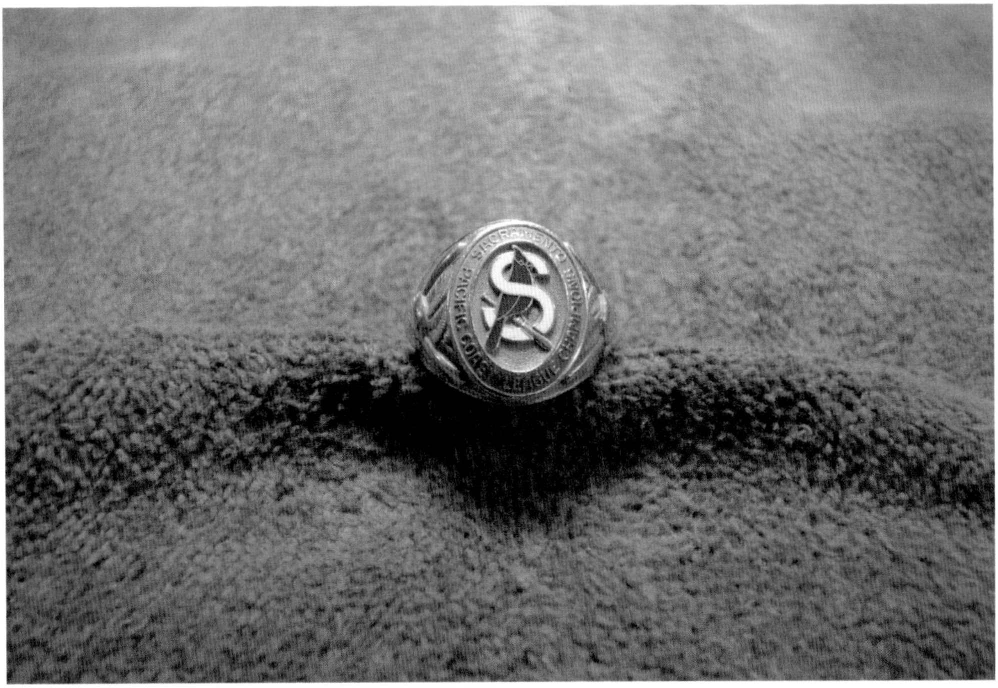

The Sacramento Solons only won one Pacific Coast League championship in their two-and-a-half-decade existence. The year 1942 was the magic year for the team, and this ring represents the victory. (Courtesy of Alan O'Connor.)

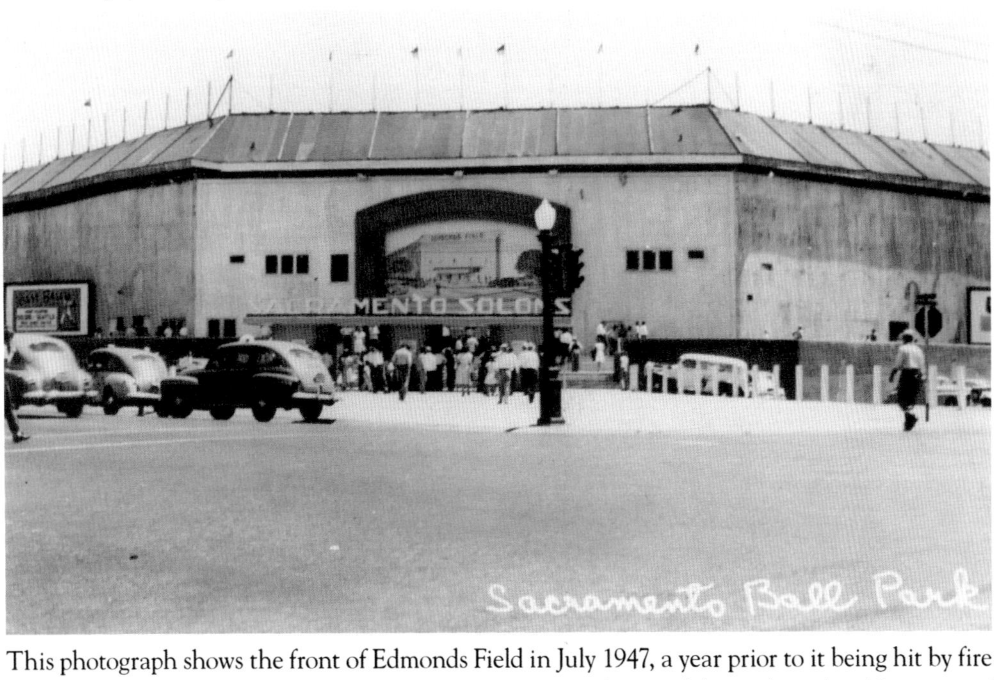

This photograph shows the front of Edmonds Field in July 1947, a year prior to it being hit by fire and burning to the ground. It shows a busy box office and part of the parking lot. (Courtesy of Sacramento Public Library, Sacramento Room Special Collections.)

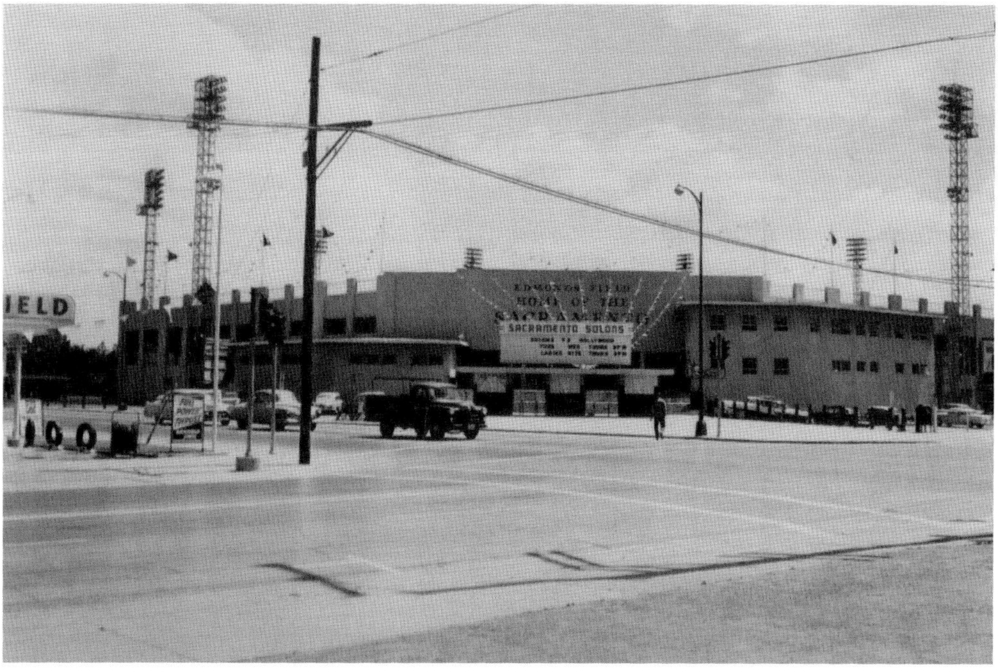

This c. 1955 photograph of the entrance to Edmonds Field was taken from across the street. (Courtesy of Sacramento Public Library, Sacramento Room Special Collections.)

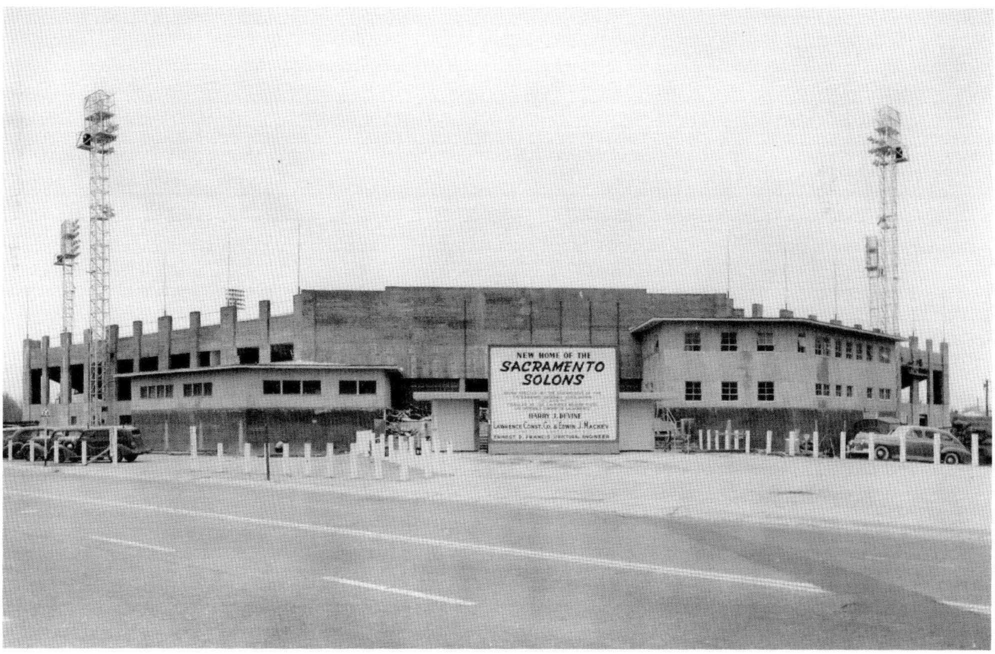

This March 1949 photograph shows the main entrance to Edmonds Field while it was being rebuilt following the 1948 fire. Note the light towers surrounding the field. The Solons were the first team in the Pacific Coast League to play night games—as far back as 1930—beating the major league by five years. (Courtesy of Sacramento Public Library, Sacramento Room Special Collections.)

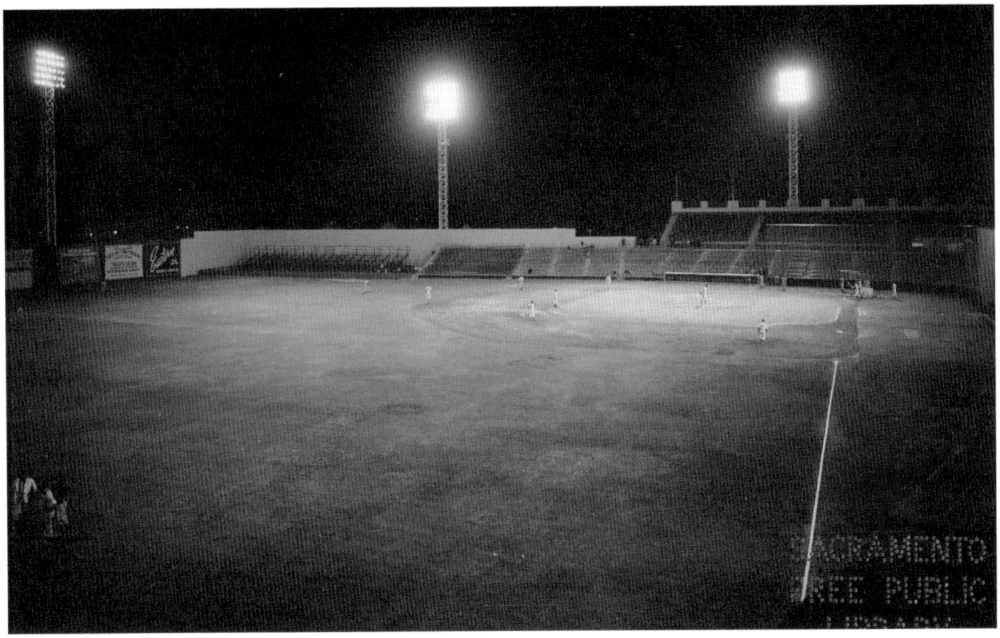

This night game at Edmonds Field was played in March 1949, after recently reopening following the destruction of the field by fire in 1948. This photograph was probably taken during pregame warm-ups, as there are only a few fans in the grandstand and weekday night games typically drew large crowds. (Courtesy of Sacramento Public Library, Sacramento Room Special Collections.)

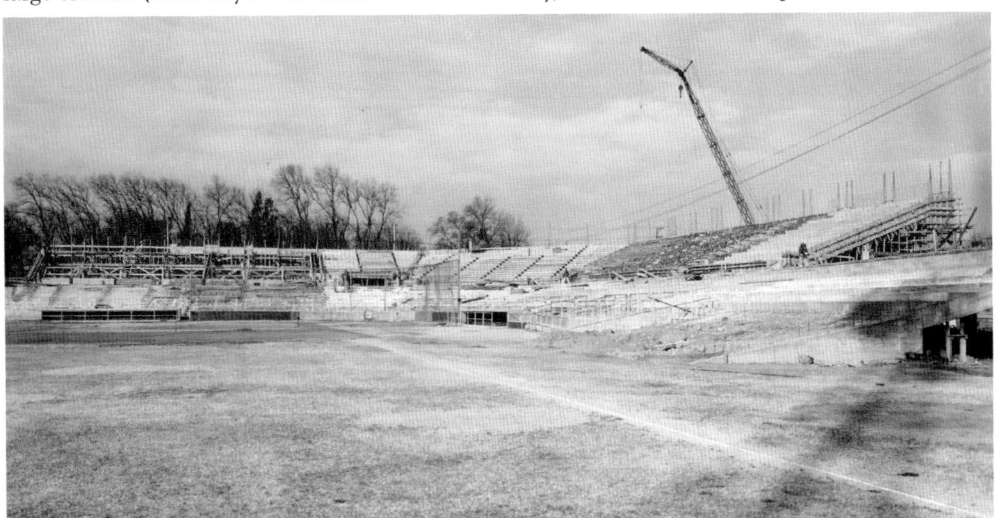

This photograph show Edmonds Field at the corner of Riverside Boulevard at Broadway on July 24, 1948, after the July 11 fire. The fire, likely started by a carelessly tossed cigarette, destroyed the park on July 11. Several years later, *Sacramento Bee* columnist Stan Gilliam "confessed" to starting the fire when he dropped a burning cigarette through the grandstand where he was sitting; the confession, however, remains in doubt. (Courtesy of Sacramento Public Library, Sacramento Room Special Collections.)

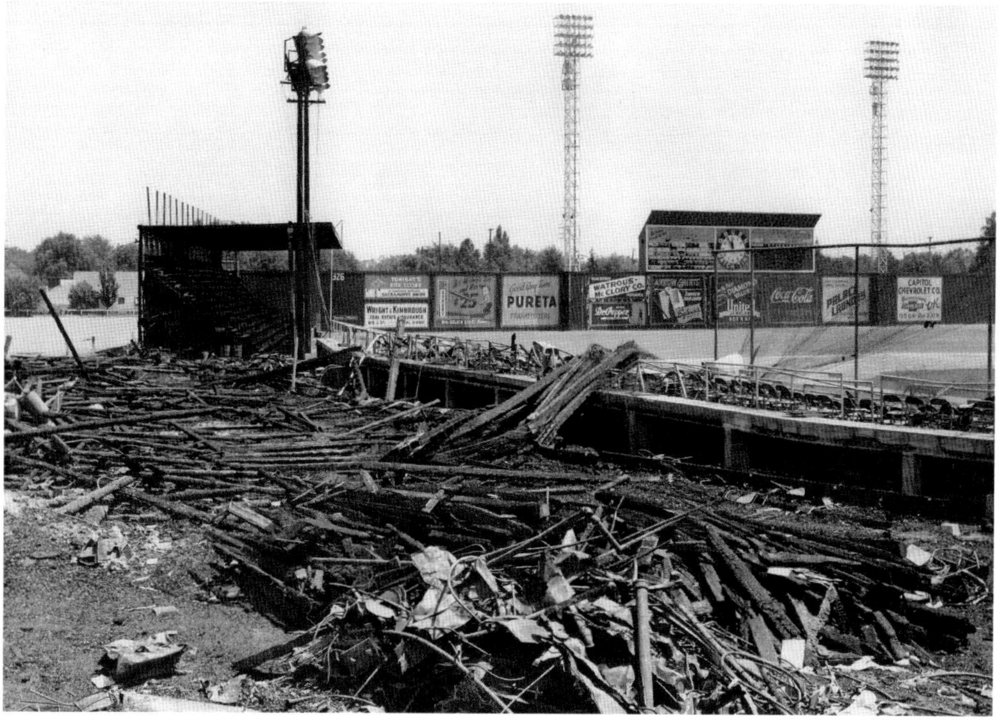

This July 24, 1948, photograph shows another view of the remains of Edmonds Field after the fire several days before.

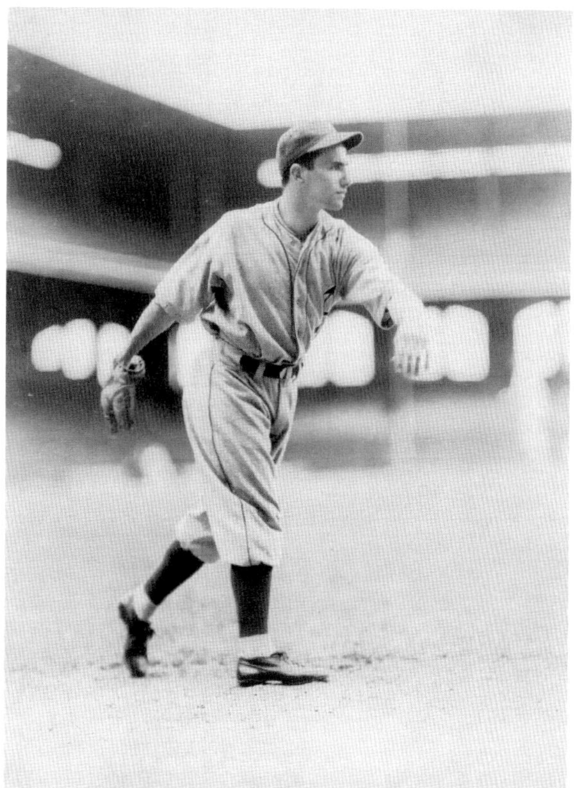

This c. 1929 photograph of Tony Freitas shows him warming up before a game. Tony Freitas was born May 5, 1908, in Mill Valley, California, and made his professional baseball debut at age 20 with the Phoenix Senators of the Arizona League in May 1928. A left-handed pitcher and outfielder, he pitched more than 5,500 innings over his 33-year career with a respectable career earned run average of 3.27. He played for the Sacramento Solons for all or part of 15 seasons, including 1942, the only year the Solons won the Pacific Coast League championship. (Courtesy of Tim Armstrong.)

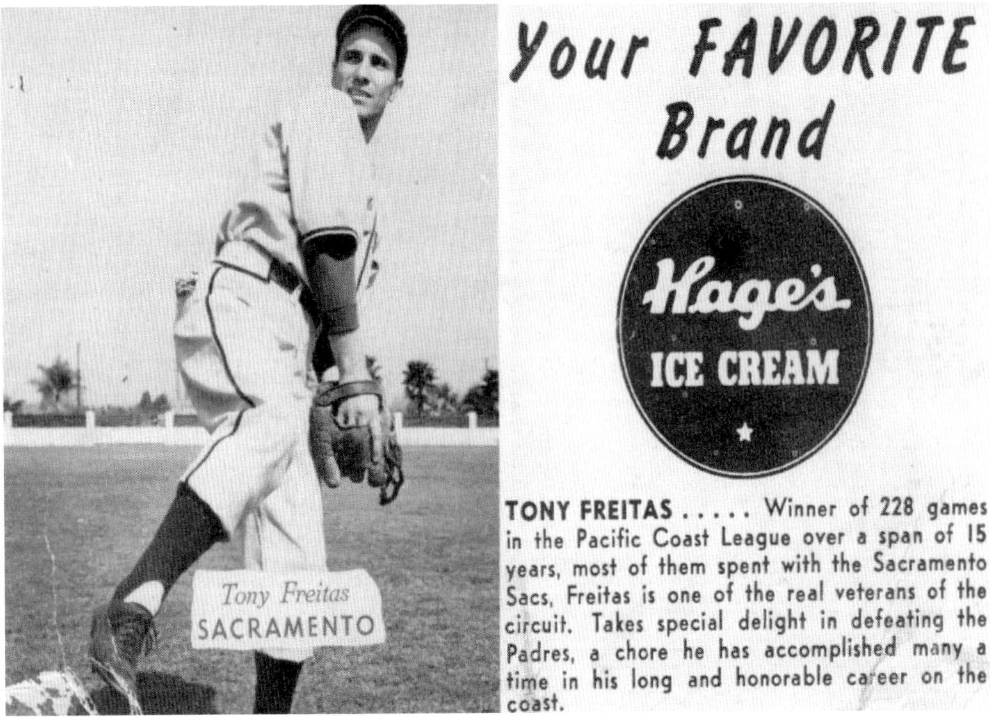

Baseball trading cards have been popular for decades. These photographs show the front and back of a baseball card featuring Tony Freitas of the Sacramento Solons. Most baseball cards during the first half of the 20th century featured a picture (sometimes a photograph, other times in drawing) of a player on one side and an advertisement on the back. This one advertises Sunbeam bread, which had a local bakery in Sacramento. The card was sponsored by the Hage's Ice Cream Company and provides a very brief synopsis of his accomplishments as a Sacramento Solon. (Courtesy of Alan O'Connor.)

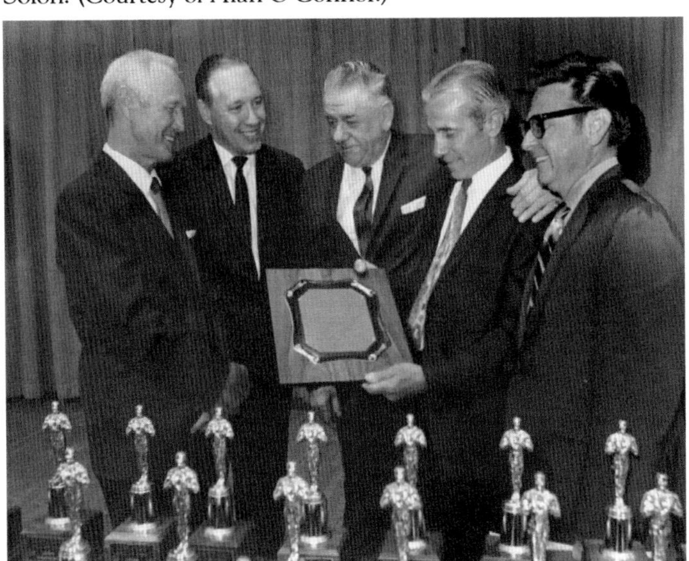

Here, former Sacramento Solon Tony Freitas receives a plaque on his entry into the Sacramento Athletic Hall of Fame. Pictured are, from left to right, Earl McNeely, former player and owner of the Sacramento Solons; Bobby Feller; Freitas; and Mike Cardenas. (Courtesy of Tim Armstrong.)

In its September 1981 issue, *Sacramento Magazine* included a section on the Sacramento Solons. This cover photograph shows Tony Freitas walking "into the past," with his bat on his shoulder and glove in his hand. (Courtesy of Tim Armstrong, reprinted with permission of *Sacramento Magazine*.)

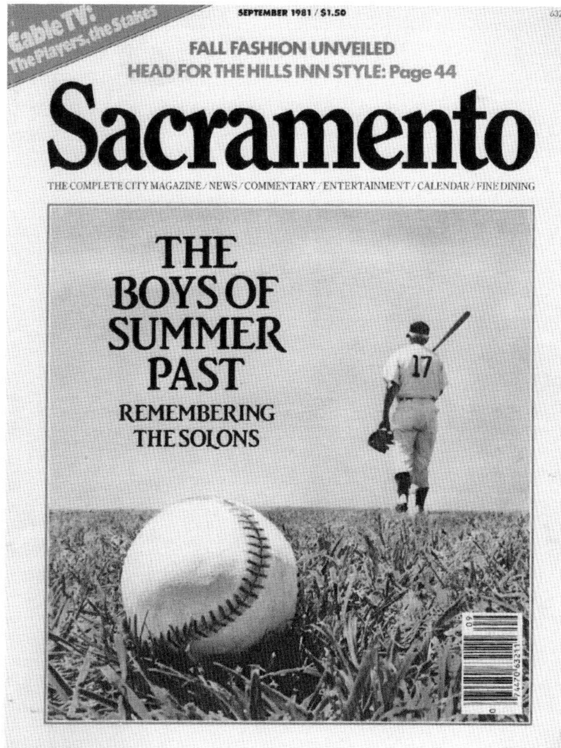

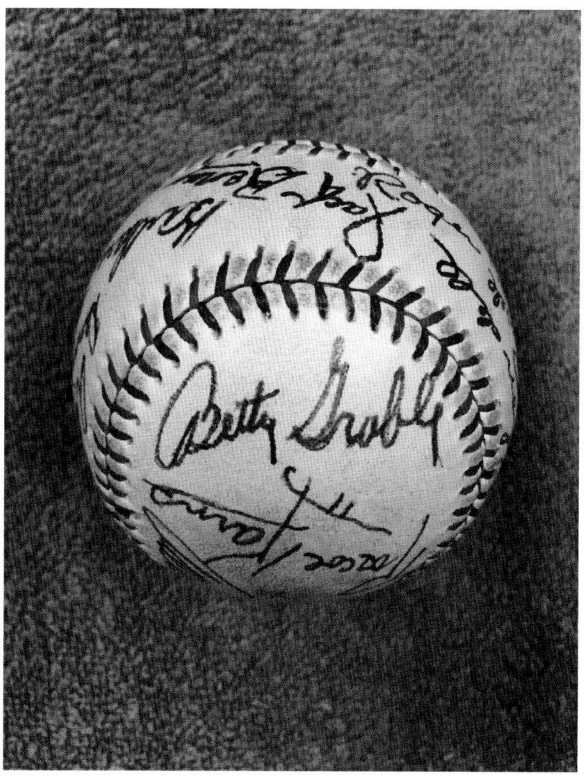

During the heyday of the Pacific Coast League, the Sacramento Solons regularly traveled to Southern California for games with the Hollywood Stars and Los Angeles Angels. The players often dined at the famed Hollywood Brown Derby, and many of the players were asked for autographs by stage and film stars. Tony Freitas carried a ball with him, and when the stars came to the table for player autographs, he got theirs in exchange. (Courtesy of Tim Armstrong.)

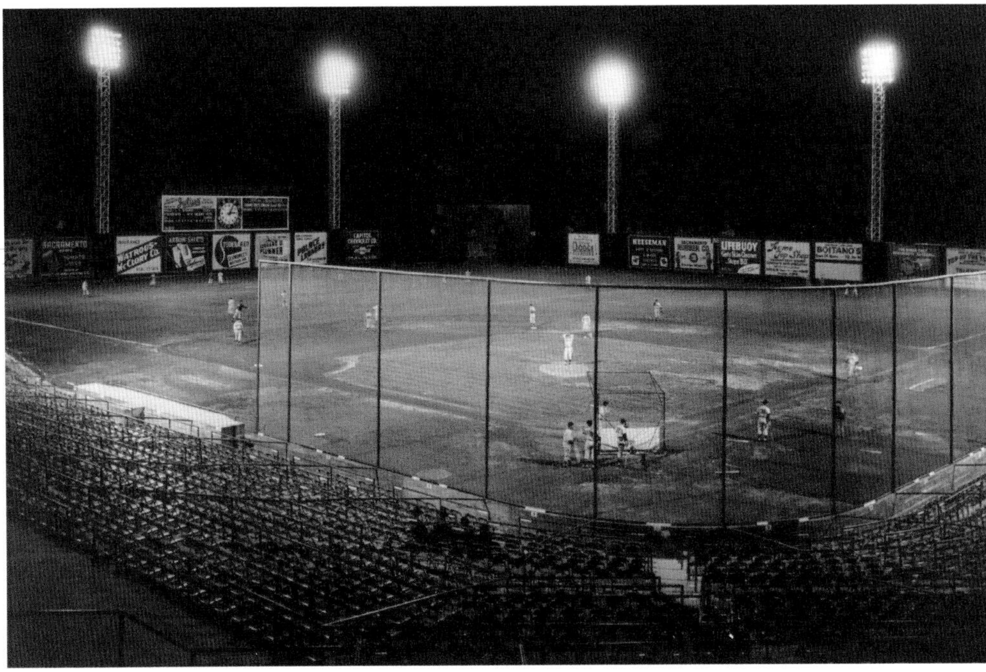

This c. 1950 photograph shows batting practice before a game at Edmonds Field. (Courtesy of Keith Davila.)

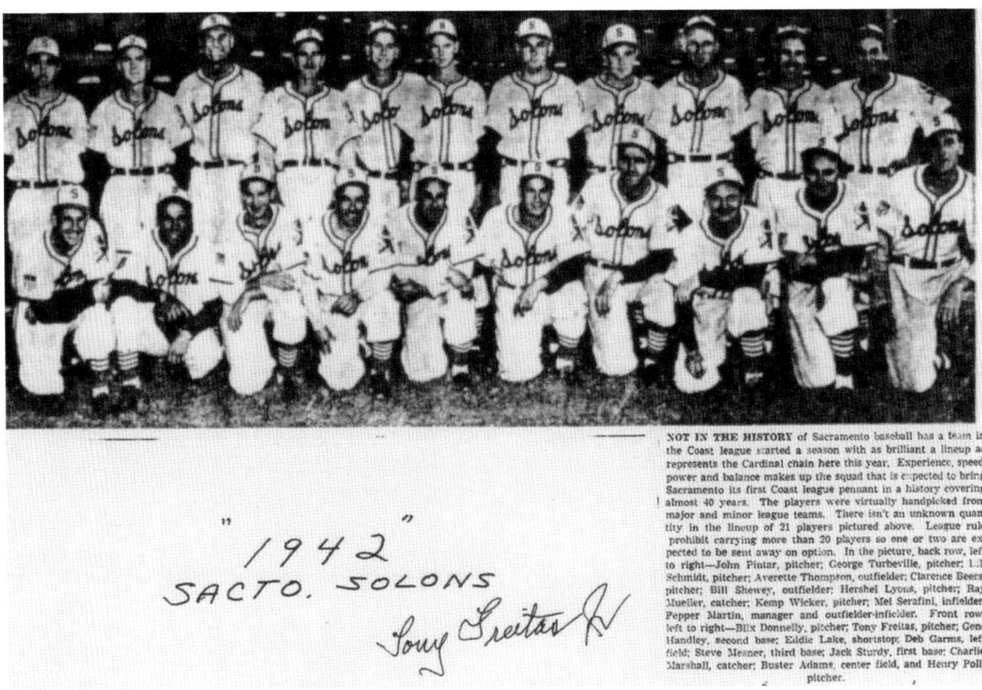

NOT IN THE HISTORY of Sacramento baseball has a team in the Coast league started a season with as brilliant a lineup as represents the Cardinal chain here this year. Experience, speed, power and balance makes up the squad that is expected to bring Sacramento its first Coast league pennant in a history covering almost 40 years. The players were virtually handpicked from major and minor league teams. There isn't an unknown quantity in the lineup of 21 players pictured above. League rules prohibit carrying more than 20 players so one or two are expected to be sent away on option. In the picture, back row, left to right—John Pintar, pitcher; George Turbeville, pitcher; Bill Schmidt, pitcher; Averette Thompson, outfielder; Clarence Beers, pitcher; Bill Shewey, outfielder; Hershel Lyous, pitcher; Ray Mueller, catcher; Kemp Wicker, pitcher; Mel Serafini, infielder; Pepper Martin, manager and outfielder-infielder. Front row, left to right—Blix Donnelly, pitcher; Tony Freitas, pitcher; Gene Handley, second base; Eddie Lake, shortstop; Deb Garms, left field; Steve Mesner, third base; Jack Sturdy, first base; Charlie Marshall, catcher; Buster Adams, center field, and Henry Polly, pitcher.

This 1942 newspaper photograph shows the Solons the only year they won the Pacific Coast League championship in their 25-year history, when all their home games were played at Edmonds Field. (Courtesy of Tim Armstrong.)

This 1974 Solons scorecard illustrates the fact that the scorecards had not changed much since the 1950s, other than a bit more modern artwork and a price increase from 15¢ to 50¢. The artwork may have lightened up a bit, but it still had the always present advertisement at the bottom and two pages to keep track of the players' performance during the game. (Courtesy of Sacramento Public Library, Sacramento Room Special Collections.)

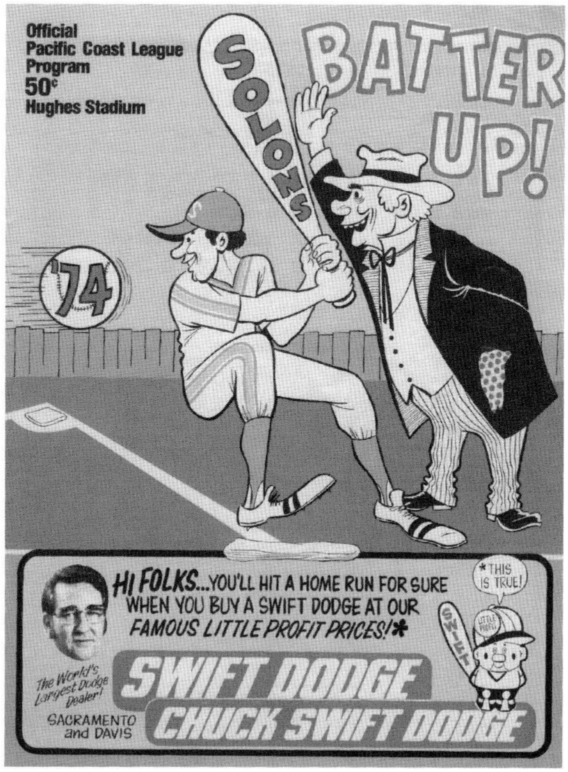

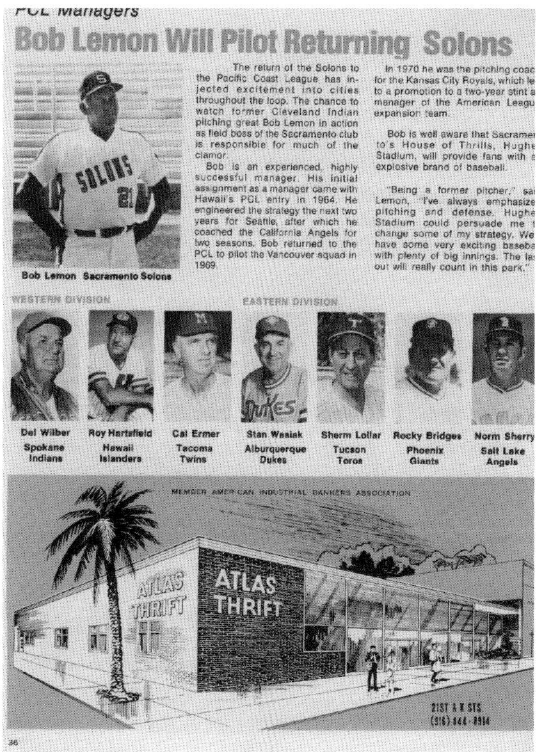
PCL Managers

Bob Lemon Will Pilot Returning Solons

Bob Lemon Sacramento Solons

The return of the Solons to the Pacific Coast League has injected excitement into cities throughout the loop. The chance to watch former Cleveland Indian pitching great Bob Lemon in action as field boss of the Sacramento club is responsible for much of the clamor.

Bob is an experienced, highly successful manager. His initial assignment as a manager came with Hawaii's PCL entry in 1964. He engineered the strategy the next two years for Seattle, after which he coached the California Angels for two seasons. Bob returned to the PCL to pilot the Vancouver squad in 1969.

In 1970 he was the pitching coac for the Kansas City Royals, which le to a promotion to a two-year stint a manager of the American Leagu expansion team.

Bob is well aware that Sacramer to's House of Thrills, Hughe Stadium, will provide fans with explosive brand of baseball.

"Being a former pitcher," sa Lemon, "I've always emphasize pitching and defense. Hughe Stadium could persuade me change some of my strategy. We have some very exciting baseba with plenty of big innings. The la out will really count in this park."

WESTERN DIVISION

Del Wilber, Spokane Indians
Roy Hartsfield, Hawaii Islanders
Cal Ermer, Tacoma Twins

EASTERN DIVISION

Stan Wasiak, Alburquerque Dukes
Sherm Lollar, Tucson Toros
Rocky Bridges, Phoenix Giants
Norm Sherry, Salt Lake Angels

MEMBER AMERICAN INDUSTRIAL BANKERS ASSOCIATION

ATLAS THRIFT

21ST & K STS
(916) 444-8914

36

The inside of this 1974 scorecard highlighted the new Solons manager, Bob Lemon. Lemon was a native Californian. He started his professional baseball career at age 17 when he was signed by the Cleveland Indians organization, and he spent his entire playing career with the Indians and their minor league clubs. He was a seven-time All-Star and helped the Indians win the World Series in 1948. He retired from playing after the 1958 season. His managing career included the Triple-A Hawaii Islanders, the Vancouver Mounties, and the Sacramento Solons. Following the Solons, he managed in the major league, where he led the New York Yankees to a World Series win in 1978. He was inducted into the Baseball Hall of Fame in 1976. (Courtesy of Sacramento Public Library, Sacramento Room Special Collections.)

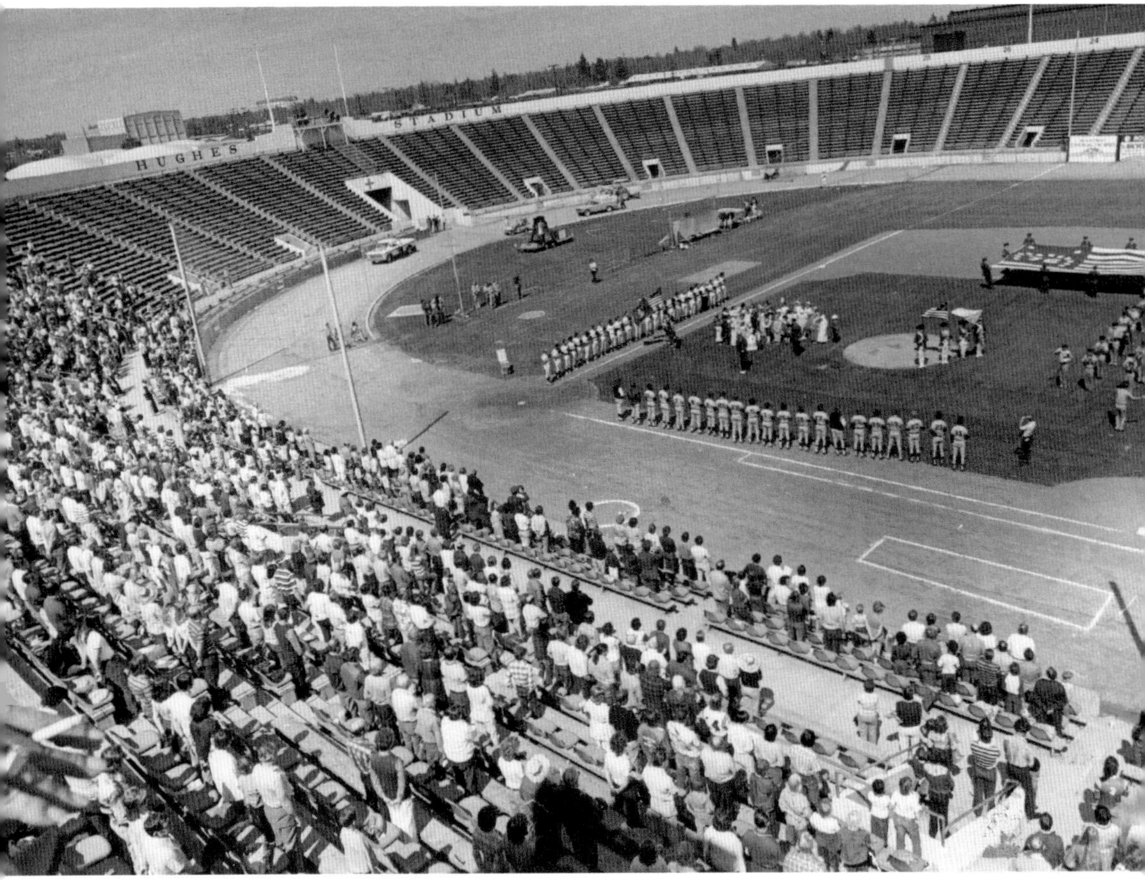

This photograph of Hughes Stadium shows the reason hitters liked to play in Sacramento. The Solons played at Hughes Stadium, built for football, from 1974 to 1976. The left field fence measured 251 feet from home plate, in contrast to the 325-foot left field fence at Raley Field today. (Courtesy of Alan O'Connor.)

6

Sacramento River Cats

2000 to Present

For most of the last three decades of the 20th century, Sacramento was without professional baseball. The Solons tried to regain a footing in the late 1970s but struck out. In 2000, that all changed when the Sacramento River Cats came to town. Art Savage purchased the Vancouver Canadians in 1998 and moved them to Sacramento. A contest was held to name the new franchise, and "River Cats" became the official moniker for the Sacramento team. During their first 15 years, the River Cats were affiliated with the Oakland Athletics as their Triple-A affiliate team. During that time, they won two Triple-A championships (2007 and 2008), four Pacific Coast League championships (back-to-back PCL championships in 2003 and 2004 and again in 2007 and 2008), and 11 PCL South Division championships (2000, 2001, 2003, 2004, 2005, 2007, 2008, 2009, 2010, 2011, and 2012). They set league-wide records for attendance every year during their first eight years and then again from 2012 to 2015. In 2015, their first year as the San Francisco Giants affiliate, they averaged more than 9,330 per game.

Raley Field, the River Cats' home field, is one of the few professional sports facilities in the nation built without a public sector contribution and is considered a crown jewel of minor league baseball. It sits along the Sacramento River across from the state capital, and it spurred new residential and commercial building in an old run-down industrial area of West Sacramento. The naming rights for the facility were sold to Raley's, a longtime family-owned supermarket chain in the Sacramento area, and has remained Raley Field ever since.

The River Cats continue to draw sellout and near-sellout crowds. Raley Field has year-round events, including festivals, soccer and hockey games, concerts, and holiday celebrations.

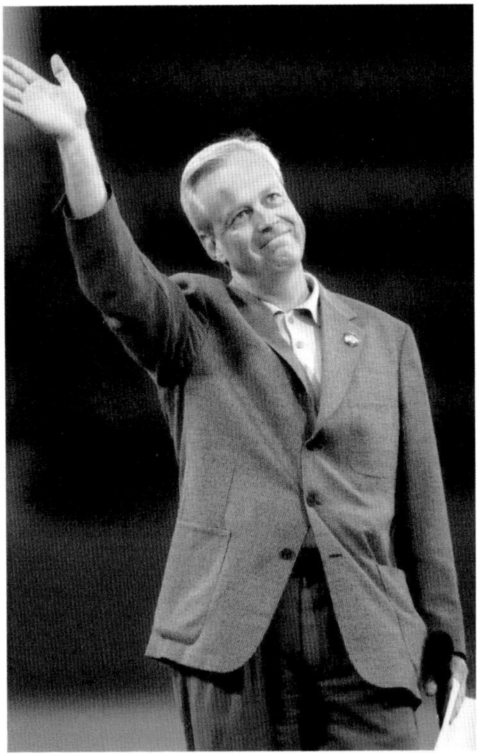

This July 3, 2000, photograph shows a smiling Art Savage, which is how fans and friends found him most of the time. With a microphone in hand, this image was taken during one of the many times he addressed the crowd from the field before a game.

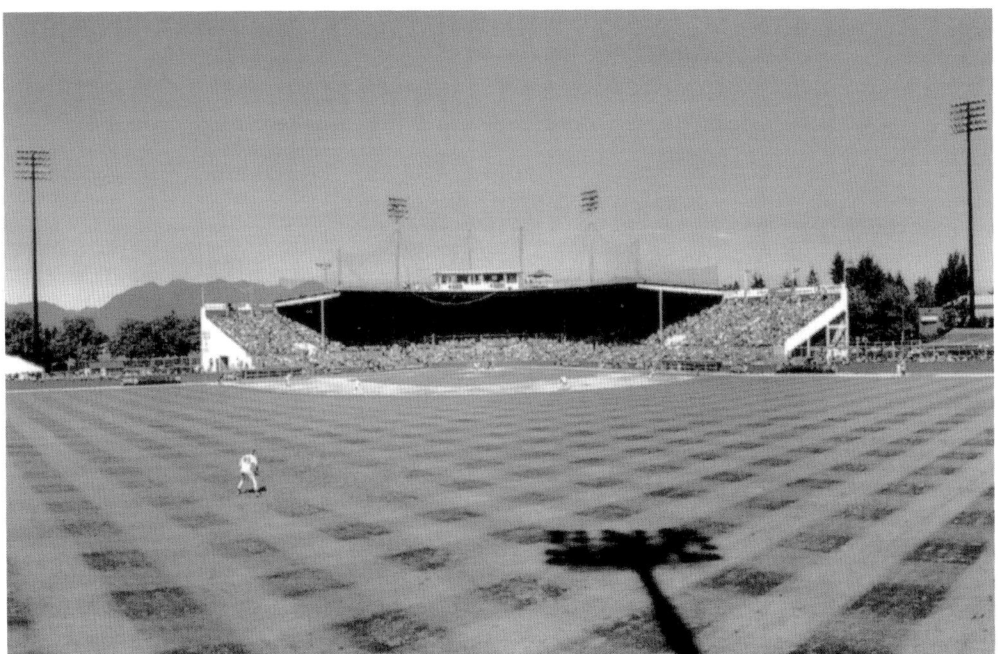

The River Cats moved from Vancouver in 2000. From 1978 to 1999, the team was known as the Vancouver Canadians and played at Nat Bailey Stadium, shown here during an afternoon game. (Courtesy of Sacramento River Cats Baseball.)

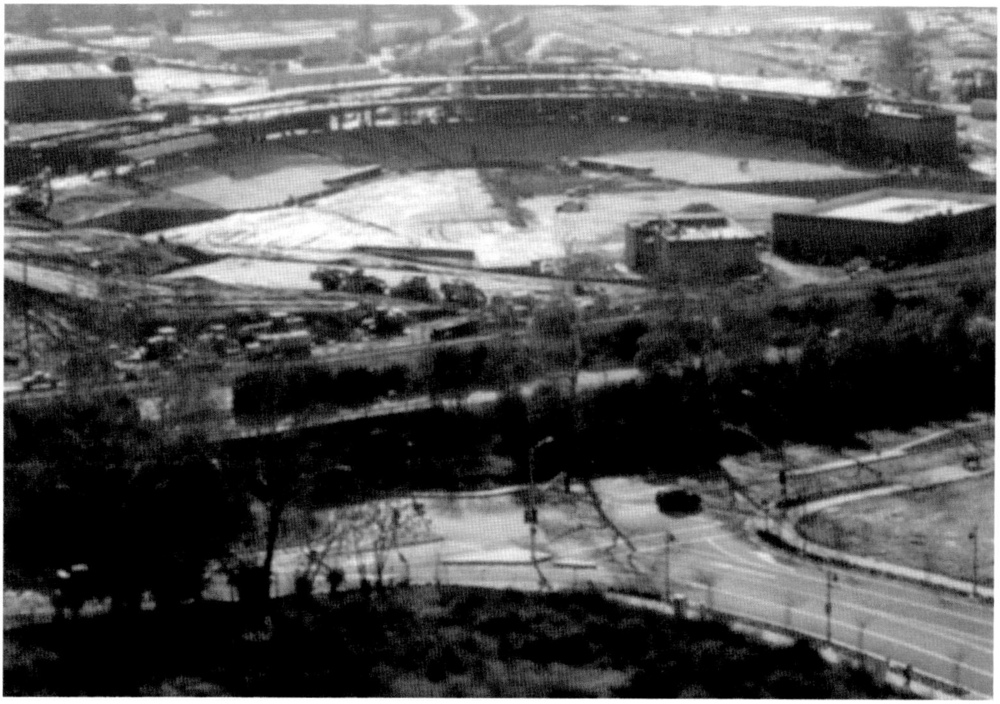

The initial construction of Raley Field took place between 1999 and 2000. The buildings in the top left corner of the photograph were eventually removed to make space for parking. (Courtesy of Sacramento River Cats Baseball.)

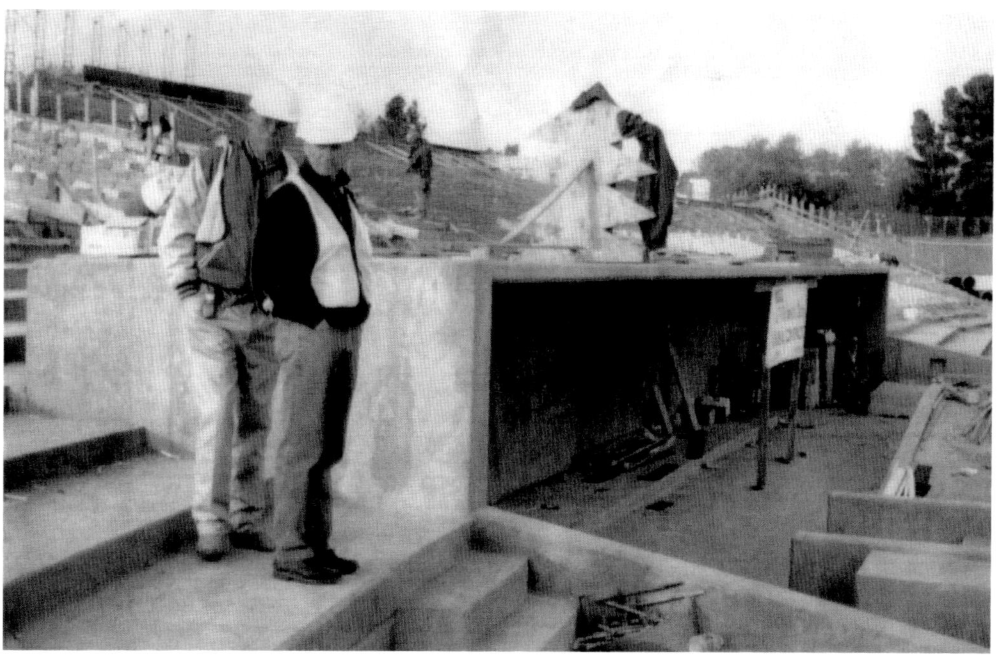

This 1999 photograph shows the third-base dugout during Raley Field construction. (Courtesy of Sacramento River Cats Baseball.)

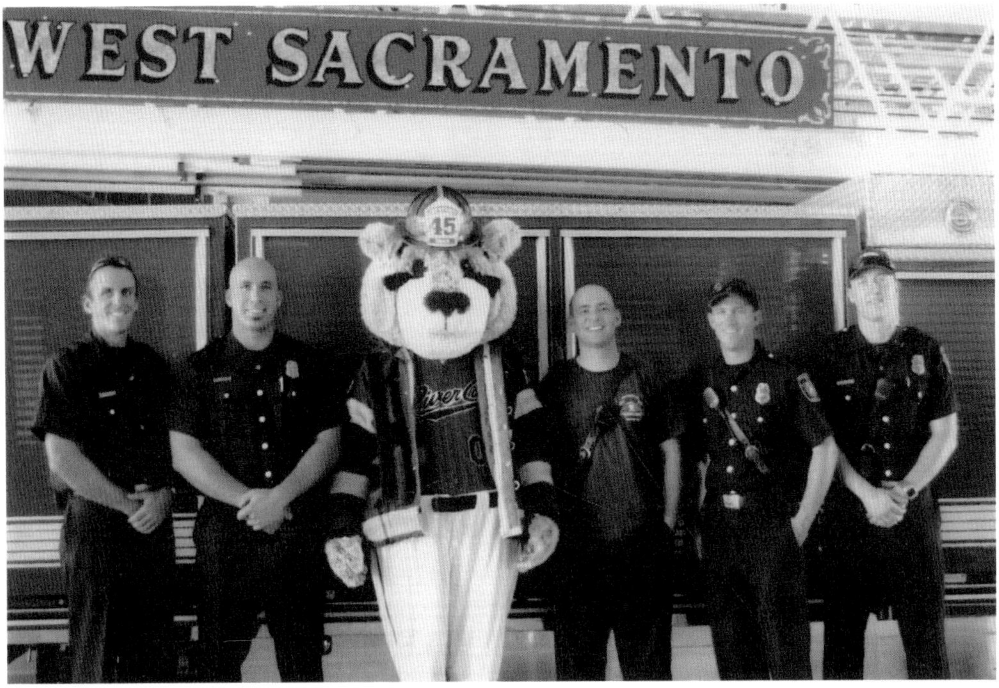

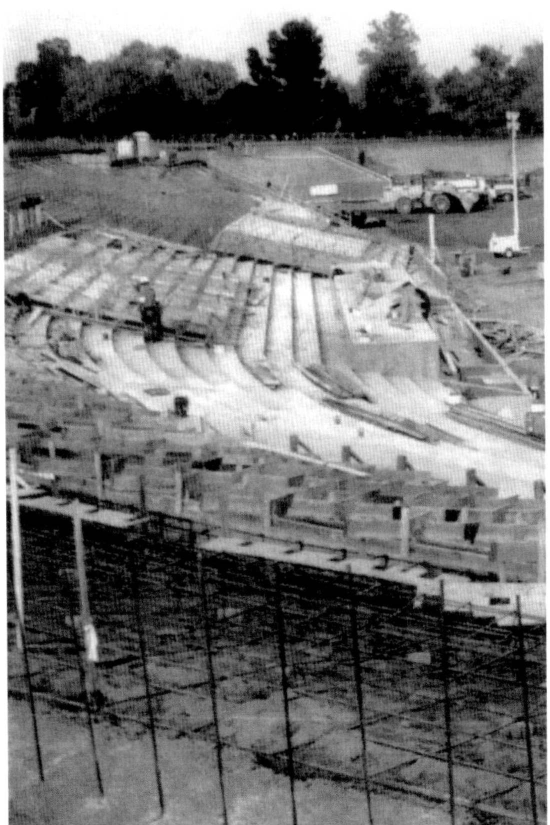

This photograph shows Dinger, the River Cats mascot, with five West Sacramento firefighters during one of the many community outreach projects in which the River Cats participated. Pictured from left to right are Ian Gilmour, Jeff Bohnet, Brenden McTighe, Dinger, Miguel Actmirano, and Marco Pasquera. (Courtesy of Sacramento River Cats Baseball.)

Here, construction takes place looking from home plate down the third-base line. (Courtesy of Sacramento River Cats Baseball.)

Pictured here is the 2000 inaugural season scorecard. Scorecards are now included in the game program. The program is no longer sold; it is given free to the fans as they enter through the gate. (Courtesy of Sacramento Public Library, Sacramento Room Special Collections.)

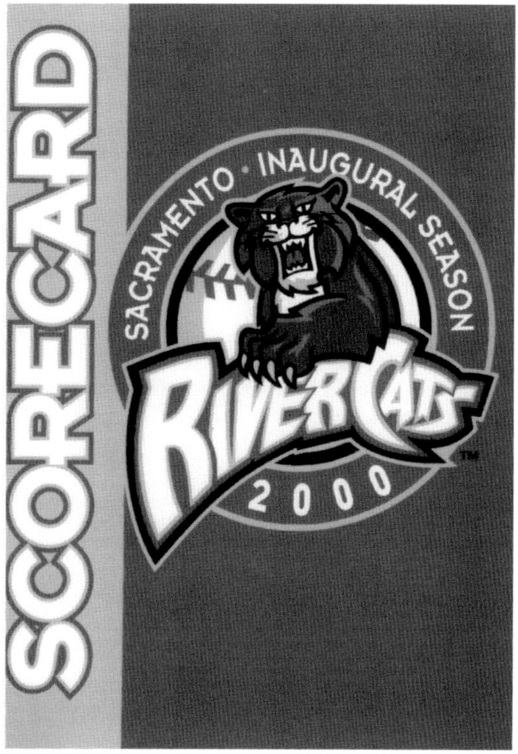

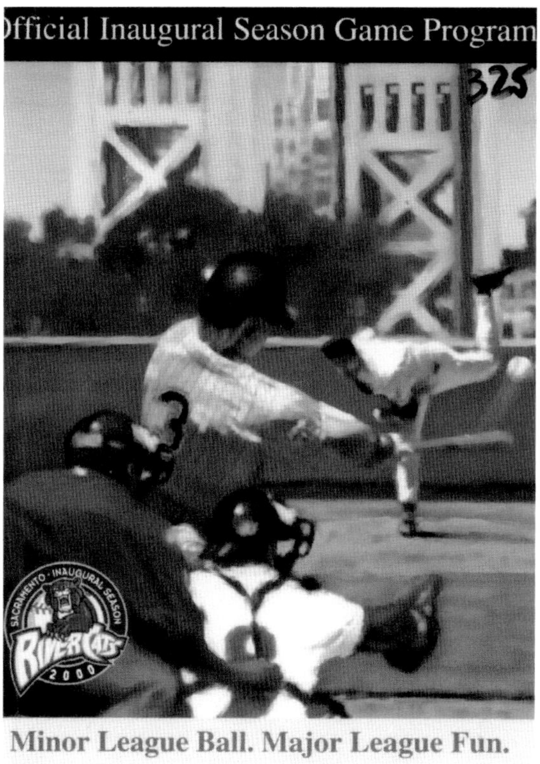

This program for the Sacramento River Cats inaugural season in 2000 proclaims the River Cats as "Minor League Ball. Major League Fun." Prior to 1958, when the New York Giants moved to San Francisco, minor league baseball was all that was available to fans in Sacramento and the West Coast. That did not mean the level of play was substandard. Then, as now, players moved between minor league teams and major league teams on a regular basis. (Courtesy of Sacramento Public Library, Sacramento Room Special Collections.)

SACRAMENTO RIVER CATS

2001 TEAM ROSTER

As of May 8

MANAGER: BOB GEREN (53) **HITTING COACH:** ROY WHITE (6) **PITCHING COACH:** RICK RODRIGUEZ (27) **ATHLETIC TRAINER:** WALT HORN

PITCHER (11+1)	POS.	B/T	HT	WT	DOB	BIRTHPLACE	RESIDES	2000 CLUB (S)
BELITZ, TODD	LHP	L/L	6-1	218	10-23-75	DES MOINES, IA	SPOKANE, WA	DURHAM, SACRAMENTO, OAKLAND
BOWIE, MICAH	LHP	L/L	6-4	210	11-10-74	WEBSTER, TX	NEW BRAUNFELS, TX	IOWA, W. TENNESSEE
HILJUS, ERIK	RHP	R/R	6-5	230	12-25-72	PANORAMA, CA	NORTHRIDGE, CA	TOLEDO, DETROIT
IRELAND, ERIC	RHP	R/R	6-1	170	3-11-77	LONG BEACH, CA	LONG BEACH, CA	ROUND ROCK
JONES, MARCUS (DL)	RHP	R/R	6-5	235	3-29-75	BELLFLOWER, CA	YORBA LINDA, CA	VISALIA, SACRAMENTO, OAKLAND, MIDLAND
LANKFORD, FRANK	RHP	R/R	6-2	190	3-26-71	ATLANTA, GA	ATLANTA, GA	SACRAMENTO, MODESTO ®
MILLER, JUSTIN	RHP	R/R	6-2	200	8-27-77	TORRANCE, CA	TORRANCE, CA	MIDLAND, SACRAMENTO
RATLIFF, JON	RHP	R/R	6-4	195	12-22-71	SYRACUSE, NY	CLAY, NY	SACRAMENTO, OAKLAND
REYES, CARLOS	RHP	S/R	6-0	190	4-4-69	MIAMI, FL	TAMPA, FL	SAN DIEGO
SCHRENK, STEVE	RHP	R/R	6-3	215	11-20-68	GREAT LAKES, IL	PARRISH, FL	PHILADELPHIA, SCRANTON
VASQUEZ, LEO	LHP	L/L	6-4	193	7-1-73	LA ROMANA, D.R.	LA ROMANA D.R.	MIDLAND
VIZCAINO, LUIS	RHP	R/R	5-11	170	6-1-77	BANI, D.R.	BANI, D.R.	SACRAMENTO, OAKLAND
CATCHER (2)	**POS**	**B/T**	**HT**	**WT**	**DOB**	**BIRTHPLACE**	**RESIDES**	**2000 CLUB (S)**
MCKAY, CODY	C	L/R	6-0	207	1-11-74	VANCOUVER, B.C.	SCOTTSDALE, AZ	MIDLAND, SACRAMENTO
WILSON, TOM	C	R/R	6-3	220	12-19-70	FULLERTON, CA	LAKE HAVASU, AZ	COLUMBUS
INFIELDER (5+1+rehab)	**POS**	**B/T**	**HT**	**WT**	**DOB**	**BIRTHPLACE**	**RESIDES**	**2000 CLUB (S)**
ELLIS, MARK	INF	R/R	5-11	180	6-6-77	RAPID CITY, S.D.	RAPID CITY, S.D.	WILMINGTON, WICHITA
HART, JASON	1B	R/R	6-3	225	9-5-77	WALNUT CREEK, CA	SPRINGFIELD, MO	MIDLAND, SACRAMENTO
HINSKE, ERIC (DL)	3B	L/R	6-2	225	8-5-77	NEENAH, WI	MENASHA, WI	WEST TENNESSEE
LANE, RYAN	2B	R/R	6-1	185	7-6-74	BELLEFONTAINE, OH	BELLEFONTAINE, OH	TULSA
ORTIZ, JOSE (rehab)	2B	R/R	5-9	177	6-13-77	SANTO DOMINGO, D.R.	SANTO DOMINGO, D.R.	SACRAMENTO, OAKLAND
SALAZAR, OSCAR	SS	R/R	6-0	155	6-27-78	MARACAY, VZ	MARACAY, VZ	MIDLAND, SACRAMENTO
SANTANGELO, F.P.	OF	S/R	5-10	165	10-24-67	LIVONIA, MI	EL DORADO HILLS, CA	LOS ANGELES, SAN BERNARDINO
OUTFIELDER (5+1)	**POS**	**B/T**	**HT**	**WT**	**DOB**	**BIRTHPLACE**	**RESIDES**	**2000 CLUB (S)**
ABAD, ANDY	RF	L/L	6-1	184	8-25-72	PALM BEACH, FL	JUPITER, FL	OSAKA (JAPAN)
CHRISTENSON, RYAN	OF	R/R	6-0	191	3-28-74	REDLANDS, CA	APPLE VALLEY, CA	OAKLAND
ENCARNACION, MARIO (DL)	CF	R/R	6-2	210	9-24-77	BANI, D.R.	BANI, D.R.	SACRAMENTO, MODESTO ®
JENNINGS, ROBIN	OF	L/L	6-2	210	4-11-72	SINGAPORE	PARK CITY, UT	SALT LAKE, LOUISVILLE
PIATT, ADAM	OF	R/R	6-2	218	2-8-76	CHICAGO, IL	MISSOURI CITY, TX	SACRAMENTO, OAKLAND
ROSARIO, OMAR	OF	L/L	6-1	170	1-14-78	SANTO DOMINGO, D.R.	SANTO DOMINGO, D.R.	VISALIA, SACRAMENTO

This 2001 Sacramento River Cats roster identifies each team member along with his height and weight, date of birth, birthplace, current places of residence, and the team(s) he played for in the previous year. This format has not changed over the years and still appears in current programs. (Courtesy of Sacramento Public Library, Sacramento Room Special Collections.)

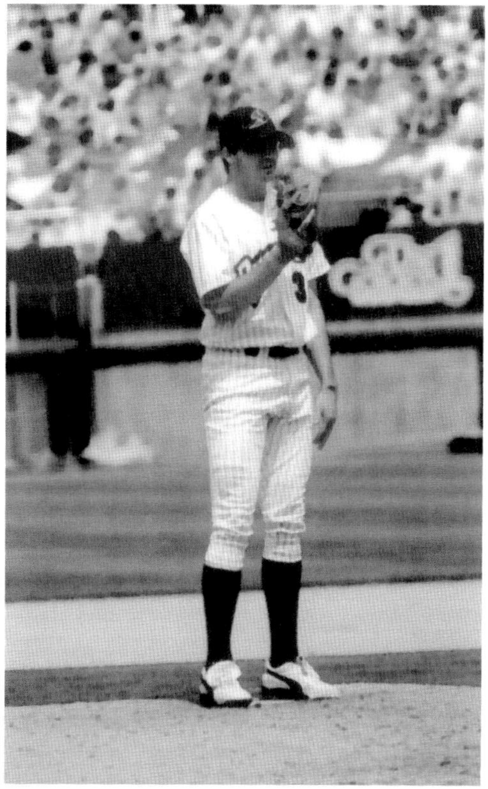

Twenty-two-year-old Barry Zito, a future Cy Young Award winner, three-time major league All-Star, and *Sporting News'* American League Pitcher of the Year, takes the mound for the River Cats in their inaugural season. (Courtesy of Sacramento River Cats Baseball.)

By June, things start heating up in Sacramento. The race for the PCL pennant is underway, and temperatures begin reaching 90 degrees. These photographs show the front and back side of a fan given to people as they entered the park around 2000. As the advertisement on the fan shows, it was paid for by funds from California's Proposition 99, passed by voters in 1988, which among other things imposed a 25¢ per pack excise tax on the sale of tobacco cigarettes within California. (Both, courtesy of Sacramento Public Library, Sacramento Room Special Collections.)

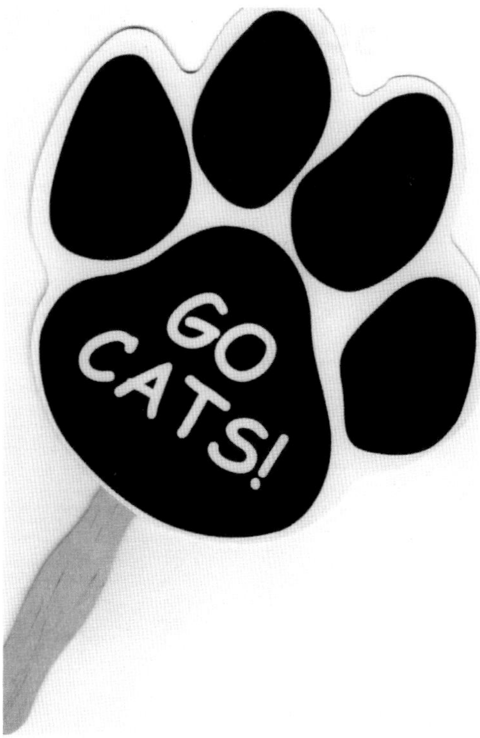

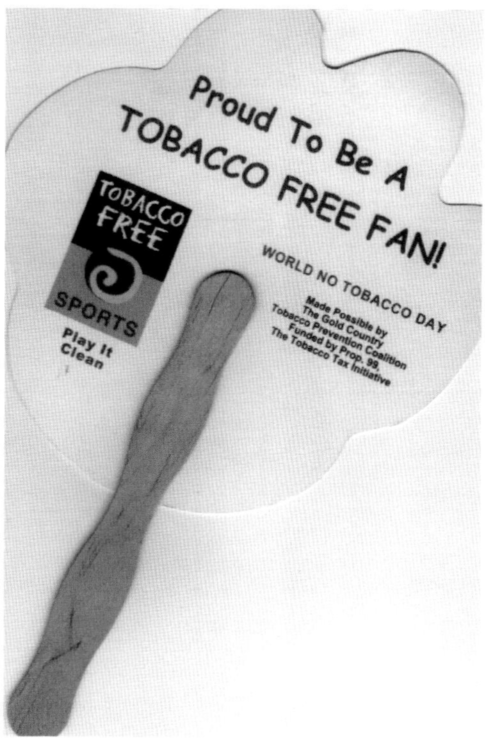

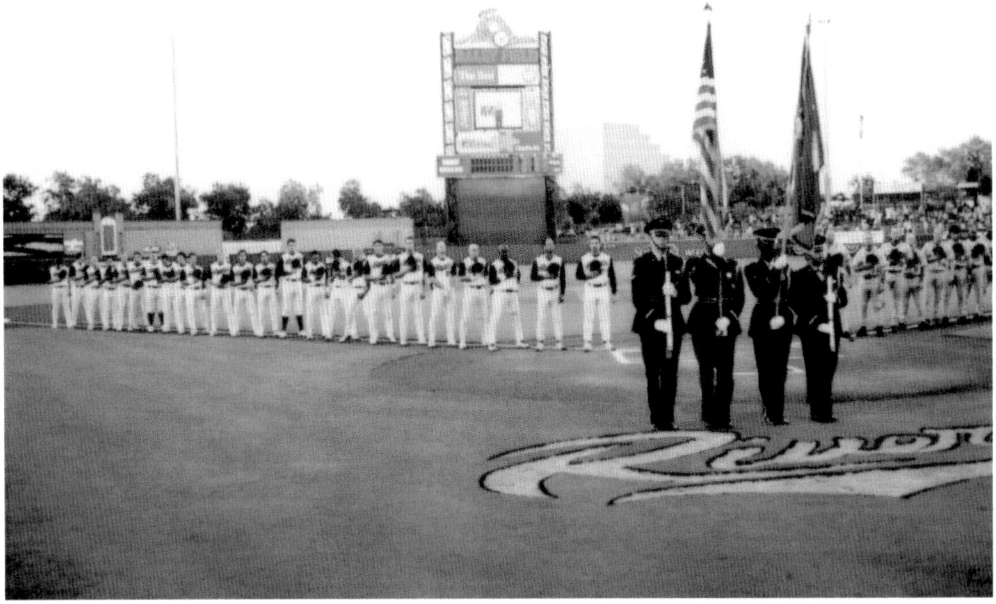

This 2004 photograph shows the National Anthem being played during the opening day ceremony, with the River Cats lined up on the third-base line in front of their dugout and the visitors lined up on the first base line. The ceremony featured an Air Force color guard. (Courtesy of Sacramento River Cats Baseball.)

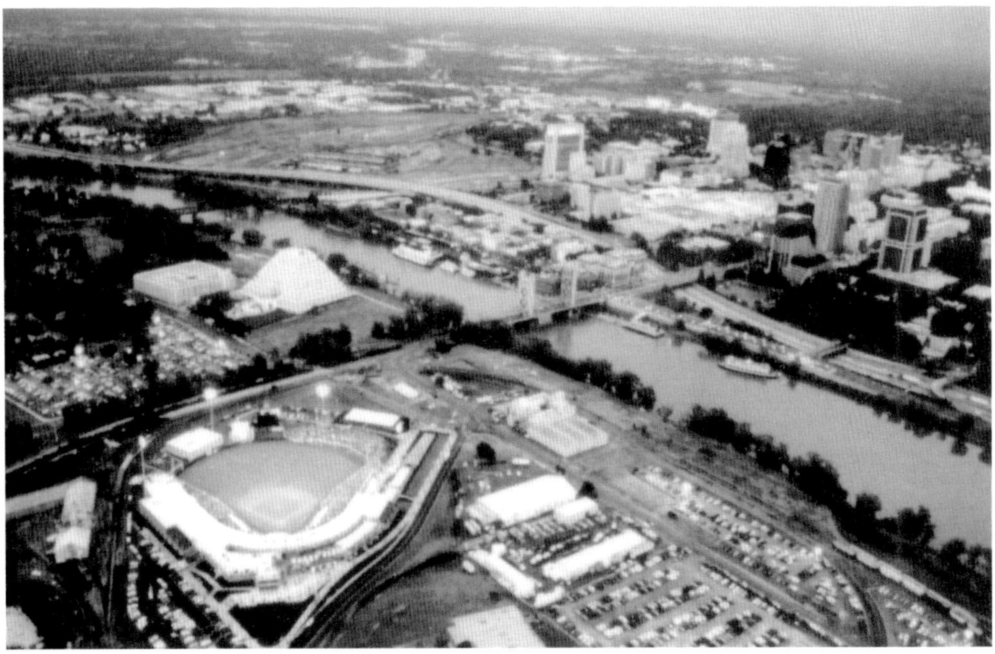

This aerial view of Raley Field during a night game shows the Sacramento River and downtown Sacramento. It is a regular photograph in the River Cats' program, which includes a short history of Raley Field and the team. (Courtesy of Sacramento River Cats Baseball.)

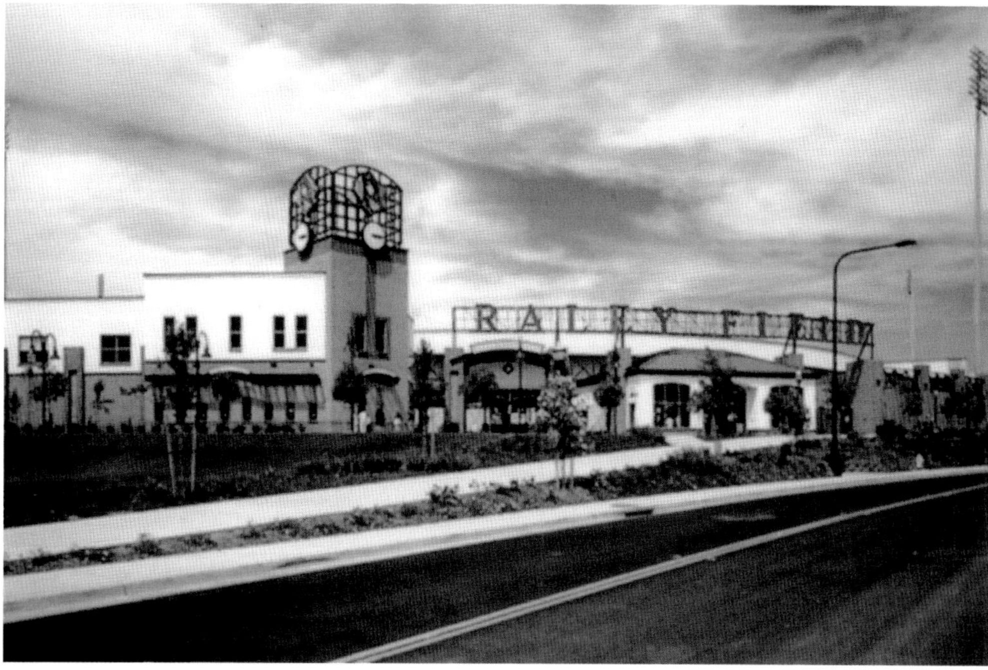

This is a photograph of Raley Field looking toward the home plate gate. (Courtesy of Sacramento River Cats Baseball.)

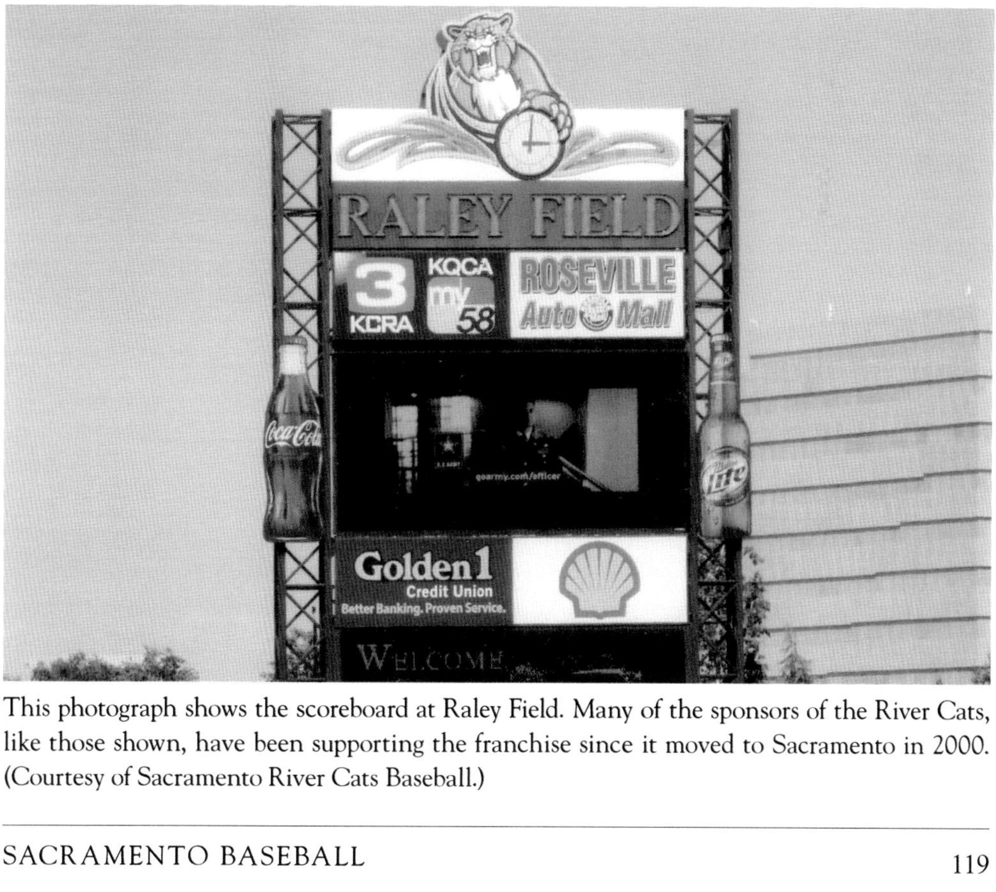

This photograph shows the scoreboard at Raley Field. Many of the sponsors of the River Cats, like those shown, have been supporting the franchise since it moved to Sacramento in 2000. (Courtesy of Sacramento River Cats Baseball.)

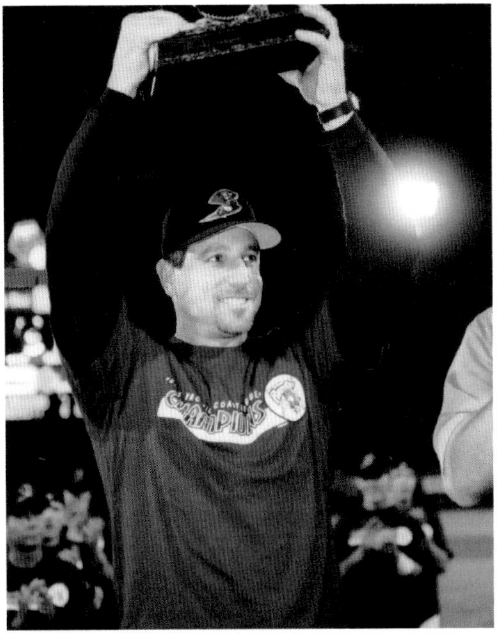

This photograph shows River Cats manager Tony DeFrancesco holding the 2003 championship trophy after the winning the final game of the series. During their first 15 seasons as the River Cats, the team had unparalleled success on the baseball field, winning two Triple-A championships (2007 and 2008) and four Pacific Coast League championships (back-to-back PCL championships in 2003 and 2004 and again in 2007 and 2008). The team has also won 11 PCL South Division championships. (Courtesy of Sacramento River Cats Baseball.)

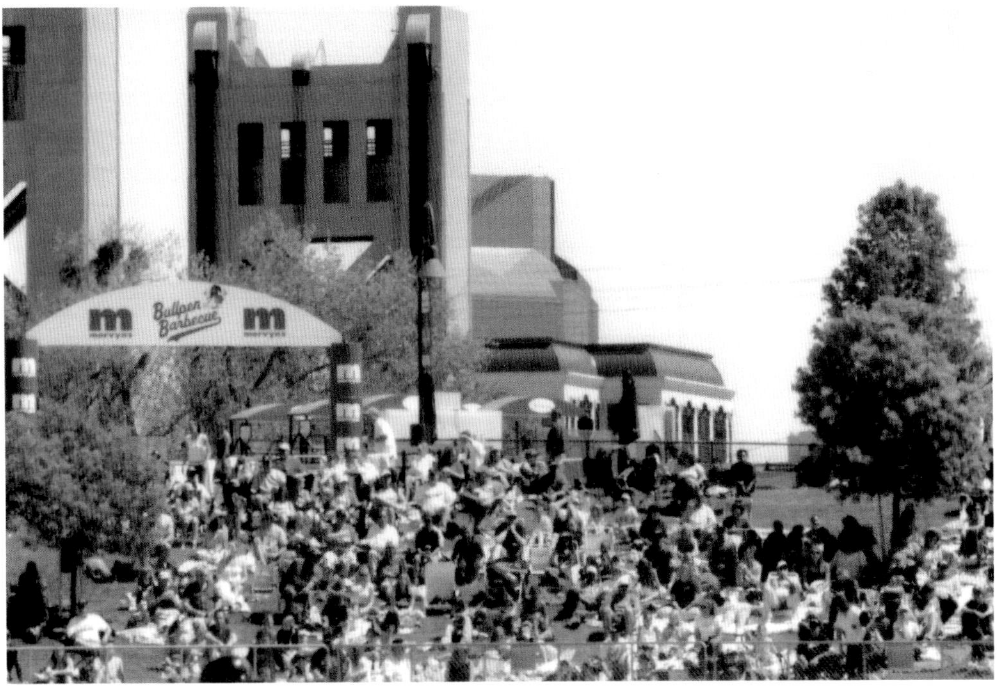

Looking toward the Tower Bridge from Raley Field's home plate, one can see many fans on the grass beyond the right field fence enjoying a River Cats game. When the field opened in 2000, the cost of a grass-area ticket was $5. Once in, a fan can spread out a blanket or sit on a low beach chair, watch the game, and hope to catch a home run ball. Although the tickets are now $10, the trees have grown and provide more shade; it is still an inexpensive way for a family to take a spring or summer outing to savor the national pastime. (Courtesy of Sacramento River Cats Baseball.)

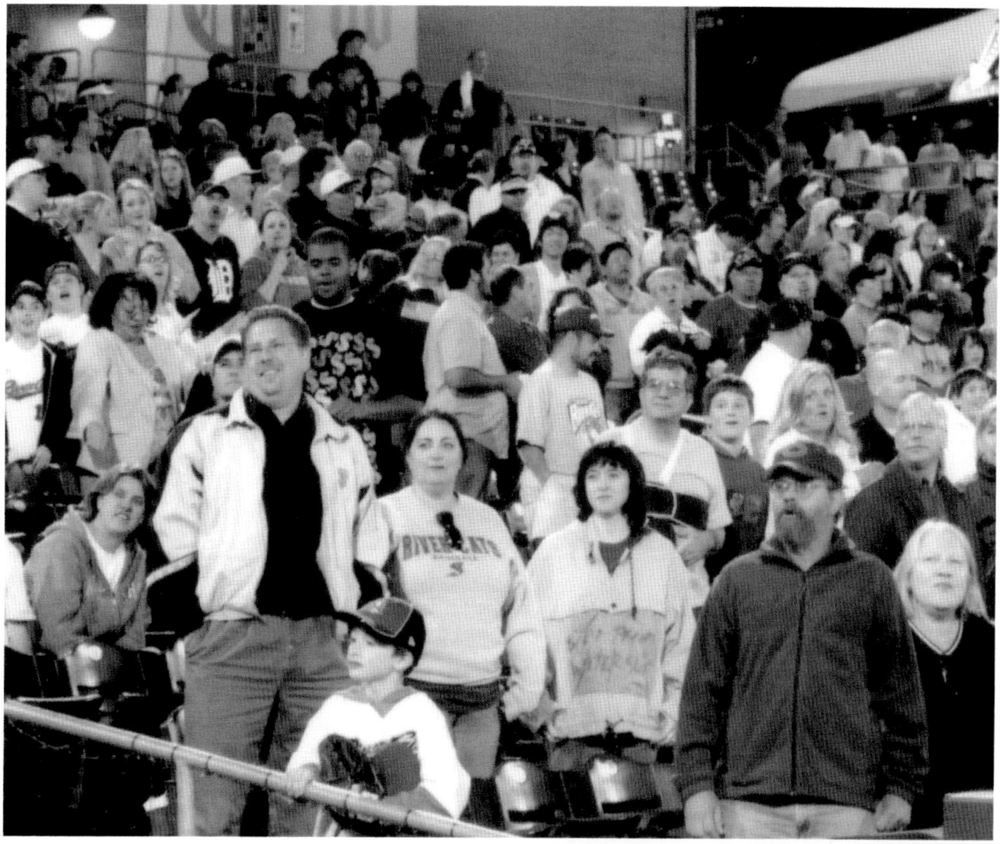

This is a photograph of the crowd at Raley Field. Fans might be on their feet because of an exciting play that just took place, or it could be between innings and one of the many entertainment activities is in progress. (Courtesy of Sacramento River Cats Baseball.)

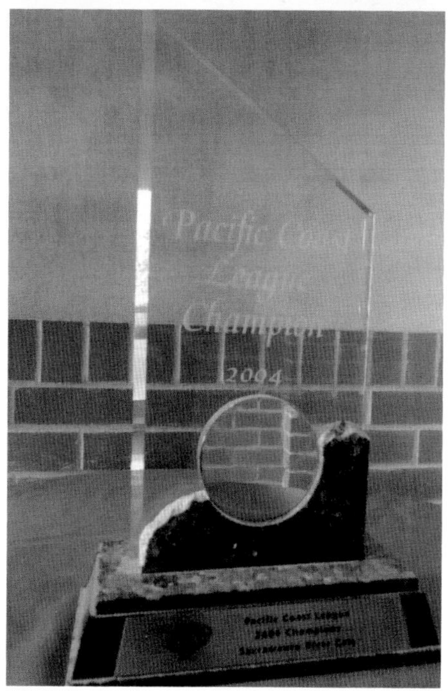

This trophy represents the Pacific Coast League championship won by the River Cats in 2004. There are 16 teams in the Triple-A Division of the PCL. In their 16-year history, the River Cats have won the first place title four times. (Courtesy of Sacramento River Cats Baseball.)

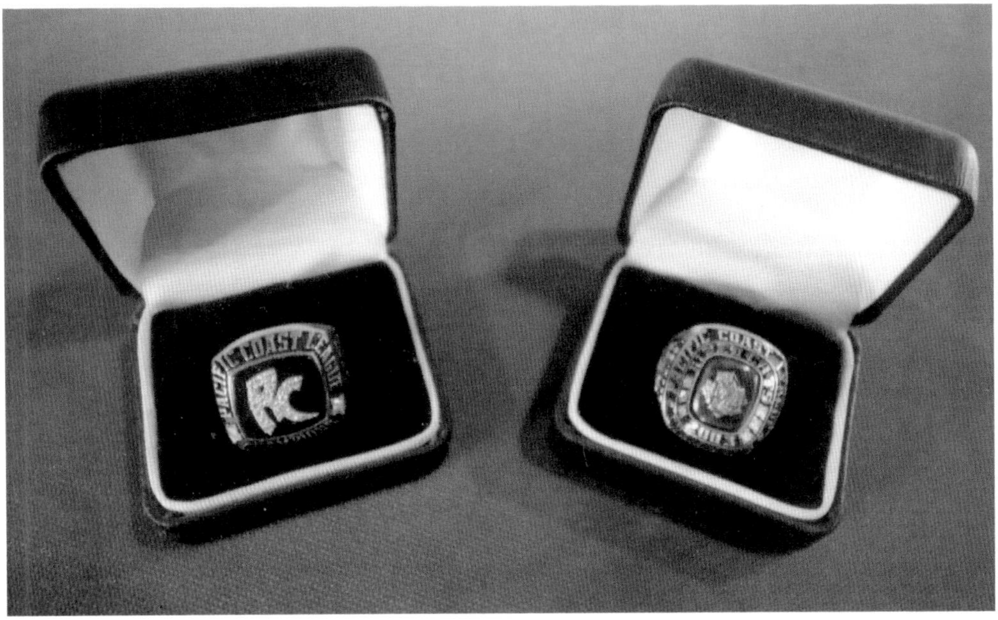

These two Pacific Coast League rings were awarded to the members of the River Cats in 2007 and 2003, respectively, for winning the Pacific Coast League championship. The River Cats claimed the Pacific Coast League title in 2003, 2004, 2007, and 2008. (Courtesy of Sacramento River Cats Baseball.)

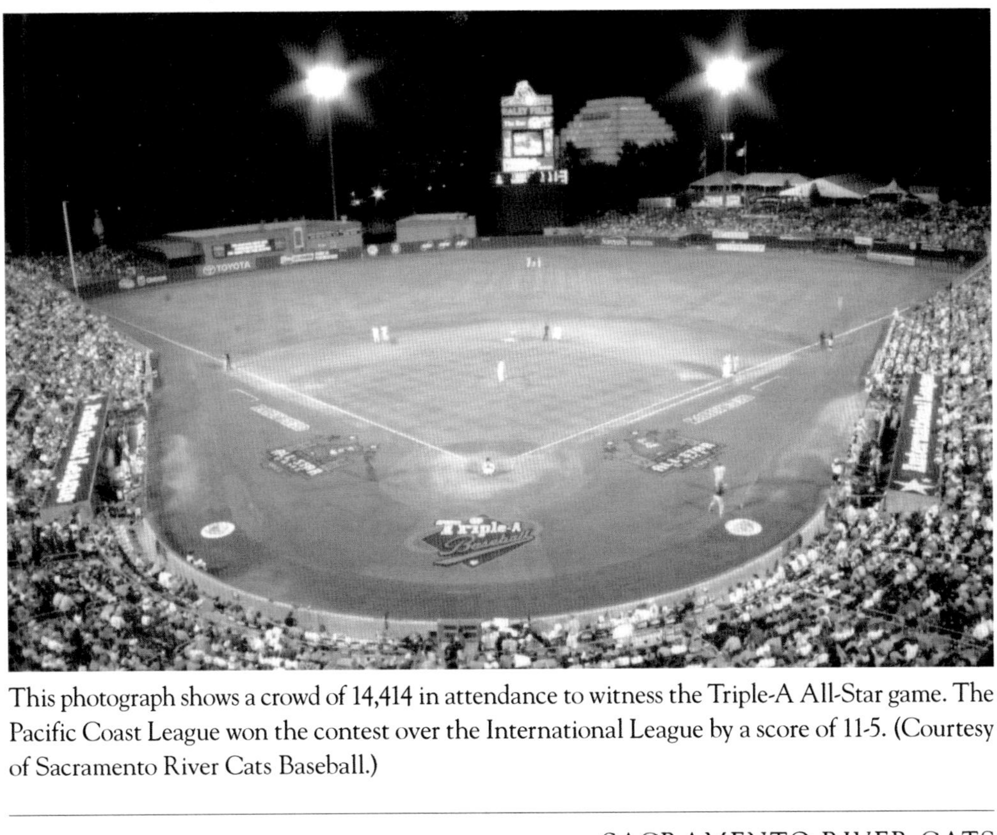

This photograph shows a crowd of 14,414 in attendance to witness the Triple-A All-Star game. The Pacific Coast League won the contest over the International League by a score of 11-5. (Courtesy of Sacramento River Cats Baseball.)

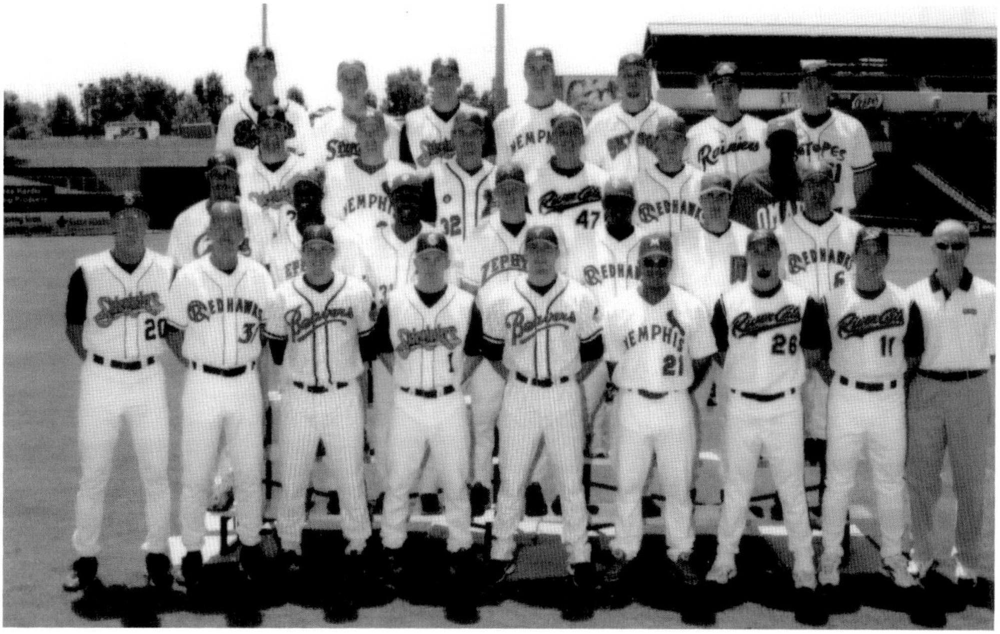

This photograph shows the 2005 Pacific Coast League All-Star team, which features three River Cats members—No. 26, outfielder Matt Watson; No. 47, pitcher Ron Flores; and No. 11, team manager Tony DeFrancesco. (Courtesy of Sacramento River Cats Baseball.)

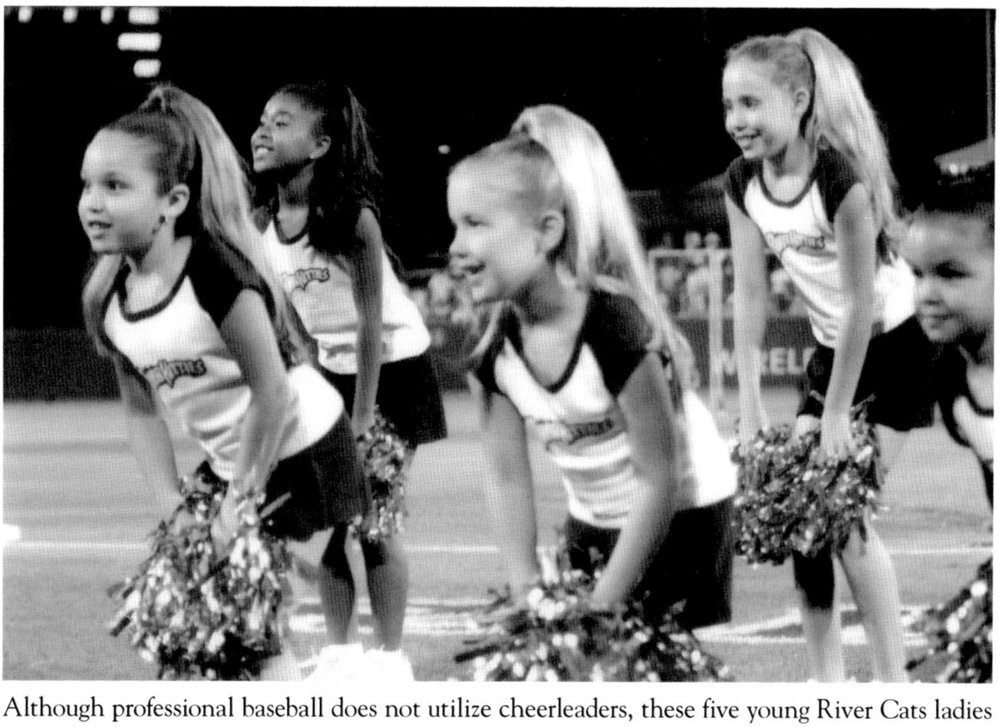

Although professional baseball does not utilize cheerleaders, these five young River Cats ladies came out to help the crowd encourage the home team at the 2005 Triple-A All-Star game played at Raley Field. (Courtesy of Sacramento River Cats Baseball.)

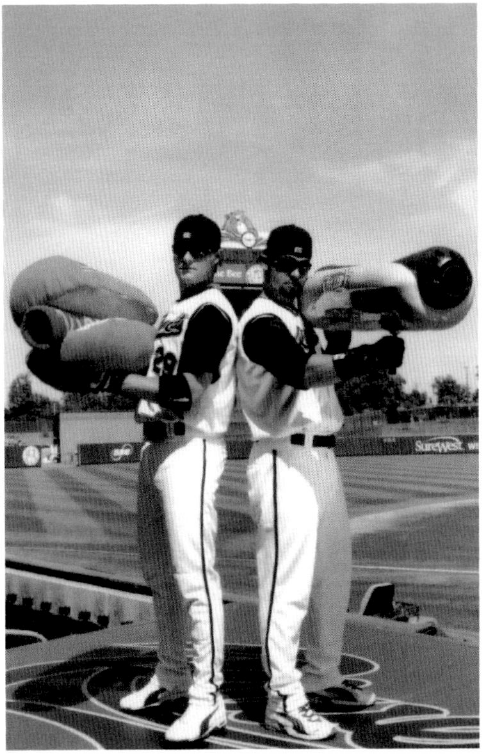

Shown in this 2004 photograph are Dan Johnson, No. 29, and Nick Swisher, No. 33, holding the River Cats canons. The canons are used between innings to "shoot" rolled River Cats T-shirts into the grandstands. (Courtesy of Sacramento River Cats Baseball.)

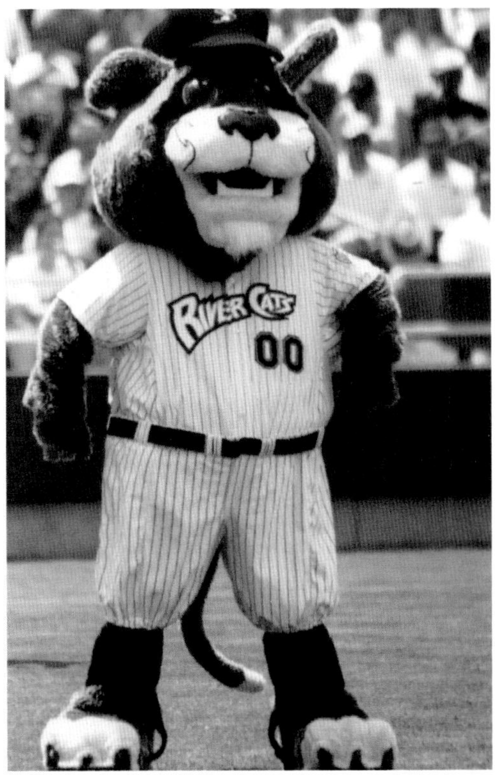

Pictured here is Dinger, the mascot for the Sacramento River Cats. Dinger makes appearances during the game, keeping the fans entertained, and when he is not at the park, he attends many community and area school events. (Courtesy of Sacramento River Cats Baseball.)

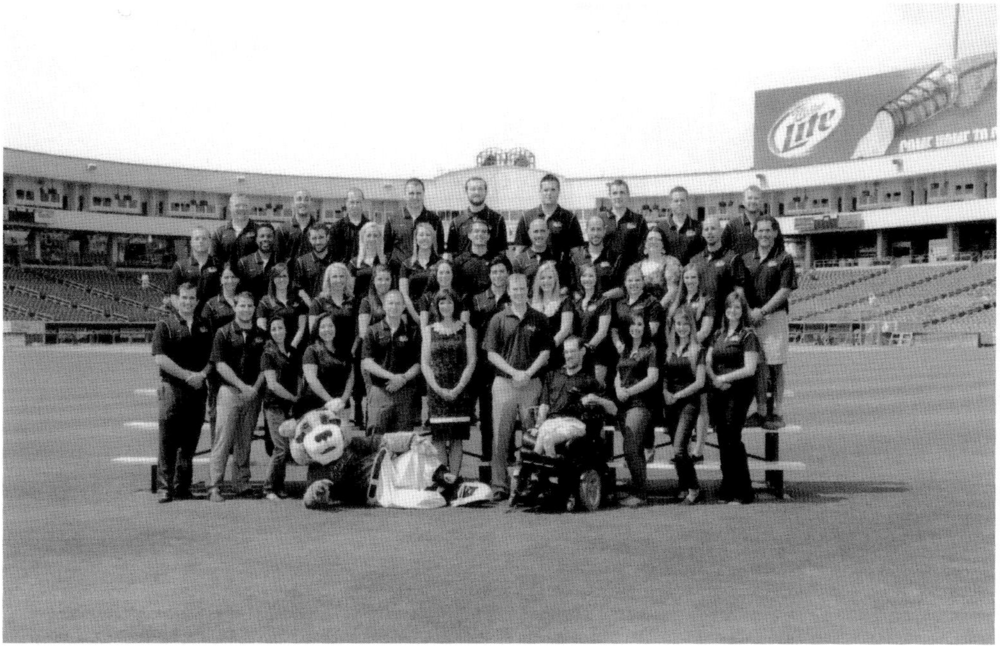

The front office team is pictured here. In the first row, at center, is Susan Savage, the River Cats owner; to her left is Jeff Savage, River Cats president, and to her right is Chip Maxson, general manager. This image includes all the people who keep the administrative part of the River Cats up and running year-round. (Courtesy of Sacramento River Cats Baseball.)

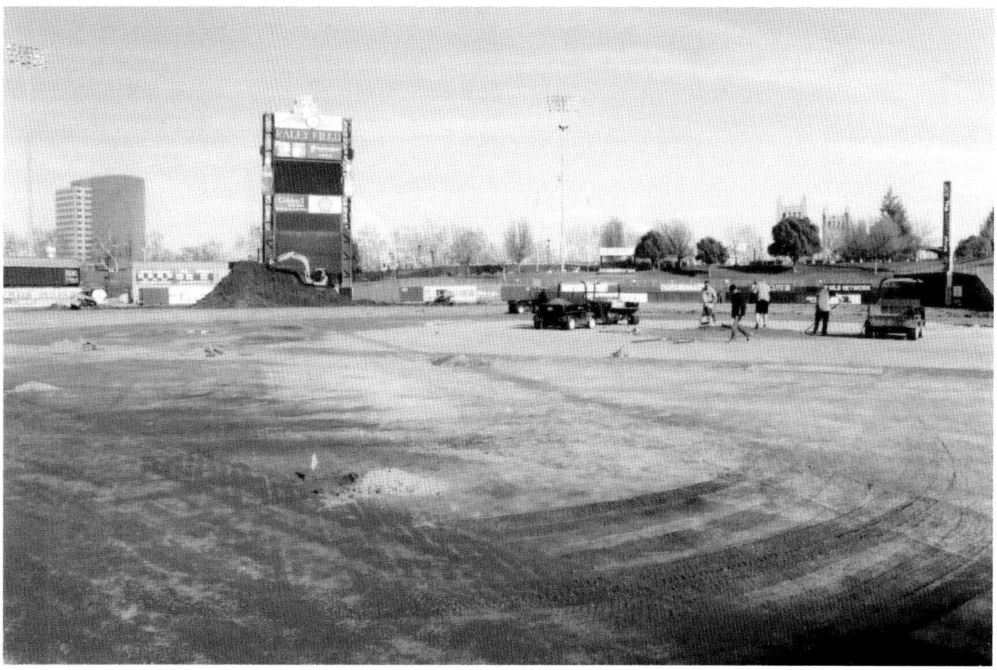

This photograph exhibits the spring 2016 refurbishment of the field, which included laying new turf in the infield and outfield and construction of sa new pitcher's mound. (Author's collection.)

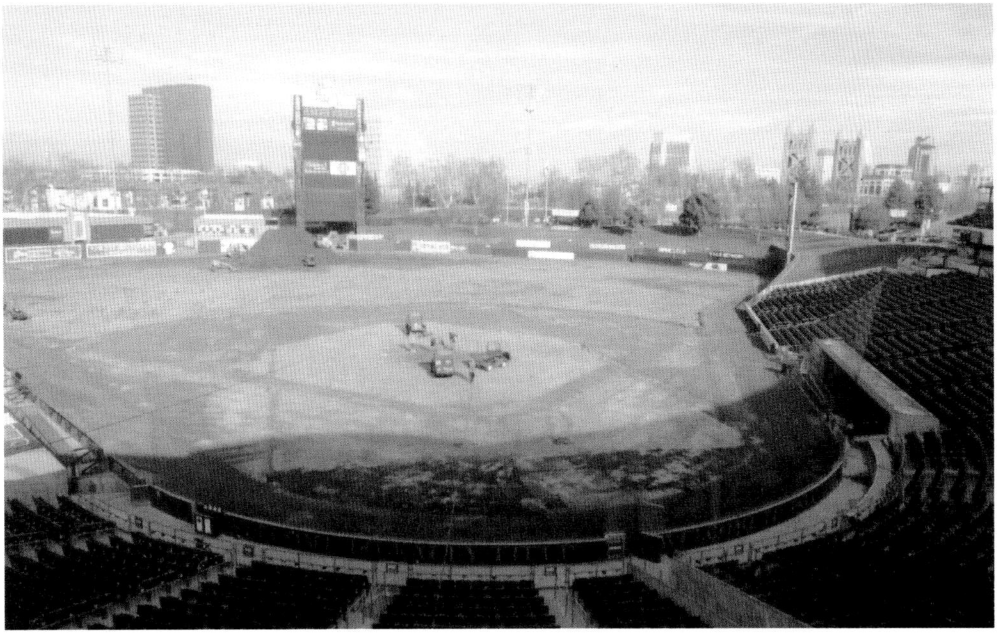

This afternoon shot of Raley Field from the press box shows the field renovation completed in 2016. During this renovation, the turf was completely removed and replaced less than a month prior to opening day.

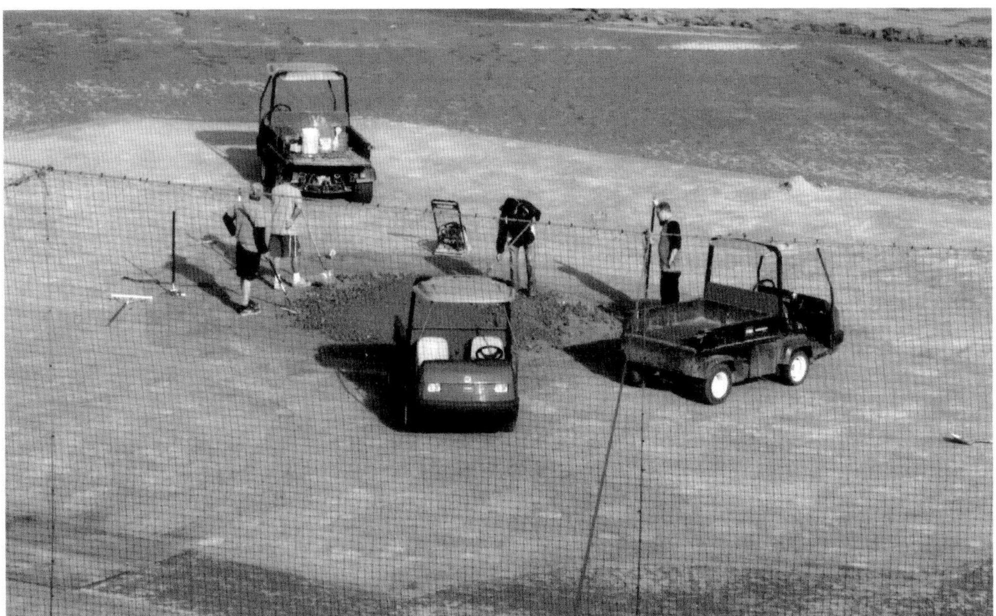

This 2016 photograph shows the pitcher's mound being rebuilt as part of the overall field restoration. Major League Baseball rules are very specific about the height and slope of the mound. The pitcher's plate—or rubber, as it is commonly called—must be 10 inches above the level of home plate and slope six feet toward home plate at a rate of one inch to one foot.

BIBLIOGRAPHY

Goode, Chris. *California Baseball: From the Pioneers To The Glory Years.* Raleigh, NC: Lulu, 2009.

Isidro, Jocelyn Munroe. *Sacramento's Land Park.* Charleston, SC: Arcadia Publishing, 2005.

Nakagawa, Kerry Yo. *Japanese Baseball in California.* Charleston, SC: The History Press, 2014.

O'Connor, Alan. *Gold on the Diamond: Sacramento's Great Baseball Players, 1886 to 1976.* Sacramento, CA: Big Tomato Press, 2008.

Snelling, Dennis. *The Greatest Minor League: A History of the Pacific Coast League, 1903–1957.* NC and London: McFarland & Company, Inc., 2012.

www.littleleague.org/Little_League_Big_Legacy.htm